Iran, Israel, and
the United States

Iran, Israel, and the United States

Regime Security vs. Political Legitimacy

Jalil Roshandel
with Nathan Chapman Lean

Praeger Security International

PRAEGER

AN IMPRINT OF ABC-CLIO, LLC
Santa Barbara, California • Denver, Colorado • Oxford, England

Library of Congress Cataloging-in-Publication Data

Rawshandil, Jalil, 1944 or 5–
  Iran, Israel, and the United States : regime security vs. political legitimacy / Jalil Roshandel, with Nathan Chapman Lean.
    p. cm. — (Praeger security international)
    Includes bibliographical references and index.
    ISBN: 978–0–313–38697–8 (hard copy: alk. paper) — ISBN 978–0–313–38698–5 (e-book)
1. United States—Foreign relations—Iran. 2. Israel—Foreign relations—Iran. 3. Iran—Foreign relations—Israel. 4. United States—Foreign relations—Israel. 5. Israel—Foreign relations—United States. 6. National security—Israel. 7. National security—Iran. 8. Legitimacy of governments—Iran. 9. National security—United States. 10. Iran—Foreign relations—United States. I. Lean, Nathan Chapman. II. Title. III. Series.
JZ1480.A57I717   2011
327.73055—dc22   2011005964

ISBN: 978–0–313–38697–8
EISBN: 978–0–313–38698–5

15 14 13 12 11   1 2 3 4 5

This book is also available on the World Wide Web as an eBook.
Visit www.abc-clio.com for details.

Praeger
An Imprint of ABC-CLIO, LLC

ABC-CLIO, LLC
130 Cremona Drive, P.O. Box 1911
Santa Barbara, California 93116-1911

This book is printed on acid-free paper ∞

Manufactured in the United States of America

To our spouses,
Parvin Roshandel (Samei) and Naïma Lean,
whose love, support, and encouragement have made
this project, and all projects, possible.

Contents

Acronyms

APA	Asian Parliamentary Assembly
BBC	British Broadcasting Corporation
CRS	Congressional Research Service
EU	European Union
GC	Guardian Council
GCC	Gulf Cooperation Council (the term "Gulf" is often used by the Persian Gulf's Arab states to define this body of water)
GDP	gross domestic product
Hamas	[Harakat al-Muqāwamat al-Islāmiyyah] Islamic Resistance Movement
HEU	highly enriched uranium
IAEA	International Atomic Energy Agency
IDF	Israeli Defense Forces
IED	improvised explosive devices
IRBM	intermediate-range ballistic missile
IRGC	Iranian Revolutionary Guard Corps
LEU	low enriched uranium
LNR	Lebanese National Resistance
MINATOM	Ministry of Atomic Energy of the Russian Federation
MOAB	massive ordinance air blast
MTC	Military Trade Cooperation
NATO	North Atlantic Treaty Organization

NEP	nuclear earth penetrators
NPP	nuclear power plant
NPT	Non-Proliferation Treaty
NUTS	new use theorists
PBS	Public Broadcasting Service
PLO	Palestinian Liberation Organization
SCO	Shanghai Cooperation Organization
SNSC	Supreme National Security Council of Iran
UNIFIL	United Nations Interim Force in Lebanon
UNSC	United Nations Security Council
WMD	weapons of mass destruction

Glossary

Aliot: Plural of Aliyah

Aliyah: Hebrew for "ascent"—a term used to refer to periods of immigration to Israel

Ayatollah: The highest clerical authority in Shi'a order. An Ayatollah is regarded a person of reference and worthy of imitation in religious matters. Since 1979, the Ayatollahs in Iran have attempted to expand their authority in political matters as well as religious arena.

Eretz: Hebrew for "the Land of Israel"

faghih: Islamic scholar

Hamas: [Harakat al-Muqāwamat al-Islāmiyyah] Islamic Resistance Movement

Hezbollah: Literally, "The Party of God," specifically the armed militia based in Lebanon. In general, those who oppose the creation of political parties on the grounds that only God can lead a party and all allegiances should be directed toward God and not a political authority.

Koran/Quran: The holy book of Islam

Mamlakhtitut: Hebrew word for "statism," "statehood"

Ostpolitik: German word for "Eastern policy"

Qods (also Quds): Special unit of Iran's Revolutionary Guard Corps (IRGC), originally taken from the word "Al-Quds" and often used to refer to Jerusalem

Shah: In this text, Mohammad Reza Pahlavi, the last monarch of the Pahlavi dynasty of Iran that was ended by the Islamic Revolution in 1979

Shia, Shiite, Shi'ite: The largest denomination in Islam after the Sunni majority. Followers of Shi'a Islam are called Shi'ite; also written as "Shiite"

Sunni: The largest branch of Islam, the majority of Muslims today Muslims

Ummah: Arabic term meaning "nation or Community of Islam"

Vali Faghih: A disputed position of Islamic jurisprudence run by the highest religious scholar, called "Faghih"

Velayat-e faghih: A system of absolute rule by a" Faghih" in a particular Islamic jurisprudence. Practically the only existing example of such system in current world is the Islamic Republic of Iran.

CHAPTER 1

Introduction

In October 2010, U.S. Deputy Secretary of State James Steinberg and Israeli Deputy Foreign Minister Daniel Ayalon released a joint statement calling Iran one of the "greatest challenges" to stability in the Middle East and reconfirmed an U.S.-Israeli effort to prevent the country from developing nuclear weapons. "While today's strategic dialogue covered many subjects, it is clear that Iran is among the greatest challenges we face today in the Middle East," a portion of the text read.[1] "Iran's continued noncompliance with its international obligations related to its nuclear program, as well as its continued support for terrorist entities, are of grave concern to our two countries and the entire international community."[2]

The statement came at a critical time for U.S. foreign policymakers. Weeks earlier, Palestinian and Israeli leaders met at the White House and Pentagon to reengage in a long-awaited series of peace talks. Making good on a promise to vigorously engage these rival states in thoughtful, diplomatic dialogue aimed at finding a solution to end the years of their bitter opposition, President Barack Obama balanced the endeavor with other pressing policy decisions, including a drawdown and removal of permanent combat troops in Iraq and an increasingly obstinate quandary in Pakistan, where the Khyber Pass—a mountainous trail that connects Pakistan to Afghanistan—was shut off as Pakistani officials protested U.S. drone strikes. For the United States, this moment was critical. With no land route into the ongoing war in Afghanistan, ground operations would be limited. Two years into Obama's first term, Middle Eastern policymaking dominated the West Wing.

Though the first days of talks between Israel and Palestine offered no glimpse of what would come, Shimon Peres, the Israeli president, offered a candid and revealing admission: peace talks with the Palestinians would "isolate Iran."[3] He said.

As the United States is trying to understand the security needs of Israel, we Israelis ourselves must understand the security needs of the United States. In our own small way we can be of help, and of help means [to] enable an anti-Iranian coalition in the Middle East. And the contribution will not be by a declaration, but if we will stop the secondary conflict between us and the Palestinians.[4]

There it was—the elusive, unspoken, but ever-so-present triangle. Its three points—Israel, Iran, and the United States—defined it, and without any one of them, it was not complete. Peres revealed the complex nature of the relationship between these three countries, evidencing that Iran loomed in the distance and was always a part of not but peripheral to the U.S.-Israeli alliance. For Iran, its growing enmity with the United States and its nuclear saber rattling was a result of Israel, lurking nearby, hoping to establish itself as the main act among other actors in the region. Like a game of political dominos, one quick move affected the entire playing field, and in a world where political leaders sought to establish dominance, mark their territory, and save their people from competing ideologies, the consequences of misplay were catastrophic.

Peres's observations revealed more than his hopes for isolating Iran. In fact, to Peres, the Palestinian-Israeli conflict was "secondary." The primary conflict was the threat of Iran and one that he and his Israeli compatriots viewed in terms of security and legitimacy—Iran posed the single greatest danger to Israeli security, and, if not thwarted, that threat would undermine the political legitimacy of the democratic state. Correspondingly, though not acknowledged by Peres, Iran was also concerned with security, though not entirely the type that dealt with protecting its borders, fending off attacks, and maintaining peace. Iran's concern was more expedient—regime security. An Israeli-U.S. alliance threatened the Iranian regime, and any discussion of dissembling the nuclear reactors and weapons that provided Ahmadinejad and his cohorts with that sense of protection would be met with fierce opposition, the stockpiles of nuclear weapons potentially deployed against aggressors.

In many ways, this book picks up where Shimon Peres left off. That is, it discusses the relationship between Israel and Iran from the perspectives of regime security and political legitimacy—the underlying mechanisms that drive the politics of both states and fuel their animosity toward each other. For Israel, the possibility of Iranian regime security does not exist. For Iran—and particularly Mahmoud Ahmadinejad—the political legitimacy of Israel may as well be "wiped off the map" with the entire country.

Since the dawn of the Iranian Revolution, Iran has developed a contentious reputation for violence and opposition, harboring ill will and deploying occasional threats at the United States and Israel. Iranian leaders recently said "that Israel 'should be dealt with once and for all' if it makes threats to countries in the region." Ahmadinejad, the leader of Iran's government, and Ayatollah Khamenei, Iran's spiritual leader, have consistently expressed opposition to the state of Israel. In 2000, Khamenei went so far as to call for the annihilation of Israel, which he described as a "cancerous tumor" of the Middle Eastern region.

Well known in the international community for its nuclear proliferation, Iran has attracted attention on multiple fronts. In addition to frequently deploying threats at Israel, the republic's nuclear enrichment efforts and, most recently, its test launch of nuclear missiles have led some to believe that if not contained, the country will wreak havoc on the security and stability of the Middle East and perhaps of the world. Also of concern, though it does not receive the spotlight that the nuclear program does, is the use of proxy groups to fight wars and engage in skirmishes on its behalf. The surrogate groups, namely, Hamas and Hezbollah, serve as an extension of the regime's strict interpretation of Islamic values and the desire to eradicate posed threats, replacing them with uniquely Islamic (and some may argue uniquely Iranian) systems of government.

The 2006 Hezbollah attack on Israel displays a greater concern for regional stability. Iran began supplying Hezbollah with weapons in Lebanon shortly after Israel's withdraw in May 2000 for a preemptive attack to be used as a deterrent for an Israeli attack against Lebanon. As Iran was supposedly transporting relief aid to victims of a recent earthquake, missiles were secretly entering the hands of this proxy group. Though the conflict ended in a cease-fire with UN Resolution 1701, Hezbollah scored high in the eyes of the Islamic world as a militia that could withstand the Israeli Defense Force (one of the most powerful military forces in the Middle East). And even though Hezbollah encompassed several causalities, its top leaders escaped unharmed, and its efforts were still dubbed as a success.

Several factors may have contributed to Iran's decision to go down the path of acquiring and developing nuclear technology and use proxy groups to fight their battles. These factors range from military concerns (Iraq's invasion and ensuing war of 1980–1988) to feelings of insecurity as a result of U.S. and European pressure over the course of the past 30 years, including economic sanctions and attempts to isolate Iran in the international arena. Most recently, and as this book discusses, their growing nuclear ambitions stem, in part, from signals that Israel that may unilaterally or in coordination with the United States bomb Iran.

American Secretary of State Hillary Clinton feared that "ignoring the threat posed by Iran will put the world in a more precarious position within six months to a year."[5] This statement indicated that the United States is, in fact, concerned that a unilateral strike by Israel could trigger yet another regional conflict in a region already stricken by two wars. If President Obama decides to stay the course for a dialogue with the Islamic Republic, changing the approach toward the Iranian government after 30 years of heated confrontation, he will likely face serious criticism from both Americans and Iranians. First, many Iranians strongly oppose Ahmadinejad's legitimacy as the president of Iran given the accusations of fraud and the turmoil following the election. Khamenei's authority has also been damaged. American negotiation and a change of approach toward Iran should not make the regime stronger and more persistent in suppressing its domestic dissidents. Second, most European leaders have openly criticized Ahmadinejad and have announced they are not going to congratulate him for winning the election. This has even forced the White House to change its language and stance on the issue. In the meantime, while it seems like Secretary Clinton is hopeful to get a response from Iran on the U.S. initiatives, several factors are making it more and more difficult. Clinton was quoted by BBC as saying,

We've certainly reached out and made it clear that's what we'd be willing to do, even now, despite our absolute condemnation of what they've done in the [June 12 presidential] election and since, but I don't think they have any capacity to make that kind of decision right now.[6]

Would a unilateral strike against Iran enhance Israeli political legitimacy? Would increased nuclear stockpiling advance Iranian regime security? What would the impacts of an eventual confrontation between these two states be, and how might such an event affect U.S. foreign policy toward its close ally, Israel? What will the future relationship between Israel and Iran look like now that Egypt, Israel's long-time regional ally, is undergoing a revolution whose results are all but certain? Though the Obama administration very much supports direct diplomacy with Iran, Israeli opposition leader Tzipi Livni believes that the Israeli strategy of diplomacy and security should include a "process to end the [Middle East] conflict and reach an arrangement that ensures Israel's defense"[7] and by isolating Hamas, which she claims "is not a partner to peace or to an arrangement with a legitimate Palestinian government."[8] In the foreign policy agenda that the Obama administration has set forth, they have stated that the best way to make progress with Iran is to offer the regime a choice: if Iran abandons its nuclear ambitions and support for terrorist organizations such as Hamas and Hezbollah, incentives, such as membership to the "World Trade Organization, economic investments, and a move toward normal diplomatic relations,"[9] will be offered. In the event that Iran chooses not to abandon its nuclear program or support for terrorist groups, the United States has declared that it will step up political isolation and economic pressure by coordinating with allies to proceed with increased sanctions. This has caused

Supreme Leader Khamenei to shift focus to the outside world (particularly toward the United States) by increasing verbal attacks and exacerbating regional conflicts in order to diminish the civil strife that is building in Iran. Iran's well-choreographed confrontations with the United States and its use of diplomacy as a stall tactic leave little hope for a peaceful end in the near future.

Chapter 2 discusses Iranian politics with specific focus on domestic issues and international relationships. Exploring the role of president versus supreme leader, the chapter discusses constitutional limits and challenges as well as more overtly contentious issues that dominate the republic, including controversial elections, oil refinement and petroleum supply, human rights, and the pursuit of nuclear weapons. Iran is the only regime that is directly ruled by clergy in the Muslim world. The preamble of the Iranian constitution states that the *faqih* (who is considered to be an expert in Islamic law) holds all the power; he is the one who has veto power over all aspects in the political system. The *faqih* is "recognized by the majority of the people at any period as best qualified to lead the nation." This displays how important the supreme leader is in influencing the politics of the Islamic Republic. Many Iranians believe the election of the president should be a legitimate decision that should bear the endorsement and reflection of the Iranian people. In the 2009 elections, even before President Ahmadinejad was declared the winner, he fully expected to get reelected despite opposition of majority population. Though the ayatollah essentially controls all political affairs within Iran, many Iranians believe that the president's viewpoints shall influence important decisions that are made for the state and thus that the people's vote should count in the presidential elections. While the protests continue after the 2009 elections, human rights violations are continuously resurfacing as opposition supporters have been arrested, killed, tortured, and reportedly raped. As exposure increases of massive human rights violations, popular discontent toward the leaders of Iran will continue to increase as well. One of the greatest and most serious causes of regional and international concerns regarding Iran is its nuclear proliferation and ambitions. Iran's nuclear program actually dates back to the 1950s and made progress through U.S. guidance and assistance until the 1970s. Iran's clandestine revival of the program was revamped in the early 1990s with the help of Russia and has since been a concern of many international players. Suspicions of Iran's nuclear program drew even more attention in 2002 and 2003 when Iran reportedly began researching fuel enrichment, claim that this was for "clean energy for environmental, agricultural, and technological purposes." Today, all evidence shows that Iran's nuclear program is stronger than ever, posing an imminent threat to the international community.

Chapter 3 discusses the dynamics of Israeli politics and seeks to answer the question, "Can Israel live with a nuclear Iran?" It will also focus on the impact that the Palestinian-Israeli conflict and other regional disputes has on the current triangular relationship between the United States, Israel, and Iran. What would the prospect of a preemptive Israeli strike be, particularly at a time when their closest ally—the United States—is engaged in two major wars. (Though combat operations have officially ended in Iraq, a vast number of troops still remain, making any future conflicts exponentially more difficult logistically.) Israel's relationship with Turkey, Iraq, and Syria are also highlighted and examined within the context of Israel's political legitimacy in a region engulfed in conflict.

Chapter 4 discusses regional politics and addresses rhetoric versus reality in the standoff between Iran and Israel. It also focuses on regional proxy groups. Who will fill the power void left by Egypt and Ba'athist Iraq? Iran has had troubled regional relations for some time now, especially with issues of human rights violations and economic sanctions, all of which are causing several countries in the region to place blame on Iran for problems in other nations. Iran is causing concerns for its own nation with the ruling of its hard-line president: "If you listen to the democratic voices of Iranians and leaders of Iran's Green Movement there is a unanimous view that Ahmadinejad's policies have severely undermined Iranian national interests and he has inadvertently better served the interests of Israel."[10] The current regime has been able to repress this social transformation, but it is only a matter of time before a major civil reform takes place. According to one scholar "Iran is now by all accounts politically repressed, economically troubled, and socially restless."[11] Additionally, since Iran has become involved in the Israeli-Palestinian conflict, the battle is no longer viewed as a war over land; it has become a growing struggle between Islamism and the West. Since the creation of Israel, several proxy groups in the region have denied recognition of Israel's sovereignty, and thus a peaceful agreement between the two groups has yet to be agreed on; a new conflict has arose over the past two decades between Israel and the proxy groups Hezbollah and Hamas, both of which are backed by Iran. Conflicts over the past decade display a greater role of proxy groups in the Israel-Hamas-Hezbollah situation. Israel has been continuously at war with Palestinian militants, including Hamas in the Gaza Strip and with the proxy group Hezbollah in Lebanon, but there are secondary players (Iran and Syria) who have had significant impact and influence for these groups by providing them with arms, training, and financial support. Today, both Hamas and Hezbollah pose an immediate threat to stability in the Middle East because of their power and alliance to defend the ummah regardless of the different Islamic sects from which the two groups originate. Even more threatening are Hezbollah's and Hamas's backers, particularly Iran, for their continued support for such violent groups. There is no end in sight for these prominent radical groups to stop their low-level attacks on Israel and remain close allies with Iran. Though Iran has created powerful alliances with Hamas and Hezbollah in order to create a strategy to "sow the seeds of the Islamic revolution" to bring Iran closer to waging war against the West and perhaps strengthening its regional power, the legitimacy of Iran's regime has come under major scrutiny. The Israeli-Palestinian conflict has caused an unstable environment for several decades, and Islamic groups that came about after the revolution are causing major issues in regional politics today.

Chapter 5 focuses exclusively on the issue of nuclear weapons. The rights to acquire sources of energy versus the risks of nuclear proliferation are discussed within the context of Middle Eastern aspirations for power. Iran's nuclear threat is causing Israel serious concern, but some sources reveal that Iran is already capable of causing immense damage to Israel if it desires to do so. Iran has claimed on several occasions that it wishes to "wipe Israel off the face of the earth,"[12] and it currently has missiles that are capable of reaching Israel.[13] Israel has stated that it considers Iran the most dangerous enemy and will consider all options to stop Iran's nuclear development.[14] While the United States has a huge influence on Israel, the Obama administration should keep these threats in consideration, particularly in the development of its foreign policy with Iran. Since President Bush labeled Iran part of the "axis of evil," proposals for engagement have gone from preemptive strike to diplomatic engagement, and the future appears to be the same. In the eyes of the Iranians who support Iran's right to nuclear energy, Iran will continue to be a nation victimized by hegemonic political and economic pressures until attention can be drawn away from Iran's existing nuclear discourse. Until then, the international community will be vigilant of Iran's nuclear developments.

Chapter 6 discusses the importance of recent conflicts on the current situation in the Middle East. These conflicts include the 2006 Hezbollah War, the 2008 Hamas War, and various other episodes of regional and international violence that directly impact the relationship between Israel and Iran. Since its inception, Hezbollah's and Israel's fates have been intertwined as Hezbollah has sought to resist Israeli expansion into Israel and Israel has sought to fight back Hezbollah. Hezbollah and Israel have been involved in a number of confrontations. From its creation until 2000, Hezbollah has carried out an extensive guerilla campaign against Israel. Israel's "Operation Accountability" in 1993 and "Operation Grapes of Wrath" in 1996 were launched in response to Hezbollah's attacks on Israeli civilians and soldiers. While these campaigns were significant, it was the early twenty-first-century campaigns that resulted in the largest political gains for Hezbollah.

According to the United States Institute of Peace, "The departure of Israeli forces from Lebanon in 2000 and of Syrian forces in 2003 vaulted Hezbollah to the forefront of the Lebanese political scene." Hezbollah's

military success against Israel has led to validation and its virtual legitimatization. During the 2006 confrontation, Hezbollah managed to resist
defeat, and the Israeli withdrawal from Lebanon resulted in increased
prestige for the Iranian-funded organization.[15] This campaign was especially significant, as Hezbollah was able to claim victory despite heavy
casualties and Israeli's heavy-handed response garnered sympathy for
the group and resulted in an increase in political power. Throughout the
campaign, Hezbollah was supported politically and financially by Iran.
According to Bickerton and Klausner, "Israelis claimed that their ultimate
antagonists were neither Hamas nor Hizbullah, but Iran and Syria, which
provided both groups with financial and logistical assistance as well as
political support."[16] While Iran may not have been a direct participant
in the 2006 Israeli campaign against Lebanon (in terms of military
involvement), it was most definitely an integral part of what allowed
Hezbollah to have such success against the well-equipped and battle-
proven Israeli forces. One account observes, "Most of Hezbollah's arms—
including modern antitank weapons and the thousands of rockets that
rained down on Israel—came from Iran (as well as Syria). Iran advisers
had spent years helping Hezbollah train and build fortified positions
throughout southern Lebanon."[17] Hezbollah had spent six years preparing
for a war against Israel and had been able to employ unconventional methods to hold its own against the perceived superior military. In addition, the
2006 Hezbollah resistance "enabled Tehran to rally Muslim opinion and
score a strategic, albeit indirect, gain."[18]

Chapter 7 discusses the concept of regime security versus political
legitimacy with regard to the complex relationship between Iran and the
United States. For the United States in particular, relations have been continuously back and forth for some time. The contentious relationship
began before the shah took the throne when the United States and the
British organized and assisted in nationalizing Iran's oil industry. After
the coup, the shah took over as the United States had pushed to overthrew
Iran's prime minister and install a government that favored U.S. foreign
policy. Looking back at U.S.-Iranian relations under the rule of the shah,
it is easy to see that the United States had a dominant presence in Iran
for many years before the revolution, and, just as many Iranians opposed
this overbearing westernization back then, this rhetoric continues today,
especially as put forth by the current hard-line Iranian president and
some of the fundamentalist groups, such as Hezbollah and Hamas. Will
the United States look backward in time and reflect on contemporary
challenges with historical musings? Will the rhetorical back-and-forth
eventuate in military action? How will the United States react if Israel
strikes Iran? How will the current foreign policy in the Middle East fluctu-
ate in the likely event that Iran continues to develop nuclear weapons?
These questions and others like them are addressed in this chapter.

Whether the stakes are Iranian regime security or Israeli political legitimacy, the growing antipathy between these two Middle Eastern nations is not likely to subside soon. Nonetheless, by uncovering the real motives for the saber rattling and political posturing that has become all too common over the past 30 years (and more pronounced than ever within the past two years), there may be a shimmer of possibilities with regard to international security.

CHAPTER 2

Iranian Politics: Domestic Issues and International Relationships

Since the dawn of the Iranian Revolution, Iran has developed a contentious reputation for violence and opposition for the United States and Israel alike. The Islamic Republic has become well known in the international community for its nuclear proliferation, its continuous violations of human rights, and its support for proxy groups in the area. The 2009 elections, which have been greatly disputed regionally and internationally, have caused Iran great scrutiny that will likely continue to make the legitimacy of the Iranian government questionable. This chapter looks briefly at the recent history of Iran's international relations and developments and explores factors pressuring and influencing regional and international politics in Iran, including proxy groups, such as Hamas and Hezbollah. We also explore several possibilities for Iran's future on the aftermath of the 2009 controversial presidential elections as Iran continues its nuclear program and support for proxy groups in two parallel tracks.

It was not always the case that Iran had such a radical view of Islamic principles. When the shah took throne in the early 1940s, Iran began turning into a modern pro-Western nation; women were banned from wearing the Islamic veil, men in governmental offices were required to wear Western clothes, women were allowed in Tehran University and were allowed to vote, and the Islamic calendar was even abolished. This pro-Western sentiment angered the ayatollah of the time, Ruhollah Khomeini, who would later overthrow the shah and reinstate Iran as an Islamic state.[1] This journey was not so easy, however. As the shah broke down the Islamic state from 1941 until 1979, Iran began developing strong alliances with the United States and Israel. By 1964, the alliance with the United States was so strong that the shah declared legal immunity to all U.S. military advisers and their families and other technical and administrative staff who committed any crime on Iranian territory. Ayatollah Khomeini cried to the Muslim people, "They [the shah and his advisers] have reduced the Iranian people to a lower level than that of the American dog."[2] He added,

> If someone runs over a dog belonging to an American soldier, he will be prosecuted. Even if the Shah himself were to run over a dog belonging to an American, he would be prosecuted. But if an American cook runs over the Shah, the head of the state, no one will have the right to interfere with him. . . . The government has sold our independence, reduced us to the level of a colony, and made the Muslim nation of Iran appear more backward than savages in the eyes of the world! . . . This is high treason![3]

Cries as such to the Muslim world, particularly those in Iran, continued by the ayatollah until antigovernment protests and violent demonstrations eventually led to what was called the "largest protest event in history—" a day when over 9 million Iranians (over a quarter of the population at that time) demonstrated against the shah.[4]

On February 1, 1979, Ayatollah Khomeini returned to Iran. That day marked the time when international relations with Iran would change forever. Khomeini proclaimed to return Iran to an Islamic state and adhere to the law of God (known as Shari'a); this would lead norms and laws to be derived from interpretations of religious texts (namely, the Koran) and by traditions of prophets. Shortly after the revolution of 1979, several Islamic fundamentalist groups, such as Islamic Jihad and the Muslim Brotherhood, were created.[5] Over time, both Hamas (which originated from the Muslim Brotherhood) and Hezbollah have evolved with the common goal to overpower the United States and Israel and spread their particular interpretations of Islam. Iran has displayed an overwhelming amount of support for these groups in order to help achieve their overarching goals. The country's support for these proxies has raised serious concerns from many within international community, and Iran's international relations have revolved primarily around its support for terrorist groups, its nuclear ambitions, and its alleged corrupt government.

For the United States in particular, relations have been continuously back and forth for quite some time. The contentious relationship began before the shah took throne; the United States and Britain organized a government coup to overthrow Iran's prime minister in order to assist in nationalizing Iran's oil industry.[6] After the coup, the shah took over as the United States pushed him into power and became a puppet of U.S. foreign policy. Looking back at U.S.-Iranian relations under the rule of the shah, it is easy to see that the United States had a dominant presence in Iran for many years before the revolution, and just as many Iranians opposed this overbearing westernization back then, this rhetoric continues today, especially by the current hard-line Iranian president and some of the fundamentalist groups, such as Hezbollah and Hamas.

Iran's nuclear threat is causing Israel serious concern, but some sources reveal that Iran is already capable of causing immense damage to Israel if it desires to do so. Iran has claimed on several occasions that it wishes to "wipe Israel off the face of the earth"[7] and has the nuclear capability of reaching Israel.[8] Israel has stated time and again that Iran poses the greatest threat to its security.[9] While the United States has a huge influence on Israel, the new U.S. administration should consider these threats in developing its foreign policy with Iran. Since President George W. Bush labeled Iran as part of the "axis of evil," proposals for engagement have gone from preemptive strike to diplomatic engagement, and the future appears to be the same.

The relationship of the United States with Iran has played a more constructive role under the Obama administration by avoiding military threats and economic sanctions, but this may not last long if the Islamic Republic continues on the path that it is on. Though the Obama administration very much supports direct diplomacy, Israeli opposition leader Tzipi Livni believes that the Israeli strategy of diplomacy and security should include a "process to end the [Middle East] conflict and reach an arrangement that ensures Israel's defense" and that isolates Hamas, which she claims "is not a partner to peace or to an arrangement with a legitimate Palestinian government."[10] In the foreign policy agenda that the Obama administration set forth, they appear to believe that the best way to make progress with Iran is to offer the regime a choice: if Iran abandons its nuclear ambitions and support for terrorist organizations such as Hamas and Hezbollah, incentives, such as membership to the "World Trade Organization, economic investments, and a move toward normal diplomatic relations," will be offered. In the event that Iran chooses not to abandon its nuclear program or support for terrorist groups, the United States has declared that it will step up political isolation and economic pressure by coordinating with allies to proceed with increased sanctions.[11] This has caused Supreme Leader Khamenei to shift his focus to the outside world (particularly toward the United States) by increasing verbal attacks and exacerbating regional conflicts in order to diminish the civil strife that is building in Iran.[12] Iran's well-choreographed confrontations with the United States and its use of diplomacy as a stall tactic leaves little hope for a peaceful end in the near future. According to Nasser Hadiyan, university professor and Iranian-U.S. affairs analyst, the current relationship with Iran and the United States "cannot be easily improved and possibility of détente is not on the horizon as a reward structure exists in both countries which encourages severance of relations and punishes those who want to improve the situation." Hadiyan believes that Iran and the United States are presently engaged in a Cold War that is characterized by continuous ebbs and flows, and until this structure changes, there is not much hope for better relations between the two nations. However, Hadiyan does believe that the Obama administration has provided a diplomatic apparatus that has a better capacity than any preceding administration to apply a policy of containment and selective relationship by trying to isolate Iran politically and enforce more economic sanctions.[13]

Iran has also had troubled regional relations for some time now with its issues of human rights violations and economic sanctions, all of which causing several regional countries to place blame on Iran for problems in other nations. Iran is causing several issues for its own nation with the ruling of its hard-line president. "If you listen to the democratic voices of Iranians and leaders of Iran's Green Movement there is a unanimous view that Ahmadinejad's policies have severely undermined Iranian national interests and he has inadvertently better served the interests of Israel."[14] The current regime has been able to repress this social transformation, but it is only a matter of time before a major civil reform takes place. According to one scholar, "Iran is now by all accounts politically repressed, economically troubled, and socially restless."[15]

Iran has set itself apart from other Middle Eastern states in a number of ways, but, historically, the country is unique: Iran is the only regime in the Muslim world that is directly ruled by clergy. The preamble of the Iranian constitution states that the *faqih* (who is considered to be an expert in Islamic law) holds all the power; he is the one who has veto power over all aspects of the political system. The *faqih* is "recognized by the majority of the people at any period as best qualified to lead the nation."[16] This displays how important the supreme leader is in influencing politics of the Islamic Republic. In addition, the *faqih* is responsible for appointing the jurists of the Guardian Council (GC), which is responsible for ensuring that all legislation and bills that are passed are in accordance with Islam. Any political candidates who run for office must be approved by the religious tests of the GC; the *faqih* even approves political candidates. A concept that is strikingly alarming in the international world is that "neither the *faqih* nor the GC is accountable to the public."[17] The disputed elections of June 12, 2009, display the *faqih* rulings to be supreme, but this has caused Iran major controversy in the international arena and even greater dismay among the Iranian people. It is the religious duty of the rulers within the Islamic Republic to ensure political obedience by entailing absolute loyalty to the *vilayet-e faqih* in the election process and other regime-sponsored events.[18]

Many Iranians believe that the election of the president should be a legitimate decision that should bear the endorsement and reflect the will of the Iranian people. In the 2009 elections, even before President Mahmoud Ahmadinejad was declared the winner, he fully expected to get reelected despite the opposition of the majority population. Though the ayatollah essentially controls all political affairs within Iran, many Iranians believe that the president's viewpoints should influence important decisions that are made for the state, and thus the people's vote should count in the presidential elections. The recent elections show the supremacy of all decisions, being based on clerical rule regardless of the majority vote. In order to unite the reformist vote against the possibility of Ahmadinejad's being reelected, Ahmadinejad's principal rival, former president Mohammad Khatami, dropped out of the race to avoid a split between the two primary reformist candidates. Khatami wanted to limit the chance of Ahmadinejad's becoming reelected and felt that conservatives would be more apt to vote for a reformist candidate and former prime minister Mir-Hossein Mousavi instead of himself. Under increasing pressure, Mehdi Karroubi, the other reformist candidate, also withdrew.[19] After the outcome of the 2009 elections was announced, several protestors took to the streets claiming fraud while security forces took down and killed several of the protesters. Iranians strongly reject President Ahmadinejad's claim to leadership, and they strongly oppose any meeting or recognition on the international level.[20] The prodemocracy movement (the Green Movement) in Iran unanimously believes that Ahmadinejad was "reappointed" after stealing millions of votes in the 2009 presidential election.[21] The turnout of the elections, to a great extent, caused the international community to view Iran's regime as illegitimate.

While the protests have continued following the 2009 elections, human rights violations continually resurface as opposition supporters are arrested, killed, tortured, and reportedly raped.[22] As knowledge of the country's massive human rights violations increases, popular discontent toward the leaders of Iran will continue to increase as well. In fact, there have been recent claims of several prominent figures publicly opposing the supreme leader, and many have openly criticized his regime.[23] Though more recent years have led the international community to become more focused on Iran's nuclear ambitions and Ahmadinejad's rhetoric toward Israel and denying the Holocaust, human rights violations will likely soon become an issue important to other democratic nations. After the 2009 elections, it would be safe to say that, in the near future, a major social movement is likely to occur in Iran. The massive uprisings following the elections show the Iranian population's true call for change, and this social movement will likely create a "strong and dynamic force to topple the current government and instill one with more socially and politically liberal policies."[24] One news agency reports that a major social movement "will effectively destroy the religious hold over politics and create, to some extent, a secular, Islamo-influenced government" and would ultimately throw out the Islam-based government that has influenced Iran for over two generations. Essentially, the Islamic Republic is potentially threatening the sheer existence of Iran by its "political malleability and ineffectiveness at defending their positions when blatant human rights violations are occurring in plain view."[25]

Throughout the revolution, it was argued that there was "no monolithic 'Islamic Ideology' that united the many diverse groups that formed the revolutionary alliance."[26] Much like today, several groups and social classes will have competing interpretations of Islam as political ideology. The Islamic world today includes over 50 nations where Muslims constitute the majority population; in Iran, the Muslim population is currently 97 percent (89% Shia and 9% Sunni). The majority of the world's Islamic population, which is Sunni, accounts for over 75 percent of the Islamic population; the other 10 to 20 percent is Shia. While the two Muslim branches (Sunni and Shia) disagree over the issue of religious versus political leadership, the majority of the world's Muslim population is united by their poor and undeveloped societies, lack of economic and military resources, and the overarching prevalence of poverty,[27] and many are urged to unite through their hatred of the West. The fundamental difference between Shia Muslims and Sunni Muslims is their belief about who the rightful successor to Muhammad is: Ali or the first three caliphs after Muhammad, including Abu Bakr. This struggle began in the AD 632 when the Sunnis and the Shi'ites disputed the rightful successor of the Prophet Muhammad. Even today, there is still an underlying struggle between Shi'ites and Sunnis (though more common and more violent in Iraq), and it is feared that this struggle may spread to Iran in the near future. There is also a major difference between Sunnis and Shi'ites in their interpretation of the hidden imam (or the twelfth iman). Today, some Sunnis believe that Shi'ites are "actually attributing almost divine qualities to the imams, and this is a great sin" because this means "associating human beings with the divinity."[28] Putting religious differences aside, Iran has called all Muslims to disregard these differences and unite against the greater infidels of the world: Israel and the United States. Iran has attempted to achieve world Islamic power by uniting Sunni and Shi'ites groups, and now many Middle Eastern states fear the "Shi'ite Crescent," spanning from Iran through Lebanon. Now the influence of "Iranian radicalism knows no boundaries, thanks to Tehran's increasingly pragmatic approach toward Sunni groups."[29]

Though Iran's population is primarily Shia and upholds viewpoints and beliefs that may not necessarily be parallel with the world's majority Islamic population, there has been a great push for Muslim unity since the 1979 revolution, particularly against the United States and Israel. Muslims across the world may have different opinions on who the rightful successor to Muhammad is, leading them to have different views of schooling and Islamic jurisprudence,[30] but this does not stop Iran senior Shia cleric

Ayatollah Ali Khamenei from urging Muslims to unite against Israel for the greater cause of Palestinians. And there may be a legitimate reason for concern regarding this exhortation. Most recently, in a three-way meeting between Iran, Syria, and Indonesia, Khamenei urged Muslim countries to take unified action to help Palestinians achieve their rights and help put an end to the Gaza siege. A top Indonesian official adds that the Asian Parliamentary Assembly, which now has 41 members and 17 countries with observer status, potentially has the power "to unify Muslim member states against Israel."[31] In addition, Khamenei also said in his speech to U.S. Secretary of State Hillary Clinton, in her first visit to the Middle East since taking office, that "support and help to Palestinians is a mandatory duty of all Muslims. I now tell all Muslim brothers and sisters to join forces and break the immunity of the Zionist criminals." President Ahmadinejad, is also calling for a "global anti-Zionist front."[32]

Additionally, Iran has held several conferences aimed at aligning Sunni and Shi'ite groups, while scholars of both groups lecture on the importance of "unity and solidarity among Muslims in the face of the arrogant powers."[33] Several Islamic countries in the area (including Syria and Lebanon) have sided with Iran in claiming that Western countries are trying to create discord among Shi'ites and Sunnis in order to steal oil and energy from Islamic nations.[34] Several Islamic nations have claimed that the United States and its allies are seeking to annihilate Islam for fear that "Islam would revive and reconstruct its previous civilization."[35] Islamic nations have united in several conventions to form a strong alliance against Western countries. One recent convention, called "The Role of Islamic Ummah's Unity in the Face of Imperialism," held in Damascus, Syria, marks the sixth conference arranged by the Islamic Republic of Iran. Though Iran is a primary concern in this Islamic unity movement, both Syria and Lebanon have become increasingly alarmed as well; while Syrian Islamic scholars declare that it is the duty of all university students to promote Islamic unity,[36] Lebanese professors point out the need for Islamic resistance to create unity among the Muslim population in order to apply new pressure to their enemies. Though Islamic nations have differences in their religious preferences, they have found common ground in their hatred for the United States and other Western countries, and while Iran may not be a complete and recognized regional leader in the area, it has undoubtedly gained acceptance in its persistent pursuit of Islamic political rule and its focus on Islamic fundamentalism.

The specifics of Iran's nuclear capabilities are discussed later in greater detail, but for the moment it is important to situate this ever-so-important topic within the historical framework that animates the contemporary dynamics of the republic's international relationships. After all, as the 2010 WikiLeaks have revealed, Iran's nuclear program is the main concern among the leaders of many Arab states who have secretly urged the

United States to intervene for the sake of Middle East security. Iran's pursuit of nuclear capabilities is nothing new. In fact, Iran's first nuclear program was established with U.S. support in the 1960s, a time during which Iranian-American relations were stable as the shah of Iran positioned Iran as an ally of the West. The Iranian Revolution of 1979 would topple the shah's government, and the new Islamic republic of Iran would not actively pursue nuclear capabilities until the mid-1990s. While Iran claimed that it was adhering to requirements of the Non-Proliferation Treaty, documents procured in 2002 by an Iranian exile group exposed a hidden Iranian nuclear program.[37] While Khatami's relatively moderate government agreed to inspections by the International Atomic Energy Agency (IAEA) and worked to resolve the nuclear issue diplomatically, Iran's position of cooperativeness would change with the election of Ahmadinejad in 2005. In 2006, Iran announced its intention to work toward uranium enrichment, and in February 2010, Iran announced its intention to begin the process of enriching its stockpile of uranium.[38] According to the *New York Times*, "On Feb. 18, 2010, the United Nations' nuclear inspectors declared for the first time that they had extensive evidence of 'past or current undisclosed activities' by Iran's military to develop a nuclear warhead."[39]

Iran's possession of nuclear weapons could be extremely dangerous for a number of reasons. It could set off an arms race in the Middle East as other states move to increase their nuclear arsenals or develop weaponry to compete with Iran's capabilities. In addition, there is the potential that the weapons may fall into the hands of a nonstate actor, either by accident or on purpose. Finally, Iran's nuclear capabilities may cause other states to act militarily to preempt an Iranian strike.[40] Acting in clear opposition to international demands, Ahmadinejad "has frustrated the West but pleased many in Iran by his refusal to give in to international demands to curtail his country's nuclear and missile development program, maintaining his view that Iran has a right to civilian nuclear energy and denying the country is pursuing nuclear weapons."[41] By acting against the will of the international community, Iran has poised itself as a symbol of anti-Westernism, in essence positioning itself as a country that will not let the West trample on the rights of people in regions such as the Middle East. In a way, this position is reminiscent of the stance taken in the 1960s by the leader of the pan-Arab nationalist movement, Gamal Abdel Nasser, in an effort to portray its stance as one for the rights of the region. While Nasser took a secular stance, Iran, a non-Arab nation, has appealed to religion as a means of uniting causes and attracting support.

It was just 10 years after Nasser's movement that Iran, along with other members of the international community, signed the Nuclear Non-Proliferation Treaty. The treaty states that any nation cannot independently seek to procure nuclear technology materials, although the treaty also specifically states that it will aid in the "peaceful use of atoms." As we have witnessed over recent years, this has been the crux of Iran's argument for enriching uranium, however disputed that may be.

It seems clear at this point that Iran is well on its way to developing and perhaps even deploying a sustainable array of nuclear weaponry even though the certainty of such notions remains ambiguous. The United States, however, has cited Iran's advancements in ballistic missile technology (i.e., the Shahab-3 intermediate-range ballistic missile), its belligerent attitude, and its clandestine actions as evidence that Tehran has a sinister intent behind its pursuit of highly enriched uranium, certainly not one of "peaceful use" related to energy concerns. The United States has also voiced concern over Iran's emerging nuclear capabilities because of its connection with various terrorist groups, as is discussed in more detail toward the end of the chapter.

Iran has denied these accusations and points to its joint project with Russia, the Bushehr nuclear power plant, as proof that it is seeking nuclear energy, not that it is seeking to become a nuclear power. Iran stands on its sovereign right to pursue technical "know-how," and it views the United States as a hegemonic power that bullies whenever it can. Reports on Iran show that it has an extensive nuclear infrastructure with over a dozen declassified sites; of special interest are the technological-academic complexes in Tehran and Esfahan, the underground enrichment facilities in Natanz, and several storage facilities, including Lashkar Ab'ad and Anarak.

Europe has indicated that diplomatic dialogue, along with diplomatic pressure, can bring about a favorable solution. Europe has also been clear that it is resistant to the idea of supporting military strikes. Meanwhile, China and Russia have been slow to act and have been even more skeptical of the U.S. position. At times, however, both countries have tentatively joined together in putting limited pressure on Iran, but Russia in particular has been apt to play both sides of the coin. For example, Russia has withdrawn its physicists from Iran and stopped construction at the Bushehr site, which is 60 percent complete, but in Munich earlier in the year, Russian President Vladimir Putin announced that he would send millions of dollars worth of antiaircraft equipment to Iran.

The United States became increasingly hostile over Iran's infractions and defiance in the winter of 2006 and early spring of 2007. Originally, Washington appeared to be on the verge of using military force, but the actions of Secretary of Defense Robert Gates have signaled Washington's return to the international community since the resignation of the former secretary of defense, Donald Rumsfeld. Although initiating a direct diplomatic dialogue cannot be proposed by either Tehran or Washington, Secretary Gates has put more emphasis on finding a diplomatic solution and has asserted support for the attempt to use economic pressure to reach a resolution to the problem, "A diplomatic solution is [the] best way to deal with Iran's nuclear program, because, 'having to take care of this problem militarily is in no one's interest.'"[42] The United States and Europe also said that they would be willing to aid Iran in the nuclear production of energy by granting them access to Russian refinement facilities,[43] but the United States still warns that military strikes will be considered if Iran does not suspend its enrichment program. To date, it is also important to note that the U.S. Navy has maintained, if not increased, its threatening posture in the Persian Gulf.

Iran, however, has stood by its policy of having a fundamental "national right" to pursue technological advancement for peaceful purposes. As such, Iran has stated that it will not necessarily concede to provisions that are not specifically mentioned in the IAEA's regulations,[44] and has charged that the West and the United Nations, the latter being controlled by the West, is acting in a discriminatory manner. As such, Iran has vowed that it will not suspend its enrichment programs, especially for an unspecified amount of time, and to assert this position, Iran has retaliated by reducing the transparency that it has previously allowed to the IAEA and its inspectors. However, during this phase of the media war, Iran maintains that it is welcoming international involvement in helping to find a reasonable solution, and recently the secretary of Iran's Supreme National Security Council, Ali Larijani, has said, "We are not interested to see any outstanding issues between Iran and the IAEA. We call for more IAEA supervision to resolve our issues."[45] Iran has also sought to outflank Washington's media maneuvers (meant to induce fear in Europe) by emphasizing that Iranian missiles do not have the range to threaten Europe and that Iran would never target such a productive business partner.[46]

In terms of escalation, Iran has been brought before the UN Security Council on the grounds that it has hindered IAEA oversight, and as a result, two relatively mild UN sanctions have been imposed on Iran since December (there is currently a stronger, third sanction pending), and as Secretary of Defense Gates said, these sanctions would force the Tehran government to "begin to face some serious trade-offs in terms of their economic well-being and their economic future for the sake of having nuclear weapons"[47] based on the hope that Iran's "third force," its young people, will pressure its government to concede. The United States has also unilaterally continued to pursue tougher "individual sanctions" with some success.

Iran has countered by saying that these resolutions will not alter Iran's course and pose no real threat to Iran's moral or its economy. "The Iranian nation does not give the slightest value to your resolution,"[48] said Iranian President Ahmadinejad at a rally in the city of Semnan on June 13, 2007. Iran has also questioned the legitimacy of the sanctions on the grounds that the Security Council has no jurisdiction over what it considers an IAEA affair, and Iranian ambassador to the IAEA, Ali Soltanieh, has said that "for every action, such as sanctions, there is a reaction."[49] Meanwhile, Muhammed el-Baradei, the head of the IAEA who, in January 2011, led opposition protests against Hosni Mubarak's regime, called Iran's stubbornness "regrettable" and "disconcerting" while also maintaining that a military attack would be "madness."

In terms of deescalation, there have been third-party discussions between the IAEA, Western European policy policymakers, and Iranian officials in an effort to diffuse the problem. So far, these talks have failed to reach any solid results, but each side has stated that "progress has been made" and that the talks should therefore continue. Talks in June of 2009 between the European Union's J. Solana and Iran ended in failure as did the most recent talks in January of 2011.[50] Despite the fact that both sides declare the necessity of meetings and follow-ups, they rarely produce tangible results and their lack of success has become predictable. The United States has expressed its impatience over these stall tactics, and Israel has joined the United States recently in saying that it "has not ruled out military action, although it also prefers a diplomatic solution."[51]

The most well-known and debated problem with the U.S. and Israeli strategy of preemption against Iran is, as this book discusses, legitimacy. The advantages of striking Iran might be great if the threat was unambiguous, but Iran's nuclear intentions are far from being unambiguous despite all the saber rattling.

To some degree, difficulty in establishing legitimacy is a problem endemic to preventive military action; as Mueller and colleagues state, "Rallying international and domestic support for preventive attacks to deal with threats that are neither imminent nor certain tends to be intrinsically difficult, and their political costs can be high."[52]

In the case of Iran, this is heightened because of the country's proximity to what many abroad feel was an "illegitimate" invasion of Iraq in 2003. This is true of Russia, China, and many Muslim nations, and it has also caused extreme tension with many of the traditional allies of the United States. As Robert Kagan writes,

Will the West still be the West? A few years ago, such questions were unthinkable.... Conflicts might divide the West from the rest, but not the West itself. That reasonable assumption has now been thrown into doubt, for it is precisely the question of legitimacy that divides Americans and Europeans today.... For the first time since World War II, a majority of Europeans has come to doubt the legitimacy of US power and US global leadership.[53]

This feeling is hardly expected to go away if the United States goes to war with Iran, being that Secretary of Defense Gates has stated openly, in response to Iran's intent, that "the reality is—we really don't know."[54] Part of the reason that the United States is struggling with this question is that the United States and Europe view the rationale for military action in different terms. Whereas many in the United States thought that "coalition building" and going through the motions of working through the UN Security Council could substitute for actual approval from the UN Security Council, most Europeans, especially Western Europeans, do not.[55]

Joanna Spear cites five reasons to explain why the United States is having trouble getting international support for enforcing nuclear nonproliferation in Iran. First, Europeans do not feel so threatened by Iran or Muslim extremists that they believe they would use weapons of mass destruction against them. Second, Europeans see Iran as an important trading partner and are especially connected to Iran's petroleum. In this regard, cooperation is always more beneficial than confrontation. Third, European security planners view proliferation through the context of regional power balances and therefore do not single out weapons of mass destruction as a point of concern. In addition, many in postmodern Europe are averse to the idea of power politics and therefore view all proliferation with a disinterested disgust. For example, many Europeans look down on Israel's weapons program as much as they look down on that of anyone else. Finally, European intelligence agencies, because of budget constraints, are often unable to independently verify intelligence claims by their U.S. counterparts, and this often breeds a certain amount of skepticism.[56] Europeans also believe that the diplomatic process and lengthy dialogues of engagement are the way to handle concerns regarding proliferation:

Europeans believe that the way forward is to engage problem states, not merely to contain them and freeze the situation into a hostile status quo. For example, during the cold war the West Germans pursued a policy of *Ostpolitik*, trying to get Communist East Germany to open up. European diplomats have adopted a "critical dialogue" with Iran. They believe that this has yielded benefits such as a decrease in Iranian terrorism in Europe. . . . There have been positive results, too, from Italy's "critical dialogue" with Libya, its one time colony.[57]

The problem of legitimacy in the case of preemptively striking Iran is that if the United States decides to defy the rest of the world and use the approach of "you're either with us or against us," the United States may well find itself permanently separated from the global community. Over the past several years, the United States has been able to partially get the international community back. For example, NATO has taken a larger role in Afghanistan and Lebanon, and Russia has temporarily withdrawn its physicists from Bushehr and was instrumental in ratifying UN sanctions against Iran. But the relationship remains weak and tense, and maybe this is rather unfortunate because many analysts believe that Iran is a much more real concern than Iraq was in 2003. As Kagan states,

Herein lies the tragedy. To address today's global dangers, Americans will need the legitimacy that Europe can provide, but Europeans may well fail to grant it. In their effort to constrain the superpower, they might lose sight of the mounting dangers in the world, which are far greater than those posed by the United States.[58]

Washington, for its part, has already used up too much of its political capital on preemptivism. All supporters of military action in Iran, whether they be unilateralists or multilateralists (who see force as the last step in a diplomatic process), assume that at some point the "duty to act" will correspond with the "ability to be effective."

An April 2010 *New York Times* article explains a deficiency in U.S. capabilities, citing the potential for Iran to become a "virtual" nuclear weapons state should it choose to do so.[59] While the Obama administration has disputed allegations of being ill prepared in regard to its Iranian policy, a recent three-page memorandum released by Secretary of Defense Robert Gates allegedly says that "the United States does not have an effective long-term policy for dealing with Iran's steady progress toward nuclear capability."[60]

Iran's nuclear ambitions have recently incited speculation and fears of an escalation of hostilities between Hezbollah and Israel—an encore performance, perhaps, of the 2006 conflict. According to Blanford, "Given the rising tensions and recent strengthening of an Iran-led alliance in the Mideast, a war between Hezbollah and Israel could expand to become a regional conflagration involving Iran and Syria, both of which support the Lebanese Shiite party."[61] In addition, Israel has made it clear that it is willing to strike Iran in a preemptive attack if it feels threatened by the development of Iran's nuclear program. If such an attack were to occur, Syria and Hezbollah would likely become entangled in the conflict.[62]

Haseeb notes that Mohammed Mohtadi, an Iranian political commentator, summarizes Iran's concern with Israel as being twofold (1) "the importance of the cause of Palestine and the Holy Land, and the impermissibility of neglecting this central issue that concerns all Arabs and Muslims" and (2) the "strategic importance of the Persian Gulf area and the Sea of Oman, as a vital artery for Iran."[63] In addition, from the perspective of Middle East relations as a zero-sum game, where one country gains power only at the expense of another's losing it, growing Israeli hegemony in the region represents a reduction in Iranian and Arab power and "is tantamount to weakening the Muslims ... in the heartland of the Islamic world."[64] From Iran's perspective (referring to the current position of the Iranian government), the presence of Israel in the region is unacceptable, representing an invasion of Muslim holy lands that must be removed.

Iran continues to express support for activities against Israel, recently saying "that Israel 'should be dealt with once and for all' if it makes threats to countries in the region."[65] Ahmadinejad, the leader of Iran's government, and Ayatollah Khamenei, Iran's spiritual leader, have consistently expressed opposition to the state of Israel. In 2000, Khamenei went so far as to call for the annihilation of Israel, which he described as a "cancerous tumor" in the Middle East.[66]

Consistent with the rhetoric of the Iranian elite, Iran has provided Hezbollah with an enormous operating budget as well as arms and training. Using Hezbollah as a tool for operating against Israel and extending its influence in the region, Iran has backed the group with a significant amount of resources. While the Shia Hezbollah has received the majority of Iranian support, Iran has also backed other Sunni and secular organizations, such as Hamas, the Palestinian Jihad, and the Popular Front for the Liberation of Palestine—General Command. All these groups are directed toward action against Israel.[67]

In February 2010, Iranian President Ahmadinejad met with the Syrian president and the head of Hezbollah, Sheikh Nasrallah, at a joint summit in Damascus that "was seen as a strengthening of the 'axis of resistance' against Israel and a snub to U.S. efforts to encourage Damascus to break its three-decade alliance with Tehran."[68] For now, the alliance against Israel seems to be strong and shows no sign of decline as Iran continues to support movements against Israeli interests by backing Hezbollah and other anti-Israeli movements.

Though proxy groups have long been central part of Iran's regional and even international military operations, it is the strength of Iran's military itself—not surrogates—that will ultimately decide whether diplomacy prevails or war breaks out. Before the 1979 Iranian Revolution, the U.S.-backed Iranian military was one of the most capable in the Middle East; however, the revolution and a series of military confrontations with Iraq have severely hampered its abilities. According to GlobalSecurity.org, "Subsequent to the end of the eight-year Iran-Iraqi conflict that decimated Iran's military capability, Iran has been in a gradual armament and military infrastructure rebuilding process."[69] Iran's military objectives appear to be concentrated on maintaining internal security and preventing the United States from expanding its influence in the Persian Gulf.[70] While the Iranian military does not appear to have the ability to carry out an effective ground force campaign and its air defense is equally deficit with only modest offensive capability, efforts have been made to increase defense spending and modernize the Iranian military.[71]

Iran's military strength remains concentrated in its strategic missile forces. On the April celebration of the thirty-first anniversary of the

Iranian Revolutionary Guard, Iran displayed its military strength in a series of war games that culminated in Iran firing five missiles of various ranges.[72] The military exercises were conducted in the Strait of Hormuz, a waterway vital to transportation of oil in the Persian Gulf.[73] Around 300 boats carrying torpedoes and guided- missiles were deployed in the naval maneuvers.[74] Iran also claims to have missiles that are capable of reaching targets in Israel as well as U.S. interests, although some analysts have disputed this claim.[75]

Iran's military capabilities seem to be focused on certain sectors, with certain programs, such as ballistics, receiving more funding and seeing more success than other areas. Even so, "Iran's military technology is second in the region only to the United States," although some Gulf Arab counties have been purchasing weapons contracts that may challenge Iran's power in the future.[76] Even with some "antiquated" military features, the Iranian military does present a substantial threat in the region, and U.S. leaders have warned of the growing power and influence of the Iranian Revolutionary Guard. Recently, U.S. Secretary of State Hillary Clinton said that she fears that Iran is moving "toward a military dictatorship" and that "the rise of the influence and power of the Revolutionary Guard poses a very direct threat to everyone."[77]

The rise of influence and power that Clinton noted comes, in part, as the result of a void left in the region by the removal of Saddam Hussein from power. The U.S. invasion of Iraq and removal of its leader provided an opportunity for Iran to fill a gap as the Iraqi check on Iranian power was removed. As Ted Carpenter and Malou Innocent note, the invasion of Iraq radically changed the power dynamic in the Middle East, and "America's removal of Saddam Hussein as the principle strategic counterweight to Iran paved the way for an expansion of Iran's influence."[78] Iran has sought to extend its influence in Iraq primarily through its support of Shia cleric Moqtada al-Sadr and of the increasingly influential Shia political parties.[79]

According to Jordan, "The deep and increasingly difficult U.S. involvement in Iraq and the creation of a Shiite majority government in Iraq have emboldened Iran to take a more assertive stance in the region."[80] While the United States may have gone into Iraq with the assumption that "Tehran would acquiesce to American dominance in the region,"[81] this assumption has been clearly dismissed, as the Ahmadinejad government, along with religious leaders who support his policies, has shown an unwillingness to relent to the demands of the United States and the desires of the West.[82] Instead, Iran has continued to pursue policies such as continuing its nuclear program and providing arms and training to groups such as Hezbollah.

Initially, Iran viewed the U.S.-led occupation of Iraq as a "crusader war" against Muslim nations and Islam; others believed that it was an imperialistic attempt to control the region's strategic reserves of oil. Iranian conservatives viewed it as a conspiracy against the Islamic regime. Suddenly, President Khatami's détente in foreign policy shifted toward a more pragmatic plan and the goal of self-preservation and self-protection. More important, the U.S. presence in Afghanistan and the occupation of Iraq affected Iran's nuclear program and the completion of the Shahab-3 missile project. The period after the occupation of Iraq saw a major shift in Iran's nuclear policy. Much as Pakistan used the Afghanistan crisis as a shield to take giant strides toward its nuclear capability, Iran seized the moment of turmoil in the international system as the most appropriate time to move at full speed toward its nuclear goals. When Khatami was elected president in 1997, Iran was probably still in search of means and ways to build a nuclear weapon, but because the process would take a long time and because Iran was vulnerable to a possible preemptive attack from Israel or the United States, it had to shift gradually from producing a nuclear weapon to producing fuel for nuclear power plants. At the turn of the century and in the post–Iraq occupation era, Iran faced severe challenges of a different nature. Unable to secure sufficient fissile material and components or a bomb, it decided to follow the longer road to developing a nuclear weapon capability indigenously.

Iran has also been willing to confront the United States in a way that few nations have been able to do so thus far without eventual military reprisal. Iranian leader Ayatollah Khamenei recently addressed a group of Iranian medical workers, claiming that the United States was making atomic threats against the Iranian people and that efforts toward nuclear nonproliferation were only a pretense for actual efforts on behalf of nuclear countries to maintain an advantage over nonnuclear states.[83] In the same speech, Khamenei promised that "we will not allow America to renew its hellish dominance over Iran."[84]

One of the ways in which Iran believes it can free itself from "hellish dominance" and propagate the security of its regime is through improved economic measures. Iran has the potential to become a formidable economic power in the Middle East; however, as it stands, it is facing little economic growth, high unemployment, and a "brain drain" as its educated youth emigrate. Rich with national resources such as oil, a relatively large geographical area, and a large population, Iran has the potential to emerge as a great power in the Middle East if inefficient domestic policies are altered to exploit its resources more efficiently. In terms of gross domestic product (GDP; purchasing power parity), Iran ranks seventeenth in the Central Intelligence Agency's *World Factbook* country comparison, followed closely by Turkey and trailing Canada and Indonesia.[85]

There are several barriers to economic success related to Iran's internal economic structure. "Iran's economy is marked by an inefficient state sector, reliance on the oil sector, which provides the majority of government revenues, and status policies, which create major distortions throughout the system."[86] In the face of such internal issues, Ahmadinejad and the Iranian legislature recently passed a number of measures designed to decrease food and energy subsidies.[87]

Iran's reliance on oil produces a relatively unstable economic situation where Iran's economic is reliant on the price of oil on the world market. The recent decline in the price of oil, averaging $55 per barrel from March to December 2009, coupled with an overall decline in the international economy, severely affected Iran's economy.[88] In 2009, the real GDP growth rate was estimated to be around 2.6 percent, far below expected numbers.[89] *Time* magazine reports that the current Iranian government has been hiding economic statistics, attempting to hide rising unemployment, inflation, and an unstable economy.[90]

While Iran may have some economic potential related to its oil resources and working population, there is evidence that Iran is experiencing an economic downturn that may result in an increase in discontent among the Iranian population. Already, there has been a perpetual "brain drain" as educated Iranians have sought employment outside Iran, unable to find sufficient employment inside the country.[91]

Economic power, coupled with other elements of hard power, such as military power, is a key determinant of state power. Other Middle Eastern nations, such as Saudi Arabia, have responded to the instability of oil markets by diversifying their economies and encouraging growth in the private sector.[92] While the per capita GDP of Saudi Arabia is more than 30 percent higher than that of Iran, Saudi Arabia saw even less growth in 2009.[93] Turkey saw negative growth and has comparable per capita GDP to Iran.[94] Looking at the other countries in the Middle East, it appears that Iran has had moderately more success. Relatively, this could put it at an advantage as it seeks regional power; however, substantial changes to the Iranian system must be made for Iran to overcome its economic problems. Substantial changes must also be made in order for Iran to overcome internal divisions. Fractures within the republic have the potential to weaken the regime and drag it off its current course.

As Iran continues to present a relatively hard-line stance toward the United States and much of the world, it faces domestic issues related to its relatively extreme measures to quell domestic opposition. Reformists, dissidents, and opposition political parties have been banned, persecuted, or given extreme prison sentences in response to their questioning of the policies of the Iranian government.[95]

Iran is an extremely diverse country with a number of cultural and ethnic groups represented throughout it. As these groups become increasingly dissatisfied with the current government and with government oppression, Iran's domestic situation requires increasingly more military attention. GlobalSecurity.org notes, "The Iranian regime continues to repress its minority religious and ethnic groups.... Consequently, some areas within the country where these minorities reside, including the Baluchistan border area near Pakistan and Afghanistan, the Kurdish northwest of the country, and areas near the Iraqi border, remain unsafe."[96]

Repressed groups, whether cultural, ethnic, or religious, pose a formidable threat to the security of the Middle East. Dissatisfaction with political, social, or economic conditions has led to the emergence of several notable factions, including the notoriously violent Taliban. In November 2010, the coalition of U.S. and Afghan forces killed a Taliban commander in western Afghanistan who was linked to Iran. A July 16, 2010, raid killed Mullah Akhtar, described by *The Long War Journal* as having "strong ties with Taliban and al Qaeda senior leaders [and] responsible for the training of foreign fighters from Iran. [Akhtar] was closely associated with Iran Qods Force."[97]

The relation between the Iran and Afghanistan remained tense throughout 2001 when the War on Terror began. Iran, which was totally disappointed with the Taliban that was created and supported by Pakistan, decided to aid the U.S.-led coalition on a raid to destroy the al-Qaeda hideouts and put an end to the Taliban government. Elements from the Northern Alliance forces of Afghanistan had long ties with and had lived in Iran for more than a quarter of a century, and Iran's influence was undeniable. Obviously Iran hoped to achieve two separate goals through helping the coalition forces: first, to make sure that the next regime in Kabul would be more Iran friendly and, second, to break the international pressures on its own regime through cooperation in a regional security setting. This calculation was not totally wrong, and soon Afghani President Hamid Karzai established relatively close ties with Iran.

However, Iran's decision did not have full support from all the factions within the Islamic Republic. For instance, certain clerics had "Talibs"[98] coming from Afghanistan to study Islam the Iranian way at some seminaries in the city of Qom. This connection has not stopped since the 1979 revolution. Iran has created a client community in Afghanistan as well as some influence, however small, within the Taliban.

It is important to note that the ideology of the Taliban has never been supported by the majority of the Iranians. Domestically, the fundamentalists within the Islamic Republic of Iran are usually blamed for favoring the rigid Taliban-style closed Islamic societies. Angry demonstrators in Iran would very often describe them as "Iranian Taliban." So, despite the fact that the idea of "Taliban" is politically undesirable for many Iranian elite, the religious Taliban is not totally rejected by the clerics. Thus, one can argue that even after the Taliban was ejected from the Afghani political spectrum, it continued its relation with at least some elements within the Islamic Republic of Iran.

Feeling trapped between enemies and adversaries, particularly after the occupation of Iraq in 2003, Iran started creating scenarios that could practically keep the enemy at bay. At various occasions Iran has emphasized inflicting damage to the United States by giving money, weapons, advice, training and support to various Shiite militia groups in Iraq, most noticeably the Mahdi Army lead by Muqtada al-Sadr. However these actions have not always served Iran's political influence in Baghdad political circles and actually increased suspicions of Iranian motivations. For the United States, though, the rise of Sadr's movement has been problematic. Their hostility towards the United States has included armed conflict with the American military: the Mahdi Army fought major battles against American forces, opened up a two-front insurgency, and fuelled the country's descent into sectarian civil war.

Iran increases the costs of the two ongoing wars at its eastern and western borders for the foreign troops who were menacing Iran and its territorial integrity. One possible way would be to play the old game of "the enemy of my enemy is my friend." While this seems to be the clear rationale, helping small groups of insurgents fight with an enormous number of foreign troops could easily endanger Iran's security even faster and thus could not have been done through official channels.

The formal government had to stay out of this business in order to stay safe. Therefore, Iran adopted a policy of formal support for the formal government of Afghanistan and continued its support for Persian-speaking Tajiks and people who were culturally attached or close to Iranians, but at the same time an indirect line through unofficial and unconventional ways was connecting Iran and Taliban (or even al-Qaeda for that matter). To implement this strategy, Iran did not need to show any official inclination of sympathy toward the Taliban. The Iranian desert areas of the southeast or northeast create a natural excuse for Iran not to intervene in the affairs of the Taliban in transporting narcotics through Iran and distributing them in neighboring states. Iran was aware that attempts to interrupt illegal drug trafficking would force the smugglers to distribute the same drugs inside Iran because they could not return them to Afghanistan. The same route could be used to transport weapons into Afghanistan or even through Pakistan in order to be distributed among the Taliban.

In the political arena, Iran and Afghanistan enjoyed good-neighbor relations, and President Karzai accepted Iran's former foreign minister, Manouchehr Mottaki, in December 2005 and talked about mutual interests. In addition, he was quoted as saying that Afghanistan "should draw assistance from Iran's experiences to boost the development drive" in the country. Karzai also added, "Afghanistan wishes further progress and development of Iran and will not let anyone drive a wedge between the two Muslim neighbors."[99]

According to the Afghanistan News Center, about the same time, the Afghan parliament speaker made the comment in a meeting with Mottaki expressing his appreciation for the Islamic Republic of Iran's hospitality rendered to Afghan refugees during the past decades and Iran's cooperation in the reconstruction of Afghanistan. He was quoted as saying, "We have left behind a very sensitive stage of our law making process, and fortunately, today representatives of all Afghan tribes and parties gather under the same roof to consult on sensitive national affairs." Qanooni, the Afghan parliament speaker, reiterated, "an Afghan parliamentary delegation would visit the Islamic Republic of Iran in near future to be benefited from the experience of the representative of Iran's Islamic Majlis."[100]

Like many friendships in that region of the world, Iran-Afghanistan relations were not flawless. In June 2007, U.S. Undersecretary of State Nicholas Burns revealed that Iran was transferring arms to Taliban fighters in Afghanistan and claimed that "there's irrefutable evidence the Iranians are now doing this and it's a pattern of activity." He described the operation as a "violation of its Security Council commitments" prohibiting Iran's arms transfer outside Iran. (UN Security Council Resolution 1747 passed in March 2007).[101]

Once again, in October 2007, the media reported that Iran was arming the Taliban with roadside bombs. For instance, U.S. Army General Dan McNeil, the commander of NATO forces in Afghanistan, implicated Iran's Quds (also known as the Qods Force) Revolutionary Guard in the delivery of roadside bombs to Taliban forces. Apparently, "more than 50 roadside bombs and timers" were discovered in trucks crossing the border from Iran in September. His allegation was based on the fact that "the observation of a number of British officers who served in southern Iraq was that [the bomb timers] were relatively common there and that they originated from Iran." So, if Iran was involved in arming Iraqi insurgency, it is natural that it is also involved in arming the Taliban. General McNeill argued, "I cannot see how it is possible for at least the Iranian military, probably the Quds force, to not have known of this convoy."[102]

The formal government of Afghanistan disagreed, and Iran also vividly rejected the accusation. For instance, Afghan Defense Minister General Abdul Rahim Wardak said that "evidence of Iranian cooperation in arming Taliban insurgents with advanced weapons is inconclusive." At the time, the Voice of America, as quoted by United Press International, said, "There are weapons and maybe some financial support and others. But to be completely clear about it I think it will take a little bit of time to come up with the right conclusion."[103]

The mystery of Iran's material support for the Taliban continued throughout 2008 when, according to BBC News, "Taliban members said they had received Iranian-made arms from elements in the Iranian state and from smugglers."[104] According to what has been quoted by the BBC reporter, the "Taliban commander and other sources in the south" of Afghanistan confirmed that Iranian weapons were being delivered to the Taliban through both "smugglers for profit" and "elements of the Iranian state donating arms." Even the British ambassador in Kabul, Sir Sherard Cowper-Coles, made the same allegation in the following statement:

We've seen a limited supply of weapons by a group within the Iranian state, not necessarily with the knowledge of all other agencies of the Iranian state, sending some very dangerous weapons to the Taleban in the south. It's a very dangerous game for Iran, a Shia state, to be supplying Sunni extremists, like the Taliban.[105]

The problem with this statement and the media report is that they are based on the confirmation of the Afghani warlord, who is in fact fighting with the British or American troops. There is no doubt that Iran has an interest in increasing the cost of war for the foreign troops in order to avoid the temptation to attack Iran, but how can one depend on the information acquired from the members of an insurgent groups directly fighting against you?

In May 2009, U.S. Secretary of Defense Robert Gates described the alarming situation in Afghanistan and predicted that the American public's support for the conflict may decline if no significant progress is seen soon. By expressing particular concern that "Tehran might step up its shipment of explosively formed penetrators, powerful roadside bombs capable of punching through even the strongest armor," he blamed Iran for "harming" U.S. interests in Afghanistan by sending weapons to the Taliban and other armed groups."[106]

Yet, again, things are different in formal relations. In 2009, Iran (in June) and Kabul (in August) witnessed two disputable elections. Karzai was among the first heads of states who rushed to congratulate Ahmadinejad's "win" despite national contestations of and demonstrations against the election. Karzai called Ahmadinejad on the phone and hoped for strengthening the relation that he described as having "expanded" during the first term of his presidency.[107] In return, Ahmadinejad did the same, even before the results of the recounts in the Afghan election were disclosed. Yet in another telephone conversation, Ahmadinejad congratulated Karzai for his "successful" reelection, describing him a "devout and competent" leader. Ahmadinejad was quoted as saying, "Iran welcomes your programs for further independence and prosperity of Afghanistan."[108] Such a relationship, it is certain, sparked the ire of nearby Israel, which as Chapter 2 discusses, has its own aspirations to become a regional power.

CHAPTER 3

Israel: Politics and People

During a recent visit to Washington, Israeli Prime Minister Benjamin Netanyahu called for the United States to consider military options against Iran. Netanyahu told Vice President Joe Biden that only a "credible" military threat would prevent Iran from developing an atomic bomb.[1] "The only way to ensure Iran does not obtain nuclear weapons is by creating a credible threat of military action against it if it does not halt its race to acquire a nuclear bomb," an official who asked not to be named quoted Netanyahu as telling Biden.[2] The Obama administration has not ruled out the possibility of military action but has made it clear that it prefers a strict diet of economic sanctions and international pressures to deal with the Islamic Republic's nuclear drive. Netanyahu, however, expressed his concern that tough sanctions would not do enough to thwart what could potentially be a disaster of catastrophic proportions. "Sanctions are important. They are increasing pressure on Iran. But so far there has not been any change in the behavior of Iran and upgrading of international pressure is necessary," he said.[3]

The impasse over Iran's nuclear program has already led to a steady round of sanctions by the United Nations and the European Union, but even some congressional leaders in the United States have questioned their impact. Netanyahu's meeting with the Obama administration came on the heels of the 2010 midterm elections that eventuated in Republican control of the House of Representatives. Republican Senator Lindsey Graham indicated that sweeping Republican victories in the House, combined with a growing feeling that sanctions against Iran were producing dead-end results, would lead to widespread support for U.S.-led military actions against the Islamic Republic. "[If Obama] decides to be tough with Iran beyond sanctions, I think he is going to feel a lot of Republican support for the idea that we cannot let Iran develop a nuclear weapon," Graham told the Halifax International Security Forum.[4] "The last thing America wants is another military conflict, but the last thing the world needs is a nuclear-armed Iran . . . containment is off the table."[5]

Despite renewed calls for military action against Iran from Israeli leaders and apparent support for such measures from Republican caucuses, the Obama administration stood firm in its commitment to more diplomatic measures. Secretary of Defense Robert Gates commented on Graham's remarks, as well as his meeting with Netanyahu, saying, "I disagree that only a credible military threat can get Iran to take the action that it needs to end its nuclear weapons program."[6] He continued, saying, "We are prepared to do what is necessary. But at this point we continue to believe that the political, economic approach that we are taking is in fact having an impact in Iran."[7]

Three weeks after the meeting between Netanyahu and the Obama administration, a bombshell emerged: WikiLeaks, an international whistle-blowing organization that publishes otherwise unavailable documents, unveiled more than 250,000 pages of private conversations between world leaders, including detailed information about Arab leaders pressuring the United States to strike Iran. While the Obama administration recoiled in anger over the release of the cables, Netanyahu and the Israeli government viewed the controversy as an advantage—an affirmation that indeed something needed to be done. "Israel has not been damaged at all by the WikiLeaks publications," the prime minister told a group of editors in Tel Aviv.[8] "The documents show many sources backing Israel's assessments, particularly of Iran." One result of the released cables was the revelation that Saudi Arabia had asked the United States to "cut the head off the serpent"—to launch a military strike to prevent the Iranians from gaining a nuclear bomb.[9] Egypt was also drawn into the controversy as reports concluded that Egyptian spies had been working to counter Iranian intelligence operations and prevent Iran from operating—namely, via Hezbollah—in Egypt.[10] The report also indicated that the United States should not limit its focus on Iran to one issue at a time, such as the republic's nuclear program, and echoed calls of other Arab states for increased pressure to stop Iran's nuclear ambitions.[11] In an unlikely concert of voices calling for increased military pressure on Iran, Israel and Arab states exhorted Washington to consider such measures.

It appears on some levels that Israel is losing confidence in the Obama administration and, with the release of the cables showing Arab support for military action against Iran, has found substantiation for its beliefs among the leaders of Egypt and Saudi Arabia. With mounting concerns that Iran will continue to remain defiant and forge new ground in its quest to enrich uranium, test launch missiles, and develop an atomic bomb, how will Israel react? Will the Jewish state reach a boiling point and engage in war with Iran, and, if so, how will this affect their relationship with the United States? While the specifics of nuclear dynamics in the Middle East are discussed in detail in Chapter 4, it is useful to consider the historical dimensions of Israel, the country's relationships with other states in the Middle East, and the complexity of the relationship with the United States. As Dana Allin and Steven Simon note in *The Sixth Crisis*, the future of Israeli-Iranian relations and the possibility of an eventual confrontation between the two states is couched in a dense web of unanswered and perhaps even unanswerable questions: the likelihood of Israel deciding to attack depends on Israeli assessments of U.S. and international resolve to block Iran's pursuit of a nuclear weapons capability; the state of the Iranian program; the amount of time a successful strike would buy to be worth the expected risks and costs (a point on which there is a spectrum of Israeli views, from six months to five years); whether Israel believes there is a clandestine Iranian program, which would lead some Israelis to conclude that an attack would buy no time at all; and the effect of a strike on the U.S.-Israeli relationship.[12]

What is clear, however, is that Israel sees its legitimacy as a regional and world power in jeopardy. In order to better understand its position, it is necessary first to consider the historical dynamics that animate that country's worldview, beginning with a discussion about the people of Israel and the role that immigration has played in the development of Israel's regional relationship and its foreign policy.

As Asher Arian has noted in his seminal text *The Second Republic: Politics in Israel*, one of the key elements in the development of any country is its population, and regarding Israel, any understanding of the country's politics must rely heavily on the demographics of its people, particularly those Israelis who have made up the Zionist movement.[13] The Zionists' main goal, after all, was to channel the world's Jewish population from the Diaspora (exile of Jews living outside of ancient Israel) to Zion (most commonly Jerusalem but in a biblical sense the lands of Israel). Zionism, in its broadest sense, is a nationalist Jewish political movement that has supported the self-determination of its people and the sovereignty of the Jewish national homeland and has sought to address threats to Israel's continued existence, political legitimacy in the Middle East, and security. The movement has been quite successful, largely because of its ability to attract the support of Jewish immigrants. In 1882, there were 24,000 Jews living in Eretz (Hebrew for "the Land of Israel"). More than 110 years later, that number had risen to more than 4.5 million, and by 2003, Israel's 5.1 million Jews constituted 39 percent of the world's Jewish population.[14] A December 2009 census shows that Israel is now home to more than 5.7 million Jews.[15] Despite the steady climb in immigration, however, the fact is that most Jews do not live in Israel. Rather, they live abroad in other countries and for one reason or another, have, over time, migrated back to the land they consider to be home. Largely, immigration to Israel was caused by outside factors. Jews were affected by political realities of the sometimes inhospitable (and perhaps even threatening) world around them. Many Polish Jews immigrated to Israel in the 1920s as a result of a boycott having been declared on Jewish industry and trade in their country of origin as well as the legislation of quotas brought about in the Johnson-Lodge Act, which limited access to a desirable country of destination.[16] In 1935, 66,000 immigrants arrived in Israel, nearly a quarter of them from Germany, as the conditions of World War II deteriorated. In 1957, a massive influx of Jews from Morocco came to Israel, feeling pressured and anxious about the emergence of nationalism within North Africa.[17]

These historical immigration patterns reveal that since the late nineteenth century, Jews have dealt with a variety of perceived threats that surrounded them. In essence, their identity during this time period was grounded largely in their search for belonging and their quest for a collective, protected home. The Zionist movement provided that sense of security within the borders of Israel. From 1882 until 1903, during what was called the first *aliyah* (Hebrew for "ascent," a term used to refer to periods of immigration), between 20,000 and 30,000 settlers came to Israel in reaction to a swell of anti-Semitism in Russia. Many other immigrants during this time fled to the United States, but the cadre of those who were Israel bound responded to the nationalist awakening among Jews in Israel who offered an ideologically inviting environment.[18] The second *aliyah* came in response to an unsuccessful Russian Revolution but, of all the *aliyot*, was perhaps the most significant. Not only did the revolution in Russia send more than 35,000 Jews to Israel, it also paved the way for a Zionist revolution and produced three top leaders: David Ben Gurion, Yitzhak Ben-Zvi, and Yosef Shprinzak, Israel's first prime minister, second president, and first chairman of the Knesset, respectively. The newcomers, building on the work of those who had immigrated before them, were successful in developing new agricultural settlements and industry that promoted a uniquely Jewish identity and culture. "Aliyah," Ben Gurion informed defense and foreign ministry officials in April 1949, was the "core interest" of the state and even took priority over defense. "The fate of the state depends on aliyah," he remarked, not necessarily on military capacities conventionally defined.[19]

Adding to the complexities, many of the settlers wanted physical labor. To their surprise, they were shut out of work as a result of Arab communities that could work for cheaper prices. As a result, a labor battle broke out, and eventually the Jewish settlers were successful, winning the support of the World Zionist Organization and farm and plantation owners, and the immigrants were able to develop a communal identity, establishing strong ties of internal cohesion that formed the basis of political organizations.[20] European convulsions of World War I led to a plethora of immigrants, mostly from Russia and Poland, in the 1920s. Their appreciation for political organization, their strong ideological motivation, and their brewing sense of nationalism magnified the influence of the growing Zionist movement. By the 1930s, Nazi Germany and a swell of anti-Semitic sentiment led to more than 80,000 Jewish immigrants, further strengthening the nationalistic Zionist movement and tightening the binds of a booming population that had been disaffected for decades. The year 1948 would unite the population even further when the declaration of independence was signed, stating in part that "the State of Israel is open to Jewish immigration and the ingathering of Exiles." The first order of the nascent state was to abolish the British restrictions on immigration and define as legal those residents who had once been "illegal" under British rule.[21] Following the creation of the state of Israel in 1948, some idealists on the left of the Zionist movement believed that Israeli leaders might seriously consider the prophetic image of a state that was "a light unto the nations," basing its policies on the principles of justice and right.[22] Yet, as Raymond Cohen notes, within a short time, given the extreme pressure imposed by its security vulnerabilities, Israel's foreign relations seemed to settle into the grooves of Realpolitik.[23] Cohen writes,

In conformity with realist assumptions, state organs and agencies were paramount, and non-state-to-state relations, increasingly prominent in contemporary North American and Western European thinking, were disregarded or subject to national considerations. Ben Gurion elevated mamlakhtiut (statehood) into a political principle. The state explained its actions by raison d'état, not human rights, the future of the planet, or some other universal good. Ends were assumed to justify means. Resort to armed force was accepted as a necessary evil. In the crunch, few Israelis disputed that economic or social welfare interests should be sacrificed to security considerations.[24]

Eleven minutes after the declaration of independence was signed, marking Israel's freedom from British Mandate of Palestine and establishing the first Jewish state, the president of the United States, Harry Truman, de facto recognized the state of Israel. He was immediately followed by Shah Mohammad Reza Pahlavi of Iran. As early as May 14, 1948, Eliahu Elath, the Jewish Agency representative in Washington, told Truman that "the Provisional Government has been charged to assume the rights and duties of government for preserving law and order within the boundaries of Israel, for defending the State against external aggression, and for discharging the obligations of Israel to the other nations of the world in accordance with international law."[25]

The relationship between Iran and Israel from that point forward was largely positive. In fact, Israel viewed Iran as an ally—a non-Arab bulwark in a region that was dominated by Arab states. David Ben Gurion, the first prime minister of Israel, explained in his "alliance of periphery" principle that Israel should seek alliances with other non-Arab states in the Middle East in order to counteract what could potentially be Arab opposition from all sides in the event of a regional conflict. [26] In fact, Gurion did not even consider Israel to be in the Middle East, at least not in terms of political similarities. "We have no connection with the Arabs," he said. "Our regime, our culture, our relations, is not the fruit of this region. There is no political affinity between us, or international solidarity."[27] Ben Gurion's suspicions proved to be accurate. Shortly after the separation of Israel from Britain, neighboring Arab states, including Egypt, Jordan, Lebanon, Syria, and Iraq, objected and attempted to block the establishment of Israel with armed force. The conflict, which had been simmering for years and with Jewish immigrants drastically increasing the Israeli population, escalated to a full-blown war, and Israel's display of military force and political power proved that whatever underlying feelings of inferiority were felt by Israeli leaders who viewed themselves as isolated among a region of Arab states were unfounded. Concurrently, Ben Gurion also developed the "alliance of minorities," noting that the majority of the inhabitants of the Middle East were not of Arab origin, referring not only to the Persians and the Turks but also to various religious minorities, such as the Kurds, the Druze, and the (Christian) Maronites of Lebanon. The aim of Gurion's approach was to foster nationalist aspirations among minority groups in order to create a strong web of allies in the midst of surrounding Arab countries. Even during this early period, more than 20 years before the threat of Iran emerged, Israel viewed its position in the region in terms of political legitimacy—the nascent state jockeyed for alliances that would create a strong foundation of political fortitude and showcase its strength as an independent state. Additionally, it is important to note and is observable from these early pulses of non-Arab alliance building that Israel, in some ways, has always been on the defense. The state, since its formation, has navigated its political aspirations from a geographic point of weakness and, as a result, has aimed to strengthen its position by reaching out to other potential non-Arab allies, namely, Iran. "We had very deep relations with Iran, cutting deep into the fabric of the two peoples," one high-ranking official at the Israeli Foreign Ministry said.[28] That relationship would prove to be valuable two decades later when, as Israel envisioned, surrounding Arab states, including Egypt, Syria, Jordan, Iraq, and Saudi Arabia, directed their aggression at the Jewish state in what came to be known as the Six-Day War.

From 1952 on, Ben Gurion repeated that though Israelis were geographically stranded in the Middle East, they were a European people.[29] This was evidenced in the events leading up to the Six-Day War and was especially seen in the Suez crisis. Egypt's plans to nationalize the Suez Canal sparked international ire. The canal was strategically important; it provided the shortest ocean route between the Mediterranean Sea and the Indian Ocean. It also eased commerce for trading nations and helped European powers to gain and govern their colonies. Britain and France, as a result, viewed the move as particularly controversial and began plans to invade Egypt. Not to be outdone, Israel soon began to develop its own plans for invasion, and after several efforts at international mediation failed, Britain and France agreed to undertake a joint intervention. By the end of October 1956, despite receiving personal messages from U.S. President Dwight Eisenhower urging a more peaceful approach, Israel too invaded Egypt and became embroiled in the crisis. Compared to Egypt, the casualties were few: only 177 Israelis were killed and nearly 900 wounded.[30] But compared to the United Kingdom and France, Israel suffered greater losses. Only 16 British troops and 10 French troops were killed; Israel had taken a hit, comparatively, but the consequences of its involvement in the conflict were far greater than it expected.

After the 1956 war, the Middle East remained unstable; without resolution to the underlying issues of the Suez crisis, there was still great concern that no Arab state recognized Israel. Syria, aligned with the Soviets, began to sponsor guerilla raids on Israel in the 1960s in an effort to deflect domestic opposition to the Ba'ath Party.[31] Having been independent for two decades (and recognized by other global actors), still no neighboring Arab country of Israel was willing to negotiate a peace agreement, let alone accept its existence. Habib Bourgiba, the president of Tunisia, said in a speech in Jericho in 1965 that the Arab world should face reality and negotiate with Israel, but this was rejected by other Arab countries, and soon Israel's involvement in the Suez crisis would isolate it further as another conflict emerged.[32]

The Six-Day War broke out in June 1967. The war was fought between June 5 and 10 of that year, and the Israelis defended the war as a preventive military effort to counter what they viewed as an impending attack by Arab nations. The war was against Jordan, Egypt, and Syria. Israel, already concerned with the potential fallout of the Suez crisis, believed that it was only a matter of time before the surrounding Arab states coordinated a massive attack on the Jewish state. Raymond Cohen suggests that Israel was pitted against "eternal enemies."[33] The Jews' long history of persecution strongly influenced Israel's perception of its enemies.

After the 1956 Suez crisis, the United Nations established a presence in the Middle East—the first of its kind. The United States was especially present at sensitive border areas and was in the region only with the agreement of nations that, acting as hosts, gave the international body consent to set up camp. By May 1967, however, Egypt indicated that the

United Nations was no longer welcome in the Suez region. Gamal Abdul Nasser, the leader of Egypt, ordered a concentration of troops in the sensitive zone. This was a provocative and controversial act, and the Israelis believed that Egypt was preparing to attack. The Egyptian army had also enforced a naval blockade that closed off the Gulf of Aqaba to Israeli shipping.

Instead of waiting to be attacked, Israel launched a successful military campaign against its perceived enemies. The air forces of Egypt, Jordan, Syria, and Iraq were all but destroyed on June 5, and two days later, on June 7, many Egyptian tanks were destroyed in the Sinai Desert, and Israeli forces reached the Suez Canal. That same day, the entire west bank of the Jordan River had been cleared of Jordanian forces. The Golan Heights were captured from Syria, and Israeli forces moved 30 miles into Syria itself.

The war was seen largely as a disaster for the Arab world as a whole and weakened Gamal Abdul Nasser of Egypt, the man who was seen as the leader of the Arabs. The war was a military disaster for the Arabs, but it was also a massive blow to the Arabs' morale. Here were four of the strongest Arab nations systematically defeated by just one nation. For Israel, there was much significance in the victory—feelings of geographic isolation and constant fear of being surrounded by Arab nations ready for war proved to be unsound. The Israeli military had flexed its muscles and handily defeated its neighboring foes.

Even so, the need for non-Arab allies was still great, perhaps even greater given the tense political climate that followed the conflict. Though Iran was not involved in the Six-Day War, Iranian leaders did reach out to Israel following their victory. Iran supplied Israel with a substantial proportion of its oil needs, and Iranian oil was shipped to European markets via the joint Israeli-Iranian Eilat-Ashkelon pipeline.[34] Trade continued between the two countries, and Israeli engineers and construction firms were present in Tehran. For Persia, the strategic value of Israel in meeting the challenges of internal subversion and regional aggression encouraged the development of closer economic bonds as well as security and intelligence cooperation. The opening of the Tiran Straits turned Eilat into a natural route for importing oil to Israel and later to Europe. In 1957, Israel began to buy Persian oil through ships unmarked with the Israeli flag. And over the years, the Israeli export expanded, and El-Al Airlines eventually opened a direct line to Tehran. "We weren't feeling insecure because of Israeli strength in the region," noted Mehdi Ehsassi, Iran's deputy UN ambassador during the 1970s.[35] "[There is] a geopolitical element in which the Iranians will feel better if the Israelis are not weak," he continued.[36] Iran, though coming to Israel's aid during this critical time, did not want the Jewish state to be weak. But the Iranian government also did not want Israel to become too strong. A balance was needed. If Israel were weak, Arab and Soviet states would be boosted, posing problems for Iran. If Israel were too strong, the question of Israeli expansionism and regional domination would come into play, especially given its vast display of power in the Six-Day War.[37] It is important to remember that Iran and Israel were non-Arab states and that both were under the protection of and had friendly ties with the United States.

During the early 1970s, relations between Iran and Israel were amicable. On October 6, 1973, the Jewish holy day of Yom Kippur, Egyptian forces began to Israel from across the Suez Canal. At the same time, Syrian troops flooded the Golan Heights, resulting in the Yom Kippur War. Israel was supported by the United States and several other Western nations. On October 17, the Arab member nations of the Organization of Petroleum Exporting Countries struck back at the West by imposing an oil embargo on the United States while increasing prices by 70 percent to the Western European allies of the United States. Immediately, the price of a barrel of oil rose from $3.00 to $5.11. The embargo was then extended to include the Netherlands, which had allowed American planes to use Dutch airfields for supply runs to the Israelis.[38] Iran, however, did not participate in the embargo and continued to supply oil to the West and to Israel. But the oil did not come without a price. The shah of Iran said at the time, "Of course [the world price of oil] is going to rise . . . . Certainly! And how . . . ; You [Western nations] increased the price of wheat you sell us by 300%, and the same for sugar and cement . . . ; You buy our crude oil and sell it back to us, refined as petrochemicals, at a hundred times the price you've paid to us . . . ; It's only fair that, from now on, you should pay more for oil. Let's say ten times more."[39]

However, the death of Abdul Nasser in September 1970, followed by the rise of Mohammad Anwar-al-Sadat, altered the shah's negative attitude toward Egypt. Unlike Abdul Nasser, the shah trusted Sadat and supported his Middle East policy. Subsequently, the October War (1973) diminished the prestige of the Israeli army. Moreover, in March 1975, Iran and Iraq signed the Algiers Accord, putting a temporary end to the Iran-Iraq conflict and ending the Persian-Israeli common support for Kurds. The incentives for close relations with Israel were less compelling in this new atmosphere, although extensive cooperation continued in various fields. But this period was also important to Israel for another reason. Since the October War in 1973, Washington has provided Israel with a level of support dwarfing the amounts provided to any other state. The period marked a great spike in U.S. foreign aid. And since that time, Israel has become the largest annual recipient of direct U.S. economic and military assistance since 1976 and the largest total recipient since World War II.[40] The total amount of direct U.S. aid to Israel amounts to more than $140 billion based on 2003 dollars. Additionally, Israel receives nearly $3 billion in direct foreign assistance each year, which is almost one-fifth of foreign-aid budget of the United States.[41]

By 1979, Ayatollah Khomeini's campaign to overthrow the shah led to a diminished relationship between Iran and Israel. After the second phase of the Iranian Revolution, Iran cut its ties to Israel and adopted a sharp anti-Zionist stance. More than 30 years later, that relationship has not improved, and over the course of the past three decades, rhetorical battles and proxy-led conflicts have marked the relationship between these two states, both competing for an advantage in their respective quests to become the next Middle Eastern powerhouse.

Without detailing the 1979 revolution and its effects on Israel (as such topics could easily span hundreds of pages), it is important to consider, for the purpose of this discussion, the theoretical dimensions of the power plays taking shape during that time. As noted earlier, Israel has always been in a position of defense, and in the Arab-majority Middle East, Iran proved to be a powerful and reliable alliance. Yet during the Six-Day War, Iran was absent—Israel fended off its Arab-state foes single-handedly and, as a result, proved that it was capable of existing apart from any major source of military aide or political partnership. "The Arab Enemy," so to speak, made Israel stronger. It provided the Jewish state with a threat to rally against and also strengthened its identity as a nation capable of taking on threats from multiple fronts. Israel's identity was, in many ways, a state that *needed* a strong enemy in order to survive—the political legitimacy of the government had always depended on its ability to thrive politically and economically in a region of "others."

Thus, as 1979 approached and it became clear that Iran and Israel would begin a decades-long period of hostility, Israel was faced with another such threat, albeit one was would not be easily conquered with a quick war. Nonetheless, the stalemate that would emerge between Israel and Iran would provide both non-Arab nations with a solid foundation on which to make their case as the next leader of the Middle East. Trita Parsi comments on the dynamics animating Iran's political maneuvers during that time:

The impact of Iran's change to an Islamic state on Israeli-Iranian relations must be seen within the context of Iran's geo-strategic imperatives as a non-Arab, non-Sunni state in an overwhelmingly Arab and Sunni environment beyond the camouflage of Islamic rhetoric and exaggerated threat depictions in order to assess the changes that the Revolution of 1977–79 brought about and the continuities that it failed to end.[42]

As Parsi observes, Iran and Israel had formed their strategic alliance based on the common threat perceptions. Even so, despite the extensive Israeli-Iranian cooperation, Iran began to distance itself from Israel in order to win regional approval and support for Tehran's ambitions in the Middle East. Backing away from Israel was, at the time, the only political maneuver that the shah could use to reconcile Iran with Arab states that were hostile toward and had battled with Israel.[43] As the revolution came to pass, Iran's leaders, influenced by their nationalistic impulses and their fervent religious beliefs, began to jockey more candidly for a regional position of power. While the shah had sought approval and political legitimacy for his hegemony through financial aid to and the military protection of surrounding Arab states, the new revolutionary regime sought the same through political Islam.[44]

For Israel, the Iranian Revolution and the ensuing chase for central power in the region caused great difficulties—particularly after years of support from their only other non-Arab ally. Though their own quest for political legitimacy hanged in the balance of having a strong enemy, the sobering reality was that after more than 25 years of investing in relations with Tehran, Iran was a crucial part of Israel's regional strategy.[45] David Kimche, the former head of the Israeli foreign ministry, said,

We had very deep relations with Iran, cutting deep into the fabric of the two peoples. It was difficult for people to accept the fact that all of this intimacy was thrown out of the window. So there were a lot of attempts during the first year after the Revolution, to see if we could revive the relations with [Iran].[46]

As history has shown, it became apparent that reviving past relations with Tehran was not possible. But beyond that—and perhaps the more important point for the discussion at hand—was that Israel emerged from the late 1970s with a strong alliance still intact though not one situated in the Middle East: the United States. Iran, on the other hand, as a result of Khomeini's rise to power, the hostage crisis of 1977, and the subsequent decline of a once-friendly relationship, was left without its critical non-Arab ally—Israel—and faced increasingly disgruntled Arab neighbors, many of whom objected to the regime's rigid interpretation of Islam and Iran's hard-line approach to foreign policy. This was an important time in international relations. It was then that the triangle—the United States, Israel, and Iran—emerged into fuller view with the United States and Israel forming what would eventually become outright opposition to the dealings of the Iranian regime. This was also a critical time in that it was the nascent stage of what is now a stalemate between the United States and Israel on the one hand and Iran on the other.

The 1970s also mark the period when the United States took an active role in the Middle East peace process, and for that reason, it is useful to consider the historical dimensions between the United States and Israel since that time in order to better understand the current challenges that come to the fore regarding U.S.-Israeli relations and the regional political dynamics of that alliance.

Since the formation of the Israeli state in 1948, five wars have shattered the Middle East.[47] Yet in the midst of a region rocked by turmoil, the underlying conflict between the Arabs and the Israelis has proved to be the most catastrophic, serving as a vehicle for potentially avertable face-offs. From the beginning, Israel's Arab-state neighbors did not accept its legitimacy and the existence of the new country was threatened. Seeking to establish what was perceived as a lack of legitimacy, Israel began vying for territory to provide itself with more strategic depth and reinforcement in the event of an attack by any one of its neighbors. But as Astrid Scharf writes, "Apart from territorial conflicts between Israel and its Arab neighbors, the Arab-Israeli conflict is a conflict of nations."[48] The settlement of Zionist Jews in Palestine and the ensuing annexation of the territory and expulsion of Palestinians was condemned by the Arab world. While they would have accepted the terms of the 1947 UN Security Council resolution to divide the territory between the two competing nations, Israel rejected the plan, and the first steps toward negotiation were taken at Camp David in 1978.[49] After 12 days of secret negotiations, Egyptian President Anwar Sadat and Israeli Prime Minister Menachem Begin signed an agreement that granted that both countries recognize one another (thus, Egypt became the first Arab state to recognize Israel) and that there be a cessation to the state of war that had existed since the formation of Israel in 1948, with the complete withdrawal of Israeli forces from the Sinai Peninsula, which it had captured during the Six-Day War in 1967. The treaty was by no means comprehensive and was met with much international scrutiny and controversy, as it was linked to a resolution of the Palestinian-Israeli conflict that was unsuccessful. Arab states, especially Palestine, balked at it, believing that such an effort was not likely to produce real, lasting results. Sadat, as a result of his participation, grew increasingly unpopular, and for 10 years, from 1979 to 1989, Egypt was thrown out of the Arab League. Astrid Scharf writes, "Like the later peace treaty between Israel and Jordan in 1994, the Egypt-Israeli relations based on the 1979 peace treaty can be described as a 'cold peace' as Arab interests are negotiated separately from the Palestinian ones."[50] What resulted was a flurry of anti-American sentiment that gave Gulf-state oil producers an ideological incentive not to buffer America's economy from the oil shock prompted by the Iranian Revolution.[51]

Following the Carter administration's efforts to broker some stability in the Middle East, the Reagan administration aimed to balance its policies in the region by advocating a strategic consensus among the Israeli and Arab allies of the United States.[52] President Ronald Reagan, in dealing with the Cold War, viewed Israel as an asset against communist expansion and, as a result, initiated a program of cooperation with Israel that involved substantial military and economic assistance. Siding with the Arabs against Israel, the Soviet Union hoped to strengthen its base and

spread the communist ideology throughout the Arab world. In supporting Israel, the United States expected little resistance from its allies in
the Gulf. They too needed American security assistance to help counter
communist expansion and a potential conflict with Iran that might not
be checked by Iraq's invasion of Iran.[53]

While maintaining the close relationship with Israel through military
and economic assistance, the administration of George H. W. Bush also
attempted to restore some balance in the relationship between the United
States and its Arab-state allies by promoting the peace process to resolve
the Palestinian-Israeli conflict. Bush, along with Soviet President Mikhail
Gorbachev, convened the peace conference in Madrid in 1990 that began
a decade of unprecedented negotiations between Israel, Jordan, Syria,
Lebanon, and the Palestinians. Following the expulsion of Iraqi forces
from Kuwait, the Bush administration believed that there was a window
of opportunity to use political capital generated by the victory to revive
peace talks between the Arabs and the Israelis. At the time of the talks,
Washington did not believe that economic incentives would play a central
part in the talks; however, Yitzhak Shamir, Israel's prime minister,
requested $10 billion in loan guarantees from the United States, putting
Bush and his administration in a precarious position of political bargaining. Opposed to the loan request, Bush's popularity (hovering above
70 percent at the time) allowed him to stand his ground, but the point
would prove to be one of contention during the talks. Even so, the
conference itself, despite tensions, was a watershed event. For the first
time, Israel had entered into direct, face-to-face negotiations with the
Palestinians, Syria, Jordan, and Lebanon. As Gregory Harms and Todd Ferry
argue in *The Palestine-Israel Conflict: A Basic Introduction*, "The symbolic
significance of the Madrid conference far outweighed its accomplish-
ments, which were thin indeed."[54] As a condition of its participation in
the conference, Israel made revocation of UN Resolution 3379, which
stated that Zionism was a form of racism and discrimination with Resolution 46/86. Israel also benefited greatly from the number of diplomatic
contacts it gained, nearly doubling the world powers it had relations with,
including many Arab countries, such as Qatar, Morocco, Tunisia, Mauritania,
and Oman.

Throughout the 1990s, relations between the United States and Israel
took various twists and turns, but the one highlight of that decade was
the Oslo Accords. The meeting between the government of Israel and
the Palestinian Liberation Organization (PLO) was the first of its kind
and was intended to be a framework for future negotiations. The accords
called for the withdrawal of Israeli forces from parts of the Gaza Strip and
West Bank and affirmed that the Palestinians had a right to self-govern
within those areas through the creation of an independent Palestinian
state, governed by the Palestinian Interim Self-Government Authority.

Additionally, the two groups signed letters of mutual recognition indicating that the government of Israel recognized the PLO as the legitimate representative of the Palestinian people, while the PLO recognized that Israel had the right to exist as a state and renounced its desire for the destruction of the state, condemning terrorism and other acts of violence aimed at accomplishing that.

Seventeen years later, in 2010, a videotape emerged showing Benjamin Netanyahu discussing the Oslo Accords. His comments, controversial and indicative of continued strained relations, appeared at a time when Washington, under the Obama administration, was beginning to negotiate peace talks of its own. Netanyahu said,

They asked me before the election if I'd honor [the Oslo accords]. I said I would, but ... I'm going to interpret the accords in such a way that would allow me to put an end to this galloping forward to the '67 borders. How did we do it? Nobody said what defined military zones were. Defined military zones are security zones; as far as I'm concerned, the entire Jordan Valley is a defined military zone. Go argue. I know what America is. America is a thing you can move very easily, move it in the right direction. They won't get in their way.[55]

What emerges from Netanyahu's remarks is the idea that, from Israel's perspective, the substantial military and economic assistance it receives from the United States has given Washington leverage over the Jewish state. Israel's legitimacy is largely tied to U.S. policy, and, historically, Israel's desire to define its own existence, shape its own policies, and present itself as a capable, powerful regional force has come as a result of the nation exerting its independence, whether militarily or rhetorically. Netanyahu's comments express that same sentiment but also add an additional tinge of arrogance. It appears that Netanyahu, in asserting Israel's ability to interpret the Oslo Accords as it desires, not as they are written, views the United States as a political pawn that can be used—when needed—to reinforce its political legitimacy in the Middle East, not as a nation that *made* Israel a legitimate global actor.

Frictions between the United States and Israel have also ensued over the attempts by the United States to maintain balance with its Arab allies while also maintaining positive relations with Israel. Lenore Martin points out that Israel continues to benefit directly from the dozen or more agreements that have established the basis for its special relationship with the United States and particularly its military cooperation with that country since 1970.[56] Under the administration of George W. Bush, that relationship continued, emphasizing, among other things, strategic cooperation in the region, joint weapons production, military exercises, and intelligence sharing. Economically, the United States supplied substantive military assistance to Israel, and the nation continues to receive favorable trade treatment through the Free Trade Area Agreement of 1985.[57] Diplomatically, the United States has protected Israel against condemnation in the United Nations, though some have argued that the Obama administration, while seeking to maintain a positive relationship with Israel, is more willing to confront it on issues it feels are in violation of international codes of conduct or are not politically salient.

At this early period, it is not possible to know what will come of the Obama administration's efforts to broker a peace agreement between the Palestinians and the Israelis. While there have been meetings aimed at reaching a consensus and while the administration (namely, Secretary of State Hillary Clinton) has indicated that Middle East peace talks are a top priority, the real concern, at least from the Israeli perspective, has been the way that the United States deals with Iran. For now, that appears to be the pressing issue at hand, whereas in previous administrations, the threat posed by Iranian nuclear programs was not a centerpiece of foreign policy initiatives.

Barack Obama's election produced a shift in Israeli views regarding policy toward Iran. In late November 2008, the head of Israeli military intelligence, Major General Amos Yadlin, said, "Rapprochement with Iran, while insisting on clearly defined parameters for the halting of the Iranian nuclear program, isn't necessarily negative. If it succeeds, it will stop the Iranian nuclear program, and, if it fails, it will strengthen the understanding that sanctions and the diplomatic efforts against Iran must be bolstered."[58] Some have suggested that Israeli threats of military action against Iran have been undercut by the difficulty in destroying the Iranian nuclear program, the economic disaster that would result in a world economy that is already on the ropes, and the likelihood that Iran would retaliate not only against Israel but also against its strongest ally—the United States—targeting its forces in Iraq and Afghanistan.[59] Still, Israel has made it clear that Iran is, as the Israeli Defense Forces have defined it, "a threat to the existence of the State of Israel."[60] The urgency of that existential threat, as perceived by Israel, and the continuing diplomatic (as opposed to military) tactics of the United States have resulted in tension between the Obama administration and the Israeli government. Part of that tension, it should be noted, also results from differences in intelligence estimates as to the nuclear capabilities of Israel.

In March 2009, General Yadlin reported to the Israeli cabinet that "Iran has crossed the technological threshold, so that reaching a military nuclear ability is only a matter of matching the strategy to the goal of creating a nuclear bomb." He continued, saying that "Iran continues to accumulate hundreds of kilograms of enriched uranium of poor quality, and hopes to take advantage of its dialogue with the West and the government of Washington in order to advance towards creating a nuclear bomb."[61] Yadlin indicated that the Iranian regime was working slowly to create

such a bomb so as to deflect scorn from the international community and
not give it a reason to take action against the Islamic Republic. Carol
Migdalovitz, a specialist in Middle Eastern affairs at the Congressional
Research Service, comments on Yadlin's presentation to the Israeli
government:

> He stated that it [Iran] is advancing toward the ability to produce nuclear weapons
> in stages, but stopping short of actually making one so that it would not be
> accused of breaking its obligations under the Nuclear Non-Proliferation Treaty. It
> will maintain the capability to build a bomb quickly once it makes the decision.
> He suggested that "The right combination of sanctions and incentives could lead
> to a change in Iran's policies."[62]

As Migdalovitz point out, however, the United States offered its own
assessments of the status of Iran's nuclear program. In February 2009,
one month before Yadlin's report to the Israeli cabinet, the U.S. director
of national intelligence, Dennis Blair, presented an annual threat assessment to the Senate Select Committee on Intelligence that outlined Iran's
nuclear project. The report noted that Iran had not restarted the nuclear
weapons design and weaponization work that it had halted in 2003, and
the same month that Yadlin reported his intelligence findings to the Israeli
government, Blair stated that Iran did not have highly enriched uranium
and would likely not have enough to produce a bomb until 2015.[63]
"Although we do not know whether Iran currently intends to develop
nuclear weapons, we assess Tehran at a minimum is keeping open the
option to develop them," he said.[64]

The discrepancy that emerges from this episode does not indicate that
there is some clandestine, sinister plot on the part of Israel to strike Iran—
differences in nuclear intelligence estimates are possible, and the threat
of Iran is much larger and more realistic for Israel than it is for the United
States. What must be considered, however, is how this scenario affects the
political legitimacy of Israel. As Asher Arian notes in *The Second Republic*,
a system is legitimate when its decisions are generally and widely
accepted as just and proper by major groups within the system.[65] With
that definition serving as a point of departure, an Israeli strike on Iran,
at least in the eyes of the United States, would not be a legitimate course
of action. The destruction that such an event would have on the region
and the international community notwithstanding, the actual intelligence
estimates of the United States do not appear to project the sense of
urgency that Yadlin and the Israeli government suggest exists. Arian
writes, "One may disagree with a decision yet concede that the decision-
making process is legitimate and those who participate in it have the
legitimate right to do so. It is important to distinguish clearly between
legitimacy and legality. The question is not only whether the decision

makers have the legal right to make the decision but whether the decision is generally accepted."[66] Arian goes on to note that "legitimacy in Israel is by no means assured simply because the government has been duly elected and constituted. Sensitive issues have the potential for polarizing the body politic."[67] Sensitive issues in Israel also have the potential for polarizing its allies—and among those issues, a unilateral strike against Iran may be considered the most sensitive of them all.

Can Israel live with a nuclear Iran? The question, loaded and complex as it may be, normally renders highly theoretical discussions about hypothetical scenarios. But the Israeli people have offered a more candid dimension to that question. In June 2009, a survey commissioned by Tel Aviv University asked whether Israelis could live with the prospects of an Iranian neighbor that has an atomic bomb. How would such prospects affect their lives? Stunningly, more than 80 percent of those surveyed said that they expected no change—their lives would go on as normal, perturbed perhaps but not interrupted. Only 11 percent suggested that they would consider emigrating to another, safer country, and 9 percent said that they would relocate to another city within Israel.[68] Additionally, only one in five Israeli Jews believes a nuclear-armed Iran would try to destroy Israel.[69] Israeli officials, however, believed otherwise.

In late September 2010, Israel's ambassador to the United States, Michael Oren, discussed the threat of Iran with *USA Today*. When asked how long it would be before Iran developed a nuclear bomb, Oren referred to the U.S. Central Intelligence Agency, saying that the organization had reported that such prospects would likely take place within a year.[70] The agency had recently discussed the prospects of an Iran bomb three months before Oren's interview, but Leon Panetta, the agency's director, said, "We think they have enough low-enriched uranium right now for two weapons. They do have to enrich it fully to get there. And we would estimate if they made that decision, it probably would take a year to get there. Probably take another year to develop the kind of weapon delivery system in order to make that viable."[71] Thus, while Oren was correct to assert that the *development* of a bomb would potentially take place with a year's time, the delivery of such a bomb to Israel or any other regional actor would not be possible at that time, as Iran did not have the infrastructure needed to project a grounded missile toward its foes. The important question to raise, then again, within these semantics regarding time lines is whether a nuclear Iran—not necessarily a nuclear Iran that is *capable* of launching their weapons but a country with a fully developed atomic bomb—is acceptable to Israel. Can Israel live with a nuclear Iran? The question was posed to Oren, who responded bluntly, "In no way should anybody be prepared to live (with a nuclear Iran). Israel's not alone in it."[72]

Concerns about Iran's nuclear program reflect the judgment that, should the Iranian regime turn to the production of a nuclear bomb, it would endanger Israel, the United States, their mutual allies, and the world. Policymakers fear that a nuclear Iran would touch off a regional arms race, embolden Tehran's aggressive foreign policy ideas, and possibly lead to the destruction of Israel, whose leaders sees its existence as hanging in the balance of Iran's future. But as Barry Posen, a professor of political science at the Massachusetts Institute of Technology notes, the outcomes are not inevitable.[73] A nuclear-armed Iran is a frightening prospect, but that it would necessarily result in a Middle Eastern arms race is unlikely. As Posen notes, if Iran acquires a nuclear weapon, only Israel, Egypt, Saudi Arabia, and Turkey could possibly congregate the resources to follow suit.[74] Of those countries, Israel is already a nuclear power, though an Iranian weapon may give Iran an incentive to go public with the structure of their program. Saudi Arabia does not have the infrastructure to produce a nuclear weapon and would require years in order to build the facilities necessary to enrich uranium. Further, it would, as a close ally of the United States, require security guarantees in order to engage in proliferation efforts. Turkey's reliance on NATO would likely mean that, as during the Cold War, it would rely on the United States for protection, and Egypt's dependence on foreign assistance renders them also unlikely to join the arms race.[75]

Regardless of whether Iran has the capabilities to deploy a nuclear bomb itself, there is little doubt among Israeli politicians that if the Islamic Republic does indeed develop a weapon, it will get in the hands of terrorist groups. Michael Oren has said, "The more immediate threat is that Iran, once it acquires military nuclear capabilities, will pass on those nuclear capabilities to Hezbollah, Hamas and other terrorist groups. So mutually assured destruction has nothing to do with that."[76] Two years earlier, Israeli Defense Minister Ehud Barak offered similar comments:

I do not belong to those who think that if Iran has a nuclear weapon it will hurry to drop it on a neighbor. Iran well understands that an act of this sort would set her back thousands of years. The primary danger is that a nuclear weapon will reach a terrorist group which will not hesitate to use it immediately. They will send it in a container with a GPS to a leading port in the US, Europe, or Israel.[77]

Some nuclear experts believe that a capable and well-organized terrorist group would be able to make a nuclear bomb without the help of a state provided that they have access to the sufficient fissile materials necessary for such an endeavor.[78] Chuck Freilich notes that only 20 to 100 kilograms of fissile material would be needed to make a bomb, and it could easily be purchased in small amounts that would make detection even harder.[79] However, with the state assistance of an actor like Iran, the difficulties of the process would be significantly reduced or even eliminated completely.[80]

Presently, al-Qaeda appears to be the only terrorist organization that may be able to develop nuclear weapons of its own, although the group probably does not have the necessary capabilities.[81] Even so, it is known that al-Qaeda has attempted to obtain nuclear technology and materials, including highly enriched uranium, since the early 1990s. The groups ringleader, Osama bin Laden, has declared that it is al-Qaeda's "holy duty" to use nuclear weapons against the United States and expressed their desire to kill 4 million Americans—carnage that is possible only through the deployment of nuclear weapons. Sketches and diagrams of improvised nukes were found in several al-Qaeda hideouts, and some of the terrorist group's leaders have even hinted that they have acquired them.[82] Freilich outlines several of the possible ways in which a terrorist organization such as al-Qaeda could wind up with a nuclear weapon. Among them are direct government supply (potentially by Pakistan, North Korea, or Iran with Syria in the long term), illicit sales by rogue elements operating in governments, the loss of control over existing nuclear stockpiles in the event of a regime collapse (Pakistan), insufficiently guarded facilities (Russia), and the rise of radical new regimes.[83]

What, then, would occur if a bomb did land in the hands of a terrorist group whose sacred mission was to attack Israel? It would take only one small bomb detonated in a precise and strategic way to have devastating consequences of apocalyptic proportion. For example, a 20-kiloton nuclear bomb would result in tens or hundreds of thousands of casualties in the immediate aftermath, those numbers increasing drastically as subsequent wafts of radiation spread throughout the area.[84] Chuck Freilich also notes the impact that an attack would have not only on the Israeli people but also on the Israeli state:

Although Israel as a state would survive, the consequences for its national resilience, economy, and security would be dramatic; indeed, many may choose to flee the nation following such an attack. Moreover, this scenario is based on the "rosy" assumption that only one nuclear bomb was detonated and that none of Israel's neighbors decided to take advantage of its dramatically weakened state to launch a potentially devastating conventional attack. Indeed, those contemplating nuclear terrorism against Israel might intentionally wait until they could deploy two or more such bombs before doing so. This would enable terrorists to multiply the devastation and threaten Israel's existence, or to hold it hostage and dictate terms between the first use and a threatened second one.[85]

The consequences of an attack on Israel by a terrorist organization with nuclear weapons would, as Freilich has hinted at, devastate the political and economic systems of the country such that it could never become the regional power its leaders hope it would. What is the future of the balance of power in the Middle East? Can Israel rise to the top of the hierarchy with the threat of nuclear Iran (or armed terrorist groups) lingering nearby?

To be sure, Israel exerts a powerful influence on the Middle East. Its military, economic, and political capabilities are significantly higher than any other actor in the region.[86] And Israel has the ability to define the security agenda of the region to a great degree despite being surrounded by Arab-majority states that have often worked against it. However, there are a number of complexities that must be addressed regarding the power structure of the Middle East and whether Israel's quest to be recognized as a leading force can be met with realistic aspects of what actually constitutes a regional power.

First, Israel and Iran have been isolated from other countries that may traditionally be considered as part of the regional power balance (Saudi Arabia and Egypt in particular) for two specific reasons: the Israeli and Iranian threat perceptions that have dominated discourse on Middle Eastern politics and the nuclear capabilities of both countries. During the 1950s and 1960s, Egypt may have been considered a regional power. The country's ideology of republicanism along with pan-Arabism was a legitimate threat to the survival of Arab monarchies.[87] Yet in 1970, Egypt lost its power because of an economic crisis whose negative consequences were exacerbated by the country's recent loss in the Six-Day War. Saudi Arabia gained relative strength as a result of the oil revolution in the 1970s, and today its economy remains strong. Additionally, it is the birthplace of Islam and, as a result of the spread of Wahhabi ideology, has been torn between leading the Muslim world and dealing with fringe religiopolitical groups. Moreover, the military strength of Saudi Arabia is inferior to that of Egypt, Israel, and other states in the region, making it difficult to envision how the country would lead a part of the world that dwarfs its military capabilities.

Ideology is also a useful point to consider when discussing a Middle Eastern power balance. Zionism is a highly influential, unifying ideology within the Israeli borders and is perhaps among the most unifying nationalistic ideologies in the world, but beyond Israel, Zionism loses its power and is often considered a hostile ideology by surrounding Arab states. The ideological capabilities of those Arab candidates for regional leadership are also limited in their scope. Egypt, in particular, is not viewed by other Arab states as representative of true Arab interests. As Martin Beck points out, "By concluding a 'separate peace' with Israel in 1979, Egypt neglected the interests of the Palestinians occupied by Israel."[88] Concurrently, Iran's ideological prospects are limited. Nuclear ambitions aside, the obvious Sunni-Shia schism would cause great concern among regional states, and beyond that, Iran is not a part of the Arab world.[89]

By pausing a moment to observe these nonnuclear dynamics of the possible countries vying for regional power in the Middle East, it is clear that there is not one strong and obvious state that would naturally emerge as a leader. Thus, however unfortunate nuclear military activities may be, they are, for the time being, clearly linked to Israel and Iran's quest to lead the region and set those two countries apart from other states and are vital to the regime security of Iran and the political legitimacy of Israel.

With regard to the political legitimacy of Israel and the question of the emergence of a regional leader, it is necessary to examine not only the real political and military maneuvers of Iran and Israel but the rhetorical—and symbolic—maneuvers as well. Often, things that are unspoken are more powerful than those things that are spoken, and in April 2010, this was the case. Benjamin Netanyahu was invited by the Obama administration to attend a nuclear conference in Washington. This invitation was symbolic, as it was the first time that Israel had been invited to join the select, prestigious group of attendees to discuss nuclear issues. It also effectively granted Israel a profound sense of legitimacy as a significant player in the delicate arena.[90] As Avner Cohen writes, "From a practical perspective, it will be the first time the 'good guys' will have convened to address nuclear terrorism, perhaps the greatest nuclear-related threat our generation has to confront."[91] Stunningly, however, Netanyahu refused the invitation after being told that Arab leaders would vilify Israel's nuclear policy and refusal to sign the Nuclear Non-Proliferation Treaty. The decision, it appeared, resulted from fear, a lack of trust, and a sense of isolation—signs not typically displayed by a country that hopes to establish increased political legitimacy and regional power.[92] Two months earlier, in February, Netanyahu met his Greek counterpart, George Papandreou, during a trip to Moscow and warned him of Iran's nuclear program, saying that it would set off a "a Middle Eastern nuclear arms race, where countries like Turkey, Saudi Arabia and Egypt will seek to acquire nuclear weapons."[93] Netanyahu did not mention that there are already 90 U.S.-made nuclear weapons in Turkey as part of the NATO arsenal, which no one knows what to do with because Turkey lacks the aircraft for that purpose. Moreover, Saudi Arabia lacks the infrastructure for nuclear capability, and Egypt has been debating for more than 25 years about where it will build its first reactor. In short, the urgency of a nuclear arms race does not appear to be what Netanyahu indicates it is.[94] Zvi Bar'el writes,

Here is what this bomb, which does not yet exist, has managed to do: sparked dangerous friction between China and the United States, with Washington selling arms to Taiwan in order to twist China's arm; turned Europe's missile defense program into a hostage, dependent on Russian support for sanctions against Iran; triggered a clash between U.S. President Barack Obama, who does not want sanctions against Iran that are too severe, and Congress, which seeks extensive sanctions; stirred a debate within the U.S. administration between those who think Iran should be considered a player that can contribute to stability in Afghanistan and Iraq and those who oppose that approach; and created a rift between Arab states concerned about Iranian hegemony in the region and those who do not want to be on the same side as Israel against Iran.[95]

While Israel has placed premium on keeping its nuclear program opaque, even refusing to attend a nuclear conference that would have given it legitimacy among a distinct group of "big players," Iran continues to evade the international community, perturbing world leaders by announcing the gradual enrichment of uranium and perpetuating speculation that it is in fact in the process of building a nuclear bomb. And, without even manufacturing a single atomic bomb, Iran became a regional superpower capable of influencing international policies. Iran's ability to keep the Middle East (and beyond) on their toes, constantly raising ire that at any moment it will strike, has, in some senses, already made it a regional power.

In an ironic twist, Manouchehr Mottaki, former Iranian foreign minister, said in December 2010, shortly before his dismissal, that Israel was the root cause of the conflicts in the Middle East. "The root cause of problems in the region is the existence of an occupying regime that has nuclear weapons," Mottaki noted.[96] Even so, the recent political climate of the Middle East has revolved around the "threat" of Iran, and though the country may not be respected by other states in the region, Tehran's ability to garner an enormous amount of international scrutiny and provoke policies abroad that are grounded in best guesses shows that it is in a position of power even if that power produces negative blowback.

Western intelligence is still unable to determine the specifics of Iran's nuclear program, and international sanctions seem to do little good in deterring the regime's ambitions for uranium enrichment. Even Mottaki shunned U.S. Secretary of State Hillary Clinton at a meeting in Manama, refusing to acknowledge her or speak to her—an episode that embarrassed the United States and showed that Iran's regime, however seemingly belligerent it may be, answers to no one but itself.[97] In December 2010, Iran's Foreign Ministry Spokesman Ramin Mehmanparast called on the world's major powers for a new constructive approach toward Tehran, saying, "Western countries had better make use of the Islamic Republic's powerful presence and the cooperation of other independent countries to compensate for the policies which have resulted in crises and tension in different parts of the world."[98] Iran said that it would not negotiate over its right to enrich uranium, indicating that it controls the narrative of nuclear politics.

Justin Elliot of *Salon* magazine noted in early December 2010 that Israel does, in fact, have a long history of incorrect calculations regarding Iran's nuclear program—just as Netanyahu and other Israeli leaders have sounded alarms in recent months about what they see as a growing problem, their rhetoric may be considered as part of a long pattern of accusations, none of which have borne out exactly as they described them. In October 1992, Shimon Peres warned that Iran would be capable of producing an atomic bomb by 1999, saying that "Iran is the greatest threat [to peace] and greatest problem in the Middle East . . . because it seeks the nuclear option while holding a highly dangerous stance of extreme religious militants."[99] In 1995, Benjamin Netanyahu wrote in his book *Fighting Terrorism: How Democracies Can Defeat the International Terrorist Network* that "the best estimates at this time place Iran between three and five years away from possessing the prerequisites required for the independent production of nuclear weapons."[100] In 2003, a high-ranking military officer told the Knesset Foreign Affairs and Defense Committee that "Iran will have the materials needed to make a nuclear bomb by 2004 and will have an operative nuclear weapons program by 2005."[101] Then in 2010, reporter Jeffrey Goldberg, reporting on the Israeli view of the Iranian nuclear program, wrote that "Iran is, at most, one to three years away from having a breakout nuclear capability (often understood to be the capacity to assemble more than one missile-ready nuclear device within about three months of deciding to do so)."[102] Despite the years of prediction, on the part not only of Israel but of the United States as well, one thing is certain: no one knows when Iran will become capable of launching a nuclear missile. Theories and speculations about a time line have become imbued within discourses of state leaders and lawmakers often for the specific purpose of achieving some political agenda or strategy. Nuclear weapons aside, Iran is still able to wreak havoc on the Middle East through various other outlets, and much of that havoc has, in past years, been directed at Israel. The country's concerns over Iran's nuclear program are valid, but even more relevant to the security of Israel and the future of its political legitimacy in the region are the contemporary threats it faces from proxy groups. While these groups are discussed in detail in Chapter 6, the interregional conflicts that they have participated in and their tactical mission to bombard Israel, in particular, are discussed in Chapter 3. Israel's role as a regional power is affected by the interregional conflicts that have occurred in recent decades, most notably those fought by Hezbollah and Hamas. Acting with the support of Iran and targeting their aggression at Israel, these surrogate groups have attempted to eat away at Israeli political legitimacy and have added an element of security to the Iranian regime by fighting battles on its behalf. Some have suggested that the groups also serve as a distraction from Iran's nuclear plans; while Hezbollah and Israel go head-to-head, attention is diverted from the Iranian regime, which, not long after such battles are over, announce new steps in their efforts to enrich uranium.

CHAPTER 4

Regional Politics and Proxy Groups

In November 2010, a senior Israeli intelligence official announced that Hamas rockets with a range of 80 kilometers were capable of reaching Tel Aviv. The threat of violence, he warned, was serious, and Egypt was to blame. "Egypt can stop all this smuggling of weapons within 24 hours if they want to do it," he said, speaking on the condition of anonymity.[1] By his calculations, Egypt had not taken an aggressive stance against arms smuggling, and the network of tunnels between the border of the Sinai Desert and the Gaza Strip hosted a booming weapons transport operation. The statement, which resonated throughout the international community, emphasized the complex nature of regional conflicts and the revived focus on proxy groups that have come to define the volatile and sometimes violent relationships between these actors. Just four days before the announcement, Israeli forces stormed the home of Hamas legislator Mahmoud Rahami, arresting him and saying only that he had been involved in "suspicious activities."[2]

In late October 2010, Nigerian authorities seized 13 containers of weapons from Iran. The weapons, headed for Gambia, included a cache of artillery rockets that, if placed in the hands of highly trained militants, could accurately hit targets more than five miles away, killing everything within about 40 feet. Insurgent fighters in Afghanistan and Iraq have used similar rockets against U.S. troops.[3]

Nigeria's secret service intercepted the container at the port of Lagos—an area believed to be part of a new smuggling route from Iran to the Gaza Strip. The arms shipment was camouflaged as building material after it was unloaded from an Iranian ship that had docked at the port for a few hours, unloaded its cargo, and continued on. "[On] opening the first container, the service operatives discovered rocket launchers, grenades and other explosives; the weapons were concealed among crates of floor tiles," Nigerian State Security Service spokeswoman Marilyn Ogar said.[4]

Israeli officials accused Iran of attempting to smuggle the weapons into Gaza, placing them in the hands of militants who would fire them across the border into Israel. However, questions were raised about why Iran would ship weapons into Gambia—an unexpected destination. In order for the package to have reached Gaza, it would first have needed to be trucked across Nigeria into Chad and Sudan and ultimately through Egypt.[5] But no matter the logistics regarding the package's shipment, what emerged from the incident was a certainty among Israelis that the arms were intended to be used against them and that Iran would proceed, at all costs, to supply militants with the necessary arms they needed to work on behalf of the Islamic Republic. What also emerged was the premium that Iran has recently placed on its foreign policy initiatives in Africa. The 2011 revolutions in North Africa only add to Israeli uneasiness. With Hosni Mubarak now out of the picture, the future of continued peace between Egypt and Israel is not certain and there is much speculation that widespread demonstrations in the Arab Maghreb may result in increased anti-Israeli sentiment (During the February 2011 protests in Cairo, some activists held up pictures of Mubarak with the Star of David drawn over his face; they later burned the pictures in an expression of anger). Over the course of the past two years, Iran has upped the ante in its efforts to court new African allies, especially as the United Nations and Western nations have increased sanctions on Iran over its contentious nuclear program. In the process, Iran sought to identify weak regimes in Africa whose tumbling economies would provide Tehran with an opportunity to influence an alliance. Nigeria and Gambia have been targeted, though the results were not what Iran had hoped for, as the recent arms shipment was discovered and reported to the United Nations. Nigeria's decision to report the findings of the shipment won praise from Israel, whose leadership, contended that, once again, Iran was traveling down a dangerous path—one that would ultimately lead to disaster in Israel. "They made almost no concessions to the Iranians an acted with great determination," an Israeli security source told Haaretz News Agency.[6]

In addition to Nigeria, Gambia also turned on Iran, cutting all diplomatic ties with the country. "All government of The Gambia projects and programmes, which were [being] implemented in co-operation with the government of the Islamic Republic of Iran, have been cancelled," the Gambian Foreign Ministry said in a statement.[7] The relationship between Gambia and Iran became closer after Gambia's president, Yahya Jemmah, was elected in 1994, and the African country has been among those developing nations that defended Iran's right to nuclear power. The blow dealt to Iran as a result of the expulsion of Iranian diplomats loosens its grip on the African continent. Though the weapons shipment never reached Hamas in the Gaza Strip, the affair served as another reminder to the international community that Iran's leadership will seek whatever avenue possible to supply Hamas and will continue to use proxy groups in the region to act on its behalf, perhaps as a diversion from its own nuclear ambitions—particularly as Ali Akbar Salehi, Iran's nuclear chief, takes the reigns of the Foreign Ministry.

Hamas is an offshoot of the pan-Islamic Muslim Brotherhood movement, which began in 1987 to address the Palestinian nationalist movement. Its acronym is short for *Harakat al-Muqawama al-Islamiya*, and its meaning—"strength," "bravery," and "zeal"—is organized to define Palestinian nationalism and to reclaim the land that is now considered Israel (land that is considered Islamic *waqf*).[8] Hamas is a mainly Sunni group that is strategically organized with a military and a political wing, each very different as to their nature of duties but closely intertwined. At its inception, Hamas had little to do with Iran primarily because of Iran's support for its rival Palestinian Islamic Jihad and also because Iran was focused on rallying support for Hezbollah in southern Lebanon during this time. After the 1991 Gulf War, however, the relationship between Iran and Hamas took a turn; Hamas's leader met with the Islamic Republic's supreme leader, and shortly after, both Hamas and Iran proclaimed that they shared an "identical view in the strategic outlook toward the Palestinian cause in its Islamic dimension."[9] Iran then pledged to give Hamas $30 million per year and promised to provide Hamas with weapons and military training in Iran, Lebanon, and Sudan. After a string of events (the second intifada, the American invasion of Iraq, and Hamas's electoral victory) in the early 2000s, Iran began to realize that Hamas could help legitimize Iran's government and help the Islamic Republic succeed in becoming a dominant regional power. Short thereafter, the Hamas-Iranian relationship began to switch from a "lukewarm relationship into a full-blown alliance."[10]

Though former Israeli prime minister Ariel Sharon has declared that peace is impossible without full eradication of Hamas and other resistance groups that are opposed to the peace settlement, Iran has contended that it will continue to support Hamas until the collapse of Israel. President Mahmoud Ahmadinejad told an Iranian news agency that it is the "religious and national duty" of Iran to stand behind the Palestinian nation "until the big victory feast which is the collapse of the Zionist regime."[11] Hamas has recently been labeled as the largest Islamic group for the Palestinian community,[12] and Iran openly continues to provide support for Hamas in order to promote nationalism and Islamic unity for Muslims. In turn, Hamas has reaffirmed its agenda with Iran to advance radical Islam and "defend the rights of Islamic Iran."[13]

Throughout this relationship, Iran has gained leverage over Hamas as being the group's main financial supporter. Iran's funding to Hamas has increased over the past few years (particularly following the 2006 elections), and by November 2006, it is claimed that Iran has provided over $120 million in aid to Hamas. In addition, in December 2006, Hamas's interior minister said that Iran pledged to give the group $250 million to help pay the salaries of civil servants, Hamas security forces, and the families of Palestinians who have lost their homes in the Israeli occupation.[14] A prominent lawmaker in Iran adds that there have been discussions that consider "setting up a common fund of participating nations to channel the donations."[15]

The Middle East in general and the Persian Gulf[16] in particular are highly volatile regions of the world where threat perceptions create a security dilemma. In these regions, security tends to be directly associated with the political stability of the states, their military and security agenda, and their status within the international community. Countries situated around the Gulf are practically engaged in a vicious circle of competition, and their relations are best described by the security dilemma paradigm.

The Persian Gulf states, as noted by Bjørn Møller, face "the uncomfortable dilemma" by placing the survival of their people "at risk" if they stick to some "tangible values as sovereignty" or by choosing to defend themselves (regime security) through heavy investments in military might paid by "the inevitable expense of economic development."[17] While regime security is definitely an important factor, another permanent variable in the security situation of the region is the role historically played by external players. Regime security is enhanced by the hard-currency income, mainly from oil, in a region of *rentier states*, yet it is seriously associated with power structure, leadership dynamics, and the often complex process of decision making. The entire game is also interconnected with the role of external players and the legacy they leave behind or the perception they create among the countries of the region. From this follows—and here Iran serves as an example—that national interest and national security are compromised with regime security, and regime security can also mean the security of one single person at the top of a hierarchy.

In the post–Cold War era and in the absence of two great rivals, perhaps game theory and zero-sum game theory have lost some relevance, but the more vulnerable states of the Persian Gulf still need to shelter behind a superpower in case a war breaks out. This situation has brought the United States into the picture, reinforcing the triangular relationship between Israel, Iran, and the United States.

The fact that the United States is the offshore balancer of the region, particularly the balance between Iran and Israel, makes the security environment much more complicated. The case of Iran is even more unusual since it provides a complex political pattern that does not exist elsewhere in the region—that of an Islamic Republic.

Looking at the political map of the Persian Gulf, we find that most of the hereditary monarchies in the region are in this body of water. What appears to be different is Iran, where an Islamic Republic has existed since 1979, but, unlike what one may expect from a *republican system*, the new Islamic Republic of Iran has not evolved Iran's government beyond life-long leadership, though it did do away with the hereditary factor. The "supreme leader" technically receives his (and it can only be a *he* in the Islamic Republic) lifelong appointment from a group of Islamic experts.[18] Despite the fact that even traditional monarchies adhere to Islam, the idea of monarchy was un-Islamic in Ayatollah Khomeini's mind, and he argued that the just ruler should be a trained Islamic jurist. "Since Islamic government is a government of law, knowledge of the law is necessary for the ruler, as has been laid down in tradition." That is, he wrote, the ruler "must surpass all others in knowledge" and be "more learned than everyone else."[19]

As much as Ayatollah Khomeini knew about Islamic jurisprudence, he was probably not a security expert and definitely not conversant with the security situation in the Persian Gulf and the region in general. He was a skilled populist who successfully mobilized large parts of the population against the shah's regime, but his statements while in exile do not reflect a well-developed national security doctrine. His idea of exporting the Islamic Revolution was one of the first destabilizing factors that worked to the detriment of interstate relations in the Persian Gulf. Had he been more knowledgeable about the basics of security and not pursued a revolutionary path at all costs, he might have taken a different approach to the West and perhaps avoided the war with Iraq.[20]

However, the Islamic Revolution did not entirely abolish the tradition of a leader-for-life system. In fact, an even more powerful spiritual-religious leadership replaced the omnipotent shah. The constitution of the Islamic Republic of Iran gives the leader vast direct and indirect authority and power in a number of crucial areas, ranging from the judiciary to national security. When Khomeini was the leader, this was very much a de facto acknowledgment of his theological and political status. With his successor Ali Khamenei, the need arose to institutionalize as much as possible the decision-making potential of the position. Thus, his word can virtually substitute for the law and take precedence over or entirely change decisions made on all levels of the state bureaucracy, leaving few formal—virtually none in reality—instances where his position on any given issue can be challenged.[21]

This applies to all decisions involving the state, even those formally in the purview of the president of the republic. A good example is the nomination of Rahim Mashaaei[22] by Ahmadinejad as his first vice president for parliamentarian affairs. In 2008, Mashaei had publicly announced, "Iranian people are friends of the Israeli people." His statement met the strong disapproval of high-ranking clerics and, following a public rebuke by Ayatollah Khamenei, forced him to reaffirm his loyalty to the guidance of Khamenei in all policy-related matters. In 2009, after the presidential elections, Ahmadinejad renominated Mashaei as vice president. This created a dispute among the conservatives, and once again Ayatollah Khamenei intervened. This time, he issued a decree to Ahmadinejad that he initially ignored: "Without any delay the removal or acceptance of Masha'i's resignation must be announced by the president."[23]

In the political arena, several other examples can serve to underscore the centrality of the leader in the foreign policy decision-making process. Almost all foreign leaders who visit Iran also visit the supreme leader. Ahmadinejad usually accompanies the guest to the leader's office and sits in during the meeting. While this per se does not appear to have a meaning, it is in fact an authorization from the leader for Ahmadinejad's negotiations with the guest. In other words, the visiting head of state is reassured that promises to him by the government have the support of the leader and can, therefore, be considered valid. This and innumerable similar cases, like the nuclear issue, show the supremacy of the leader in sensitive decisions directly related to Iranian security issues.

The leader has a vast network of advisers and consultation groups, such as an adviser in issues related to higher education and Iranian universities, another in armed forces, and yet another (or even a group of advisers) in relation to international, economic, or security issues. Some of these advisers switch from positions in the president's office to that of the leader and vice versa. For instance, when in 2005 Ahmadinejad emerged as a presidential candidate, Saeed Jalili, who was then in his early forties and "worked as a deputy to the foreign minister in European and American affairs," served as close adviser to Ahmadinejad's presidential campaign.[24] At the same time, Ali Larijani served as the head of Iran's Supreme National Security Council and as the country's top nuclear negotiator on nuclear issues. After Ahmadinejad's election, Larijani resigned and was immediately replaced by Saeed Jalili, who appeared to have little or no experience in nuclear negotiations. In some other cases, former top military or Revolutionary Guard commanders or former foreign ministers are appointed to advise the supreme leader. The list of most recent advisers includes Yahya Rahim Safavi, former chief commander of the Iranian Revolutionary Guard Corps (IRGC; pasdaran in Persian); Ali Akbar Velayati and Kamal Kharrazi, both former ministers of foreign affairs; and even midranking clerics, such as Mohammad Mohammadian (head of the supreme leader's Office of University Affairs). The list of advisers now contains more military than civilian names, and this is a reflection of the growing importance and influence of the military (including the Revolutionary Guard) in decisions made by the leader, particularly on issues related to security, defense, and the nuclear program.[25]

It looks like a recent statement made by U.S. Secretary of State Hillary Clinton that Iran is becoming a military dictatorship is based on an in-depth examination and interpretation of this network of advisers and their impact on the decisions recently made in domestic and international situations, including the pursuit of nuclear technology. However, Clinton sees a different dimension of the influence of the military over the supreme leader. In her words, the supreme leader is now under the full influence of the Revolutionary Guard to the point that it is approaching a military dictatorship: "We see that the government of Iran, the supreme leader, the president, the parliament, is being supplanted and that Iran is moving toward a military dictatorship. That is our view."[26]

The Arab leaders of the Gulf closely watch the political developments in Iran and are constantly mindful of their social and political ramifications. The slightest change in Iran can spread to the gulf and create insecurity. While the "disagreement over the name" seems to be primarily "symbolic,"[27] what the Arab leaders of the gulf definitely do not like to see is the hard-line clerics resuscitating their territorial claim over Bahrain. When in 2009 one of Khamenei's key advisers called Bahrain the fourteenth province of Iran,[28] Bahrain halted negotiations with Iran over planned gas imports. Iran's claim to Bahrain comes back every now and then and triggers distrust and suspicion of Iran's regional goals. It also "serves as a catalyst for sharpening Arab-Iranian polarization in the area."[29]

Iran has a complicated system of decision making, especially in matters related to foreign policy. As Mohsen Sazgara, one of the founders of the IRGC, succinctly put it, after Ayatollah Khomeini passed away, "Ayatollah Khamenei gradually has created a bureaucracy to consolidate his power over Iran's military, intelligence and foreign policy."[30] Within the Iranian power grid where the leader is central, the decision-making circles remain completely opaque. One can argue that the leader operates within a network of mainly military advisers, but it is unclear who makes or influences the decisions; usually, the president of the Islamic Republic of Iran is the one who makes the public announcements. In fact, he might be talking about decisions he has not made himself or might in fact disagree with. It is therefore fair to say that while he can take initiatives to solve problems with Iran's neighbors or create new problems, he is not the source of the decision making. His part is limited to announcing the modality and tactics of putting those decisions into operation. This can be verified in almost all incidents during the past 30 years no matter who was the president.

As Abbas Maleki, former deputy foreign minister of Iran under Velayati, put it, the leader's "word is final in the more significant matters of foreign affairs." Some critical foreign policy decisions taken in the past 20 years by him include the following: "1—Iran's stance of neutrality during the allied attack on Iraq in 1991; 2—The non-intervention in Afghan internal affairs (even after the killing of nine Iranian diplomats in Mazare Sharif by the Taliban in 1998); and 3—The support of the Palestinians in the Arab-Israeli conflict."[31] These decisions were made while three different presidents were in power: Rafsanjani, Khatami, and Ahmadinejad. While this continuity and consistency could be interpreted as evidence of the consensual nature of the decision making in Iran, one can also see the limits of such consensus by looking at the existing power struggle between the supreme leader and the former presidents or presidential candidates. What is completely missing in this quasi consensus is the role of the minister of foreign affairs.

Toward the end of Rafsanjani's second term, there was a shift toward the Arab neighbors in the Persian Gulf followed by Khatami, but it was under Ahmadinejad that the Gulf Cooperation Council (GCC) invited Ahmadinejad to speak at the December 2–3, 2007, summit of the GCC leaders in Doha, Qatar, "marking the first time an Iranian president has been invited since the GCC was formed in 1981."[32] In Katzman's words, Ahamdinejad "reiterated a consistent Iranian theme," requesting the gulf countries to form a regional security system including Iran and excluding "outside powers."[33]

Practically, and also by definition, several centers of power, such as the parliament's National Security and Foreign Policy Committee, influence the supreme leader and his advisers in international affairs. In this often highly informal process of consultation, legislation is modified before being passed. This is particularly important regarding legislation related to Iran's security and foreign relations, and here again one can argue that their existence means a structural hope for the future, but by precedent and history, they have had only nominal value and minor influence in the decisions made by the system. A good example is the stalemate over Iran's nuclear issues and Iranian-U.S. relations.

Iran's presidents in general are powerless if they oppose the leadership's ideas about foreign policy and become, at best, spokespersons if they are obedient to the supreme leader. In fact, they will be empowered to speak on behalf of the leader, who draws the pattern and instructs them about major foreign policy issues. By definition, the president is only the second man in the system and heads the executive power. As described by Maleki, the critical decisions are made by the leader, who receives his advice not from the government's Foreign Ministry but from a group of experts in international relations. The supreme leader also selects his men for some key positions, such as in the Ministry of Foreign Affairs, the Ministry of Defense, or the Ministry of Islamic Culture. In 1997, Khatami resisted maintaining Velayati for a fifth term in his position as foreign minister but finally agreed with Kharrazi, who was the head of the Iranian delegation to the United Nations.[34] Khatami had to nominate Kharrazi because Khamenei would not agree with anyone else. It is worth mentioning that Ayatollah Khamenei has kept all the previous foreign ministers (Velayati and Kharrazi) as his personal advisers in international affairs.[35]

Khamenei's vision for extending Iran's influence across the Middle East can be found in a statement he made concerning Hamas and Hezbollah. Khamenei believed in the value of proxy groups and saw them as a way of exerting indirect pressure against Israel. According to him, wars fought by Hamas and Hezbollah "reflect the spread of the Islamic Revolution's principles."[36] "The events in Gaza, and before them the 33-day war in Lebanon, when the Zionist entity's army and its U.S. equipment failed to defeat the unarmed people, reflect the spread of the Islamic revolution's principles," he said.[37]

Hezbollah was born out of the alienation and repression of the Lebanese Shias, a group that had been largely excluded by the Lebanese government and that "had long suffered discrimination under dominant Sunni Muslim rule."[38] While the rest of Lebanon was prospering economically, "the Shiites remained locked in a time warp, the underdogs of the population."[39]

In the early 1960s in Lebanon, the foundation was laid for the development of Hezbollah as a product of "an active clerical movement that served to re-invigorate Islam's key principles."[40] The movement was spawned by a group of religious clerics who had received religious enlightenment from religious schools in Najaf, Iraq, and had returned to Lebanon to initiate a movement to incorporate Islamic teachings into a more dominant role in Lebanese life. The movement was initiated and influenced by religious scholars, including Imam Mussa al-Sadr, Ayatollah Muhammad Mahdi Shamseddine, and Ayatollah al-Sayyed Muhammad Hussein Fadlallah. Under the influence of such clerics, the Islamic movement grew from a modest group of a few faithful to a larger and more influential movement.[41] According to Jaber, the Shia in Lebanon during the 1960s "continued to trail behind the rest of the country" and lacked not only government representation but also "the basic necessities of modern life, such as schools, hospitals, roads and running water."[42] The Islamic movement sought to remedy these problems and give the Shia in Lebanon some degree of representation. Al-Sadr, an Iranian educated in Najaf, was influential in the Islamic movement in Lebanon, quickly rising to a leadership position. Al-Sadr founded the Lebanese Islamic Higher Council in 1967 and the Movement of the Deprived in 1974 and succeeded in mobilizing the Shia masses and pushing the Lebanese government toward reform.[43]

The 1979 Iranian Revolution saw great support from this strong Islamic base in Lebanon, with demonstrations expressing support for the movement led by Ayatollah Khomeini. According to Qassem, the emergence of Ayatollah Khomeini to power in Iran solidified a relationship between the nascent group and Iran, as "Ayatollah Khomeini was designated the leading religious authority, and the inquisition began into the appropriate means of liaising with the Islamic Revolution's leadership."[44]

The Shia group Hezbollah (also referred to as Hizbollah, or Hizballah, and the Party of God) was born out of the Israeli invasion of Lebanon in 1982.[45] The group consisted of various Islamist groups uniting under the "Manifesto of the Nine," a document that outlined various objectives and gave authority to Ayatollah Khomeini.[46] Qassem outlines the three pillars of Hezbollah that form and dictate the role and objectives of Hezbollah as (1) belief in Islam, (2) jihad, and (3) jurisdiction of the jurist-theologian (al-Wali al-Faghih).[47] Each of these tenets dictates a particular responsibility of the movement to the spread of Islam and the individual's responsibilities as a good Muslim. As the jurist-theologian, Khomeini was the supreme theological leader of Hezbollah; thus, Hezbollah was responsible to Khomeini, who provided spiritual direction and oversight as well as substantial resources to fund the movement. After Khomeini's death, Imam Khamenei was placed in the role of jurist-theologian and continues to supply the movement with direction, spiritual leadership, and support as well as fulfilling his position as the supreme leader of Iran.

Iran was supportive of the nascent Islamic organization in terms of military training, provision of arms, and diplomatic support. When the Israelis invaded Lebanon, 1,500 Iranian Revolutionary Guards were there "to support Lebanon's confrontation with Israel, primarily through military training and the provision of necessary infrastructure."[48] Training camps were set up in the Bekaa Valley, where the group would establish its early base of operations.[49] Early on, Hezbollah members had been connected to the Lebanese National Resistance, a movement led by Amal but diverted from the secular tenets of the movement, embracing, rather, the Islamic direction of Iran. The Lebanese National Resistance served as an umbrella organization for the group until it announced its official existence in 1985.[50] According to Jaber, "Hezbollah's initial goal was to launch a revolt against the Israeli occupation, which would eventually grow to embrace the task of ridding Lebanon from the presence of Western forces and influence. These aims would be conducted under the banner of Islam, the sponsorship of Iran and with the blessing of Syria."[51]

In the beginning, Hezbollah faced difficulties in attracting support among the Lebanese population. The problem was not in its inability to attract Shia Lebanese to its cause of resistance but rather in the southern population's heavy losses as Israel struck out at Hezbollah. As Jaber explains, "It was not that the southerners were averse to the concept of resistance itself: they had, after all, growing to live with it and had participated in its activities. The problem was that they were angered at having to bear the brunt of the reprisals, as well as taking huge losses in operations that were more often than not doomed."[52] There was also growing bitterness among the population, as areas of southern Lebanon under Hezbollah's influence were drastically transformed as strict interpretations of Islamic law were imposed.[53] Unpopularity resulting in the imposition of strict Islamic law and Hezbollah's military failures would eventually be reversed in military successes and Hezbollah's provision of services to the Lebanese Shia population.

In addition to its inability to gather momentum among the population, Hezbollah faced a high number of casualties in battles with Israeli forces. One of the most significant confrontations that resulted in heavy Lebanese losses occurred in 2006 when Hezbollah's kidnapping of two Israeli soldiers escalated into a full-blown war between Israel and Hezbollah. While Hezbollah claimed victory in the conflict, the war would result in over 1,200 casualties and would leave parts of Lebanon destroyed.[54] The war between Israel and Hezbollah lasted 33 days and resulted in the displacement of around 1 million people.[55] The leader of Hezbollah, Sheik Hassan Nasrallah, apologized for the effects on the Lebanese people, saying that he would not have ordered the raid and kidnappings had he realized that Israel would respond with such actions.[56] Even as the outcome of the conflict resulted in heavy and unexpected losses, Hezbollah would emerge from the conflict with heavy support and growing legitimacy, as will be described later.

In September 2010, the Washington Institute for Near East Policy released a report indicating that a future conflict between Israel and Hezbollah—a rerun of the 2006 war—would likely be much worse. Jeffrey White, a veteran of the U.S. intelligence establishment, warned of the greater regional impact that a future conflict would have. According to White, if a second Israel-Hezbollah war erupts, it will not resemble the war of the summer of 2006 but rather will span a large majority of Lebanon, Israel, and Syria and possibly draw Iran into the conflict. In addition, it would involve major military operations, result in significant casualties (particularly among civilians), and devastate infrastructure throughout the region. White maintains that Israel's strategy in such a war would be to implement a fundamental change in the military balance and crush Hezbollah, although he says that such would not be viewed by the Israeli military or government as a "final victory."[57] The Israeli military strategy would include combined arms operations (land, air, and sea) with the purpose of destroying Hezbollah's weaponry and land forces in the south of Lebanon. Israel may also aim to prevent the war from creeping into Syria by deploying threats, perhaps of a nuclear attack, and mobilizing forces to give the impression that it is ready for a fight. Beyond a war of words, or rhetorical saber rattling, Israel would make it clear that it fully intends to attack Syrian troops who come to Hezbollah's aid.[58]

Hezbollah's goals, on the other hand, will include an array of missiles and rockets launched against Israel's borders in an effort to hit the Israeli Defense Forces near Lebanon. Syria's air force will attempt to block Israeli fighters from crossing through Syrian airspace and attempt to intercept them over Lebanon.[59]

If indeed Syria is directly drawn into the fight, its focus will be to preserve the Assad regime, not necessarily helping Hezbollah in Lebanon. Thus, with Syria fending for its own political life and the security of its own regime, Iran will begin to support Hezbollah and Syria with arms. It is not certain that Hamas will enter the fight, especially considering that Israel may use the opportunity to bring about the collapse of its hold on the Gaza Strip, the report noted. White noted in his assessment that the Israeli Defense Forces will occupy parts of Lebanon within weeks of a war and possibly all the Gaza Strip. He said that it will be the most serious war that Israel has been involved in since 1973 and that Israel must emerge victorious. If Israel is serious about its actions and is willing to live up to the long history of saber rattling in the region—if Israel is willing to incur the price of war, that is, the massive casualties, the potential for economic stagnation, or, worse, collapse—it will succeed. Hezbollah will be broken, and Syria's regime will be irreversibly weakened. As a result, Iran's future activities in the region will be damaged as the influence of its allies diminishes.[60]

The potential for conflict between Hezbollah and Israel dates back to the formation of the Hezbollah itself. After all, Hezbollah was created primarily as a result of the 1982 Israeli invasion of Lebanon. Since its inception, Hezbollah and Israel's fates have been intertwined as Hezbollah has sought to resist Israeli expansion into Israel and Israel has sought to fight back against Hezbollah. Hezbollah and Israel have been involved in a number of confrontations. From its creation until 2000, Hezbollah carried out an extensive guerilla campaign against Israel. Israel's "Operation Accountability" in 1993 and "Operation Grapes of Wrath" in 1996 were launched in response to Hezbollah's attacks on Israeli civilians and soldiers. While these campaigns were significant, it was the early twenty-first-century campaigns that resulted in the largest political gains for Hezbollah.

According to the United States Institute of Peace, "The departure of Israeli forces from Lebanon in 2000 and of Syrian forces in 2003 vaulted Hezbollah to the forefront of the Lebanese political scene."[61] Hezbollah's military success against Israel has led to validation and its virtual legitimatization. During the 2006 confrontation, Hezbollah managed to resist defeat, and the Israeli withdrawal from Lebanon resulted in increased prestige for the Iranian-funded organization. This campaign was especially significant, as Hezbollah was able to claim victory despite heavy casualties and Israeli's heavy-handed response garnered sympathy for the group and resulted in an increase in political power. Throughout the campaign, Hezbollah was supported politically and financially by Iran. According to Bickerton and Klausner, "Israelis claimed that their ultimate antagonists were neither Hamas nor Hizbullah, but Iran and Syria, which provided both groups with financial and logistical assistance as well as political support."[63]

While the outcome would solidify the status of Hezbollah in Lebanon, the initial Israeli response had been supported by some in the pro-American Lebanese government as well as Arab governments, including Saudi Arabia, Egypt, and Jordan, "which were increasingly worried about Shiite and Iranian influence in the area."[64] The relationship between the Lebanese government and Hezbollah had always been somewhat frigid, and there was some speculation that Lebanon had hoped that Israel's 2006 campaign against the group would result in the destruction of the Shia Hezbollah. This fear may have been somewhat realized, as the outcome would indeed perpetuate Hezbollah's political status and would therefore ensure Iranian influence in the area. While moderate Arab support at the onset of the war had been against Hezbollah, "as Lebanese casualties mounted, so did the support for Hizbullah throughout the region because of Arab and Muslim anger."[65] When the war ended with both the Israeli military and Hezbollah claiming victory and Lebanon sustaining significant losses in terms of civilian casualties, civilian displacement, and damage to infrastructure, it appears as if it was Hezbollah that emerged with the greatest gain. As the perceived underdog in the fight, it had been able to challenge the grand Israeli military and hold its own. In the aftermath, despite heavy losses, Hezbollah emerged victorious in its own right as public opinion emerged in support of the group. According to the *New York Times*, "Hezbollah moved quickly after the war with Israel to capitalize on its enhanced political standing at home and abroad, out of a conviction that the governing coalition had effectively colluded with Israel in the hope its bombing campaign would destroy Hezbollah's militia."[66] Hezbollah became a political force after the war, gaining significant power in the Lebanese government. In 2005, the group "won fourteen seats in the 128-member Lebanese Parliament," and after 2008, the group strengthened its control of the Lebanese cabinet to 11 of 30 seats.[67]

While Iran may not have been a direct participant in the 2006 Israeli campaign against Lebanon (in terms of military involvement), it was most definitely an integral part of what allowed Hezbollah to have such success against the well-equipped and battle-proven Israeli forces. One account observes, "Most of Hezbollah's arms—including modern anti-tank weapons and the thousands of rockets that rained down on Israel—came from Iran (as well as Syria). Iranian advisors spent years helping Hezbollah train and build fortified positions throughout southern Lebanon."[68]

Hezbollah spent six years preparing for a war against Israel and had been able to employ unconventional methods to hold its own against the perceived superior military. In addition, the 2006 Hezbollah resistance "enabled Tehran to rally Muslim opinion and score a strategic, albeit indirect, gain."[69]

Lebanon's government has historically been in contention with the Hezbollah organization and continues to struggle for power against the group, which has most recently come into real political power. Growing out of a perpetual marginalization of the Shia population by the Lebanese, Hezbollah is now "one of the country's most powerful political forces."[70] In addition to its militant actions, the group "is a major provider of social services, operating schools, hospitals, and agricultural service for thousands of Lebanese Shiites."[71]

As Hezbollah has come into political power, there has been a recent discussion as to the future of the militant wing of the organization and, specifically, the disarmament of the Hezbollah military wing with some in the Lebanese government calling for Hezbollah to nationalize its military wing.[72] In 2008, the group's military actions in West Beirut "eroded the group's credibility"[73] when Hezbollah used its military to size western Beirut in what the government called a "bloody coup."[74] This has raised questions about the means by which Hezbollah obtains the necessary weaponry to cause such destruction.

According to a Congressional Research Service report, both Iran and Syria have "played significant roles in arming, training, and financing Hizbollah (and to a lesser extent Hamas) and have used the Lebanese Shiite organization as a proxy to further goals in the region."[75] The Iranian contribution to Hezbollah has ranged from military training to armament to monetary aid. Estimates of Iranian monetary contributions range from tens of millions of dollars to hundreds of millions of dollars a year. Gienger cites Pentagon estimates that "Iran has provided weapons and as much as $200 million a year to help the Lebanese militant group Hezbollah re-arm itself to levels beyond those in 2006."[76] According to the 2006 "Terrorism Knowledge Base," Hezbollah is considered a nationalist/separatist, as well as a religious, terrorist organization.[77] The U.S. government estimates that the core of Hezbollah may contain several thousand militants and activists.[78] While the U.S. Department of State considers Hezbollah to be a terrorist organization, other Middle Eastern and some Western states do not give the group this distinction.

Iran has been effective in channeling monetary support into Hezbollah that has been redirected into Hezbollah's social programs. In addition, Hezbollah steadily increased in popularity after the 2006 Israeli invasion of Lebanon, legitimizing the organization and drawing sympathy for its cause in Lebanon. Relevant to the discussion regarding the future of Hezbollah's militant wing, Iran's enormous support for the organization leads some critics of the group to "fear that Hezbollah's ideological and material links to Iran, which supplies much of the party's funds and weaponry, may be beholden to the policies of Tehran rather than the interests of the Lebanese state."[79] And Tehran's policies may aim to establish a regional balance of power—but a balance with Iran in a strong position of command.

The Iranian position of power in the Middle East has ebbed and flowed with the flux of the strengths of various Iranian empires since the seventh century, with Iranian influence extending over large parts of the Arab world at varying times in history.[80] Divided by cultural and linguistic barriers, the Iranian relationship with the Arab world has been at times tense, with the Arab world viewing Iranian moves suspiciously. According to Jordan, "Arab-Iranian tension in recent decades stems partly from Arab fears that an increasingly strong Iran will seek to reassert its past hegemony over the Gulf."[81] These fears may be validated as Iran seeks to create a regional balance of power and extend its influence through the promotion of Hezbollah and its pursuit of nuclear capabilities.

In the post–World War II environment, where the emergence of the bipolar framework instituted an era of competition between the United States and the Soviet Union, the Iranian shah was able to expand Iranian military potential with the aid of the United States. The expansion of Iranian military capabilities was viewed suspiciously by the Arab world, even as Iranian diplomats sought to validate these moves as necessary for security of Persian Gulf oil fields and tanker facilities.[82] Jordan notes that the view presented by Iranian diplomats was contradicted by Iranian military actions, as "the Shah did not hesitate to use force to seize three Arab islands in the Persian Gulf in 1971 or to give military support for Kurdish rebels in Iraq."[83]

The overthrow of the shah of Iran in the 1979 Iranian Revolution marked a turn in Iranian policy, as the entire structure of Iranian government turned from promoting modernization and Western values to promoting the traditional Islamic state. Dominated by Shia, the government sought a policy of actively supporting movements designed to export the Iranian Revolution to other parts of the Middle East.[84] In 1981, the Islamic Revolutionary Council was created as a means to "coordinate support for Islamic revolutionary groups in Islamic countries" and quickly went to work establishing support networks for movements throughout the Middle East.[85] Iranian support for revolutionary movements has taken many forms, including the production and distribution of propaganda, the establishment of training camps, financial support, armament, diplomatic support, and the provision of safe havens.[86] The Lebanese Hezbollah has received a large amount of Iranian support throughout the past decades. According to Adam Shatz, "Hezbollah provided a means [for Iran] of 'spread[ing] the Islamic revolution to the Arab world' and 'gaining a foothold in Middle East politics.'"[87]

According to Azarshab, Iran has been an ally to Arab nations despite religious and nationalist tendencies that have historically surfaced and induced conflict between the two peoples.[88] Divided by language and cultural differences, Israeli and Arab relations have managed to find common cause, and Iran has risen as an ally of Arab nations and "has been the first to express concern and support on any issue involving the Arabs."[89] Recently, it was the restructuring of the international balance of power that provided the opportunity for Iran to actively extend its influence and make efforts toward creating a regional balance of power. Nawfal calls the dissolution of the Soviet Union and the end of the "bipolar framework of international relations" the most significant change in Middle Eastern power, as Iran and Turkey became "closer to the heartland of the political geography of the Arab World."[90] While this restructuring of global and regional politics aided in promoting Iranian influence, it could also be said that the more recent 2003 invasion of Iraq was significant as well, for it resulted in the destabilizing of the region by removing the Iraqi check on Iranian power. And most certainly, the wave of North African and Middle Eastern revolutions in 2011, particularly the ousting of Egypt's Hosni Mubarak, are game changing for future relations between Iran, Israel, and the United States. The "cold peace," brought about by the signing of the Camp David Accords in 1978 and maintained by Sadat's successor, Mubarak, were never particularly popular with the Egyptian people and despite the fact that Egypt's military has promised to maintain the treaty, the uproar in the region has many Israelis worried. Israel's Deputy Foreign Minister Daniel Ayalon was among the first to express concern about the shift in the balance of power between Israel and its neighbors, directing his remarks primarily at the possibility of increased tension with Iran. "It is incumbent on all of us to make sure this period of transition, vulnerabilities and uncertainties will not be used by Iran, the ayatollahs of Iran, and their proxies in the region, whether it is Hamas or Hezbollah," he said shortly after Mubarak announced his resignation.[91] Mubarak, however popular or unpopular he may have been, was seen largely as a figure of stability in an unstable region. For Israelis, his insistence on maintaining peaceful relations, blockading Gaza, and muting criticism of Israel's treatment of the Palestinians was paramount to gaining political legitimacy in the region. After all, Egypt is the largest Arab state and has been the cornerstone for U.S. foreign policy in the Middle East. For the United States, "the devil they knew was better than the devil they didn't know." That is, Mubarak's rule, whether it was democratic or not, was preferred to that of the Muslim Brotherhood, the largest Islamist opposition movement in the country and a group whose checkered past made continued amicable relations all but certain. Peter Beinart, professor of political science at City University and a former senior fellow at the Council on Foreign Relations, notes that the Egyptian revolution marks a significant break with the strategic dominance Israel has long touted. "For a long time, countries like Turkey and Egypt were ruled by men more interested in pleasing the United States than their own people, and as a result, they shielded Israel from their people's anger. Now more of that anger will find its way into the corridors of power," he said.[92]

Already, there are dispatches from Iran that indicate the government's pleasure with Mubarak's fall. Iranian Foreign Ministry spokesman Ramin Mehmanparast said that the Egyptian revolution was a "great achievement" and that "all nations in the region have common demands which include non-interference of arrogant powers [in their internal affairs], fighting against aggression of the Zionist regime and cutting dependence on the US, Zionist regime and their allies."[93] He also warned that a "new Middle East" was taking shape, but not the kind that "American officials are dreaming of."[94] Perhaps a preview of that "new Middle East" came in mid-February 2011 when Egypt, under military rule, allowed two Iranian warships to pass through the Suez Canal. The event marked the first time since the 1979 Islamic revolution that Iranian ships have transited the passage and resulted in an immediate response from the Israeli Foreign Minister Avigdor Lieberman, who called it a "provocation."[95] Lieberman's response broke ranks with other Israeli government officials, including Benjamin Netanyahu, who sought to respond to the regional political flux with more cautious strictures. Their calm demeanor and carefully measured words were not, however, an indication that they were nonchalant about the incident. It is likely that the Netanyahu and his aides understood the gravity of appearing frightened, or even perturbed by such measures and in the face of ever-changing political grounds, the best response was one of strength and composure. Even so, it was clear that with Egypt's Mubarak out of power, Israel turned its attention to Iran, fearing that without its longtime ally, Iran may have more reason to flex its political and military muscles. Lieberman said that the passage of Iranian warships through the Suez Canal "proves that the self-confidence and chutzpah of the Iranians are growing from day to day."[96] The primary concern over the ship's passage, aside from the fact that Egypt had allowed it to occur, was that Iran would use such vessels to send weapons to Hezbollah and Hamas, the latter of which governs the Gaza strip. Both groups view Egypt's turmoil to their advantage as it gives them an upper hand in their continued fight against Israel. During the tumult in Cairo, Ayman Nofal, the senior Hamas commander, broke out of an Egyptian jail along with thousands of other prisoners and made his way through the Sinai desert, eventually arriving back in Gaza. Talking with reporters from his refugee camp home, Nofal made it clear that the Egyptian revolution revived his life's mission: "I'm anxious to get back to fighting Israel. I'm ready for the next battle," he said.[97]

Israel has been critical of the United States' handling of the Egyptian revolution, particularly in two main areas: the perceived abandonment of a loyal ally and pushing for democracy in a country that many Israelis believe is not ready for such political transformation.[98] In the event that Egypt becomes more democratic, and in the event that the other revolutions result in more Middle East democracies, Israel's longtime claim of being the only democratic state in the region—a claim by which they earned the sympathy and support of the U.S. and Europe—will be undermined. Israel will no longer be the exception in the region and cannot make the case that, amidst a sea of Islamic and Arab barbarism, it is the stable, civilized, shining beacon of Western values. The political legitimacy of Israel may no longer rest on the fact that it is democratic if other Arab democratic states emerge. Thus, Israel will be forced to renegotiate its status as a regional power, taking into consideration the possibility of increased animosity with other Arab states and with Iran. During the uproar in Egypt, just prior to Mubarak's fall from power, Ayatollah Khamenei suggested that Mubarak had betrayed his people—that the Egyptians were, as a result of Egypt's alliance with Israel and the United States, imprisoning the Palestinians. He also suggested that the protests indicated a growing "Islamic awareness" in the region.[99] From this statement, it is certain that Iran hoped to nudge the Egyptian people in the direction of anti-Israeli sentiment, perhaps encouraging the election of a government who would even reverse the policies of the American-friendly Mubarak. If the Ayatollah could succeed in making Egyptians feel like they were the victims of an American-Israeli plot, surely they would flock to the side of Iran and take a more aggressive, hard-line position in their future policies. If there was any doubt that this was the case, Iran wiped it out, suggesting that the vast displays of anger, resentment, and despair felt by the Egyptian protestors was similar to those feelings felt by the Iranian revolutionaries of 1979. Iran's message was clear: we understand your suffering and are waiting here when you are ready to join us.

Since the turn of the century, the Middle East has experienced several changes that have altered the playing field for Iran as it has sought to ascend to regional power. The U.S. invasion of Iraq altered the power structure that had contained Iranian influence to some extent. In addition, recent decades have seen the success of the Hezbollah resistance, a primary tool of Iran that has contributed to Iran's widening influence in the region. Pezeshkpour offers his assessment of the situation in the Middle East, writing,

The current situation may be summarized as follows: Arab leaders are still confused and shocked by the US invasion of Iraq and especially by the execution of Saddam Hussein; Israel's reputation has effectively been damaged by Hezbollah's successful resistance in Lebanon; and Turkey has no major influence in the Middle East. As a result, Iran has become a leader with influence throughout the region. Even on the streets of the Arab capitals, Iran's president enjoys more popularity than local heads of states.

Several prominent issues give credence to the assertion that Iran is attempting to create a regional balance of power. Recently, Iran's aggressive stance in promotion of its nuclear agenda, attempts to exploit the situation in the power void created by the U.S. invasion of Iraq, increasing military capabilities, and aggressive relations to minimize the power of Israel through its support of Hezbollah (and, in effect, assert its interest in Lebanon) are all examples of the permeation of Iranian influence in the region. However, as Iran moves to gain power, it may be limited by constraints related to its economic instability and internal divisions among its population.

Iran's main economic, military, and political partners are Germany, Italy, Russia, Great Britain, Japan, and China. In addition, the neighboring Caspian, Caucasus, and GCC states compel Iran to assume a more significant role in international politics, particularly since September 11, 2001. This year should be taken as a turning point for the Middle East. Even though in 2001 "a weakened US economy and increase in non-OPEC production had pushed the importance of oil downward,"[100] the events of September 11 followed by the War on Terror and the occupation of Iraq emphasized the importance of oil on a global scale.

This in return sent a message to countries like Iran that the West has a plan to dominate oil regions of the Middle East. In this configuration, the Caspian Sea and the Caucasus are strategically important to Iran because there again they see "the Great Game" pattern being followed one more time—and this time on the Caspian oil and gas resources. The importance of the Caspian and Caucasus for Iran is twofold: economy and security.

However, the Caspian Sea legal regime and how it should be divided between the five neighboring nations that did not exist until the collapse of the Soviet Union remains a source of conflict deadlocked for close to two decades. Unlike Iran's policy in other neighborhoods, such as Iraq or Afghanistan, Iran's approach to this traditionally Muslim neighborhood is nonideological. Thus, Iran is closer to Armenia (Christian) than to Azerbaijan (Muslim). Iran does not want to give any incentives to its Azeri minority groups and therefore aims to downplay relations with Azerbaijan. Economic exchange with the region remains low; it is directed more to Armenia than to Azerbaijan because of security concerns. Iran and Armenia have expressed readiness to cut their trade barriers.[101]

In this relation, two major projects are worth mentioning. First, Iran will finance the Armenian sector of the road and transportation in order to connect a unique transportation corridor from the Gulf to the Black Sea. China may also be a potential contributor. Beijing is, in fact, assessing the project. On the other hand, "the Asian Development Bank has expressed interest and in December 2008, ADB provided a US$1 million grant to Armenia for performing a feasibility study of the Armenian sector."[102]

The second project will deal with the construction of a pipeline for petroleum products from the Iranian refinery at Tabriz to Armenia. This project will cost U.S.$200 million to U.S. $240 million, and it will be relatively easy to implement, as up to 70 percent of the 250-kilometer pipeline will run parallel to the existing Iran-Armenia gas pipeline. A joint venture with equal shares of the two countries will be created to implement the project.[103]

Obviously, exploitation of Caspian Sea oil and gas resources depends greatly on the legal status of the Caspian Sea and can have both positive and negative outcomes for Iran. Two possible solutions are equal or proportional share of the water. In the second case, Iran's share will be less than 13 percent of the Caspian Originally, as part of the Russo-Persian Treaty of Friendship signed in 1921, the Caspian sea (technically a lake) was divided into two sectors with the resources shared between Russia and Iran (Persia). Much politics, including Russian politics of influence in its former Soviet sphere of influence, is involved here, and for the time being, solving this problem does not look to have a priority in Russia's or Iran's foreign policy. It is likely that Iran is trying to create dependencies within the region and use those economic and occasional political dependencies to break the international pressure that is currently applied to Iran. It is also likely that the reluctance on the Iranian side might be related to their intention not to create a new tension in their surrounding territories while Russia, too, is dealing with more important economic and political problems of the post-Soviet era.

Russia is part of neither the Persian Gulf nor the Middle East, but it features prominently in Iranian foreign policy and security decision making and influences U.S.-Iranian relations. The combination of Iran's geostrategic location, its importance in the world energy supply, and the policy of rapprochement pursued by President Khatami (1997–2005) has won Iran friends not only in the immediate neighborhood but also in Europe and Asia. However, ongoing disturbances and turmoil in Iran make it hard to predict the direction these relationships may take in the future.

Russia is a good example of successful Iranian diplomacy in recent years, although the two countries have a long history and often a troubled one, particularly with the occupation of 17 Iranian cities that occurred during nineteenth century. This historic hostility continued until after World War II, when the Soviets were reluctant to withdraw from Iran's western provinces and had created the independent puppet peoples' republics of Kurdistan and Azerbaijan. During the Cold War era, the shah of Iran was concerned about the ideology of Marxism being exported from the Soviet Union to Iran, and soon after the revolution in 1979, the Islamic regime rejected the Soviets on the grounds that they are the lesser of the two evils (the other being the United States) and because they had no religion.

Russia could also be viewed as an Iranian protector of sorts. For the first time in the past several hundred years, Russia and Iran do not share a common border, but this has not stopped Russia, in several ways, from helping Iran reestablish its strength after the 1978–1979 Islamic Revolution and the 1980–1988 Iran-Iraq War. First, Russia took over the task of finishing the Bushehr nuclear power plant that West Germany started prior to the Islamic Revolution.[104] The nuclear cooperation effort is fully legitimate under international law as understood by both parties, but it also constitutes a context where Russian political support can be expressed and gauged. It is exactly this political trail that can have long-term implications for regional and international security, though Russia does not see it as detrimental in any way.

For instance, according to the Russian deputy foreign minister in the 1990s, Georgy Mamedov, "Moscow called on Washington to lift sanctions against Russian companies and research institutes, imposed because the United States believed they have sent banned technology to Iran." He mentioned that "Russia's export of equipment, technology and the development of military-technical cooperation, with Iran as with all other countries, is firmly within international obligations and non-proliferation and export control agreements."[105]

However, prior to that, a report by the U.S. Central Intelligence Agency had said that the expertise and technology gained from this enterprise could also "be used to advance Iran's nuclear weapons research and development program." In a long-term strategic calculation, all countries—and Iran is not an exception—who possess dual-use technology can potentially divert the technology into military uses, threatening their neighbors or the wider international community. Regardless of the countries involved, dual-use nuclear technology is an international problem not fully addressed in the Nuclear Non-Proliferation Treaty.[106] Nonetheless, because of the important export revenue from the sales of its arms and nuclear technology, Russia offered to sell Iran another reactor in September 2001.[107]

Russia benefits from Iran's international isolation and looks at Iran like a market where it can sell its older military equipments, missile and satellite systems (including the strategic and most advanced S-300 antiaircraft missile system,)[108] airplanes, and nuclear materials. Between 1994 and 2001, Russia provided Iran with over $1 billion in conventional weaponry.[109]

Parallel to this, Iranian technicians are being taught at Russian institutes, and because of the ease of access and the lower expenses, many

Iranian students also decide to go for their education to Russia. Since 1992, Iran has had a permanent "scientific representative" in Russia and Belarus who coordinates Iranian student activities in those countries.[110] According to Mahmoud Reza Sajjadi, Iran's ambassador to Russia, 20 out of 500 Iranian students in Russia receive government scholarships,[111] though this number does not seem to include technicians and experts being trained by Russia to work for Iranian nuclear facilities. In addition, according to a Rosoboron expert, "The volume of military trade cooperation (MTC) with Iran may exceed $300 million a year."[112] This is consistent with Iran's extravagant plan to remodel its defense structure. According to Nikolai Novichkov, a *Jane's Defense Weekly* correspondent, Iran planned to reequip its armed forces before 2010 with modern armaments worth $10 billion, of which up to $4 billion could be spent on the procurement of Russian armaments."[113] However, due to international pressures, the arms deal with Russia did not go through and Russia declined sales of S-300 missiles to Iran. As a result, Iran attempted the local production of missiles they claimed to be a version of the Russian S-300s.[114] Many people wondered why Russia would jeopardize its warming relationship with the United States to arm Iran. Ed Blanche, a *Jane's Defense Weekly* correspondent, delivered the answer:

There is an apparent determination in Moscow and Tehran to build an alliance to counter U.S. influence in the Persian Gulf and Central Asian regions. If the U.S.-led campaign goes awry politically, the emerging axis between Moscow and Tehran could assume wider importance and accelerate Iran's growing efforts to improve relations with Arab states.[115]

Russia has exported millions of dollars worth of weaponry and weapons technology to Iran during the past decade.[116] Through this type of exchange, a perception has grown within the Iranian elite that this amounts to a strategic relationship, an assertion whose validity no one seems willing to candidly assess or examine. We strongly believe that this cannot be a strategic relation as long as there is no strong military component attached to it. A mutual defense treaty can make it a strategic one, but it does not look like it will happen, though it might. Ahmadinejad's failed attempt to make Iran a member of Shanghai Cooperation Organization has to some extent blunted this belief, but the Shanghai Cooperation Organization proved reluctant to give Iran full membership, and Iran has remained an observer. This proves that neither China nor Russia is willing to jeopardize its relations with the United States in order to create a strategic axis with Iran.

Russia's economic relationship with Iran is a major stumbling block for U.S. efforts to curb Iran's nuclear aspirations. If Russia does not cooperate, attempts to impose sanctions on Iran will be much less effective. The U.S. administration is well aware of the Russian role, but it appears that it is unable to bridge the gap. In a recent visit between U.S. President Barack Obama and his Russian counterparts, little was publicly said about Iran, but most news coverage did mention Iran as the least successful part of the talks. For instance, the Atlantic Council analyst had an interesting quote from the *Los Angeles Times* that describes the latest developments of U.S. and Russian views on Iran: "Russia's long-standing economic relationship with Iran has been a principal hurdle to American efforts to curb Tehran's nuclear ambitions. Although the West believes tough sanctions by Moscow would play a decisive role, Russia has continued to balk. At their news conference, Obama cited the threat of Iran obtaining nuclear weapons, but Medvedev remained silent, refraining from even mentioning Iran by name."[117]

In May 2010, Russian President Dmitry Medvedev visited Syria and met with Hamas politburo leader Khaled Mashaal. During the visit, he stated that Hamas should be included in the Middle East peace process despite Israel's opposition to the Islamist movement. "Russia doesn't view it as taking sides. That's too harsh. It's taking the middle. It wants to assume the role of the Middle East mediator," said former ambassador Zvi Magen.[118] "It believes it already has us," he continued. "We are ready to talk, and now the question is who will bring the others. The Russians seek to do it before the Americans, and for this Russia needs the Syrians and both parts of the Palestinians—including Hamas."[119] Medvedev and the Russian government do not believe that their ties with Israel and the United States will be affected by contacts with these groups that the United States labels as terrorist organizations. The discussions indicated that Russia may be jockeying for a position of global power. Russia was the first of the large global actors to recognize Hamas, and, according to some experts, the ties between Hamas and Russia are simply a matter of Russia's desire to appear as a powerful intermediary—a nation that emerges from a conflict between two groups without having invested much in a peace process that produced successful results. "They are trying to come across as a mediating factor. They didn't take a side against Israel, and, according to them, only want to solve the conflict and bring peace. According to their approach, Abbas alone is incapable," Magen said.[120] "Without Syria, Lebanon, and Hamas, it won't work, especially when America doesn't succeed in mediating. As such, they believe, Israel has no reason to be angry with them."[121]

Today, both Hamas and Hezbollah pose an immediate threat to stability in the Middle East because of their power and alliance to defend the ummah regardless of the different Islamic sects from which the two groups originate. Even more threatening are Hezbollah's and Hamas's backers, particularly Iran and its continued support for such violent groups; however, there is no end in sight for these prominent radical groups to stop their low-level attacks on Israel and to remain close allies with Iran.

For Hamas, Israeli leaders contend that they will not reach a peaceful agreement without proxy groups recognizing Israel's sovereignty; however, "Hamas would never accept Israel's existence because 'peace with Israel would undermine the very bases of their existence' and thus amount to 'political suicide.'"[122] Even so, Israel and the United States continue try to break down these proxy groups, but the end does not appear to be near. Hamas is not a one-track organization that lives by a monolithic vision with fundamentalist interests as many people assume; rather, it is an organization that has demonstrated a willingness to base its policies on cost-benefit calculations to make a political understanding with Israel.[123] According to Khaled Hroub, it would be nearly impossible to destroy Hamas because it is so deeply rooted, and even if it were to be destroyed, it would still reproduce among some percentage of the Palestinian population. As Hamas has been dubbed "the most powerful Palestinian opposition force," this likelihood of reproduction would continue to exist for Hamas until some of the "bare minimum of Palestinian rights" is achieved.[124] The complete eradication by Israel of a group that is so prevalent and powerful, with countries such as Iran providing support and backing it, would be nearly impossible. Several peace-building theorists have agreed that complete annihilation of Hamas is impractical; rather, a more strategic modification of the demands of these proxy groups may be the key to achieving a peaceful settlement. Hamas leader Musa Abu Marzuk has stated that they hope national unity talks succeed, but if the pact compromises the rights of Palestinians and if there are conditions on Palestinians principles, this will not be acceptable. Until a peaceful settlement is reached, Hamas continues to grow its base in Gaza and threaten the secular Palestinian Authority in the West Bank. Although less direct, Hamas also continues to threaten Jordan and Egypt, where a destabilized population is feared.[125] More important, Hamas and Iran will continue to render any "traditional approaches to the Arab-Israeli conflict obsolete."[126]

As for Hezbollah, "Death to America was, is, and will stay our slogan," proclaims the group's secretary-general, Hassan Nasrallah.[127] As Iran has steadily been heading toward a confrontation with Israel, Iran will likely continue aiding Hezbollah to ensure that a strategic response would result if Israel were to take action.[128] While at the same time Israel is concerned primarily with Palestinian terror, it is also preparing its military for second-strike capability against Iran if the need should arise.[129] If U.S. forces attempt to break down Hezbollah or its state sponsors, Hezbollah could potentially activate one of its cells in Asia, Europe, Latin American, or even the United States itself and could actually increase regional appeal if the United States is unable to sustain an effective counterinsurgency campaign.[130]

President Ahmadinejad has stated that Iran will continue support for Hamas's resistance of Israel because the group's success is always a source of great pride for all Muslims.[131] Until the United States or a combination of nations steps in to defeat Hamas and Hezbollah, either directly or indirectly to their state sponsor Iran, it is likely that the two groups will continue along the same path.

Much of Iran's future international relations will be dependent on its relations with the United States, and ultimately the Iranian-Israeli relationship will reflect Iranian relations with the United States (which in turn pressures the international community since it is essentially the only superpower at present). The more threatening the relationship is between Israel and Iran, the more political pressure the United States is likely to impose on the international community to increase sanctions. Some scholars have viewed the 2006 Hezbollah attacks on Israel as an indicator of future conflicts between the two bitter rivals of the Middle East and could display "future indirect confrontations between two possibly nuclear-armed nations" as Iran has aspirations of becoming a dominant power in the region.[132] There are several scenarios likely to take place within the Islamic Republic, but Iran's prominence on the international level is largely dependent on the continued support of Hamas and Hezbollah as well as its nuclear ambitions. Among some of the questions that the international community will have is whether Iran will continue providing support to these groups to further Iran's interest and whether Iran will continue to develop its nuclear program in secrecy. Among the possible outcomes for Iran on the international level, Iran's nuclear program and support for terrorist organizations will definitely be on the agenda. There is no doubt that future relations will involve confronting Iran's proxy groups, Hezbollah and Hamas, and it is likely that the United States and its allies are the only nations capable of doing so. According to one scholar, there are only four possible ways for the United States to deal with Hezbollah: confront directly through military action, coerce Lebanon to take action against the group, work through Iran, or work through Syria.[133] The best probable way for the United States to deal with proxy groups is to indirectly confront the state sponsor, Iran. Consistent diplomatic and economic pressure on Iran and Syria, coupled with "the implicit threat of military action, can successfully rein in Hezbollah." Demands that Iran and Syria outright abandon support would likely fail, but, combined with international support and additional sanctions imposed on Iran, there may likely be a change in Iran's support for terrorist groups. On the other hand, some sources have contended that even though Iran has tremendous influence over its proxy groups, it lacks the means to make a significant change in those groups' movement and goals.[134] Either way, the United States and its allies will never know what influences Iran will have on these groups to stop their violent behaviors until they truly pressure Iran to influence these groups to cease their violent behaviors.

Regionally and internationally, there is no doubt that Iran will continue to face intense scrutiny with its recent elections. Following those of 2009, a few scenarios could take place, according to one scholar: (1) Power prevails; that is, the peoples' choice succeeds, and after extended protests, President Ahmadinejad is shown to be a fraud, and Mir Hossein Mousavi win a runoff. This switch would change Iran's power (which ultimately lies in the hands of the clerics) and bring about an end to Iran's international isolation. Though this scenario seems unlikely, this situation is what happened in the Ukraine years ago. (2) Ahmadinejad survives by moderating his position. (3) Repression continues in Iran, as does international disdain. This would cause a "deepening world resolve to stop Iran's nuclear program and its sponsorship of extremists" and would increase international isolation and criticism.[135] Another scholar agrees that the first scenario may seem more likely in the event that the Green Movement continues to become stronger and completely sweep away the current regime and establish a secular constitutional democracy or in the event that the Green Movement and a technocratic faction of the IRGC collide to create new constitutional order (call this a tutelary republic).[136] Though it is unknown what is yet to come, the 2009 elections display "Iran's stranglehold over its population," and these issues are very "indicative of the great challenges Iran will face in the coming years," particularly in the role on Middle East affairs and the need for civic reform in Iran.[137] As Iran veers closer to an outright rebellion because of the alleged election fraud, it will be much easier for countries such as Egypt, Jordan, Saudi Arabia, Bahrain, and Morocco to "[find] comfort in laying blame for their domestic and regional woes on Iran and their (perceived) allies" as they have in the past. In addition, the fierce rhetoric of Ahmadinejad will undoubtedly help bolster the case.[138]

Several scholars contend that the recent elections are likely have a major impact of the development of the IRGC, which was originally founded after the revolution to defend the Islamic Republic against internal and external threats but has since expanded "into a socio-military-political-economic force" that deeply influences Iran's power structure. Some sources even contend that it has "evolved into one of the country's most influential domestic institutions."[139] Analysts differ in their opinions as to what will happen to the IRGC, but many have suggested that the "guard's rising political and economic clout has put it in a position to challenge the clerical establishment."[140] For the past 30 years, there has been an alliance with the Islamic Republic's clergy and the Revolutionary Guard, but this dynamic is changing, especially after the 2009 elections. According to Wehrey and colleagues, there are broader changes that need to take place within the IRGC, but there are likely three scenarios to evolve over the next few years. One scenario is that the IRGC would influence and appoint a supreme leader after the demise of Ayatollah Ali Khamenei, and the controlling power of the supreme leader would be removed. Wehrey and colleagues believe that the possible contender, Ali Akbar Hashemi-Rafsanjani, would be unlikely to have a long tenure in office because of his age and his unpopularity within the IRGC and that both of the young leaders who could potentially be selected (Mohammad Khatami and Hassan Khomeini) are too moderate for the conservatives, leaving them unlikely to be chosen. Therefore, leaving no suitable candidates, the IRGC would step in and select a candidate to replace the Ayatollah; this person would likely continue to support Iran's dominance in the economic and political sphere but also be less powerful than Iran's current Ayatollah. The second scenario is that the IRGC would set the stage for Khamenei's sucessor to be someone from within the IRGC. Such a candidate would likely promise progress and would place less emphasis on Islamism (but not downright abandon it). And the third scenario is that the IRGC would attempt to run the Islamic Republic without a clerical ruler. If the Iranian people began to support this change, the IRGC could then step in and begin to develop a regime similar to that of Turkey.[141]

Iran's nuclear program will also continue to be a future predictor of international and regional relations, particularly for the United States and Israel. According to some U.S. news agencies, there is an increasing possibility of a preemptive strike, as continued diplomatic efforts are making little if any progress. Though a preemptive strike could potentially wipe out the threat of Iran's becoming a nuclear state, Iranian scientists have already prepared for the possibility of a preemptive strike by equipping several of Iran's nuclear facilities with concrete structures and antiaircraft nets that would require "hundreds if not thousands of air sorties to destroy enough targets to cripple the Iranian nuclear program." In addition to the increasing growth of Iran's nuclear program, Iran has recently installed its first satellite (named *Omid*), and it is feared to be a future launch site for its nuclear weapons.[142] Other Arab nations have also become increasing alarmed as Iran seeks regional dominance. Relating to Iran's nuclear developments, some scholars claim that Iran's nuclear ambitions have caused an "arms race" in the region. Several countries in the Middle East have asserted that they too will seek nuclear energy for peaceful purposes in the event that Iran acquires nuclear weapons.[143] Though unlikely, there is still the potential for Iran to be invaded by some international consortium in the event of some major nuclear policy. Regardless, the people of the region would have two choices: follow the current administration or support the coalition armies. This joint alliance could topple the regime and stop the Islamic Republic's regional influence, but it could also bring about international terrorism. In addition, social upheaval would likely take place in the event that this happens, and there is likely to be food shortages and intense street protests that are likely to cause immense property damage and destruction and that could break out into a civil war between the mullahs (and their word of God) and the social reformists who seek change.[144] As the nuclear threat of Iran continues and the threat of civil strife in the near future, there is also the possibility for Iran to encounter a military coup, in which case the United States would likely become involved. In the event of a military coup, the United States and its allies will become the largest influence in the area. During such a coup, in any of the major target areas (the capital, the Abadan Refinery, the religious citadel at Qom, the Bandar-e-Abbas naval station and its three Soviet-made Kilo-class diesel submarines, and finally the air base at Dezful), the risk of civilian causalities is extremely high. Though this scenario may be unlikely because of the Islamic political hold that extends even into the military and into the proxy group's military branches (if necessary to be called on), there is still the likelihood of foreign assistance and aid directly to the social reformists currently in Iran, making this scenario a definite possibility.[145]

Though Iran's regime is under intense scrutiny in the international arena, it could begin to see an increase in its legitimacy as an accepted government as the popular vote and as support for proxy groups such as Hamas continue to rise. As Iran's is fast becoming a dominant leader in the region, it will continue to use these proxy groups to legitimize its government and to promote nationalism and Muslim unity. Iran has proven its ability to be a dominant force in the Islamic world by its ability to unite Sunnis and Shi'ites, and its continued support for its proxy groups, Hezbollah and Hamas, will likely increase scrutiny and international isolation for the Islamic Republic. Policymakers believe that Israel will continue to maintain its military dominance in the region with U.S. assistance, but there is no doubt that Iran will continue to threaten Israel in order to compete for regional dominance, and this threat increases as Iran furthers its nuclear ambitions. There is much reason to believe that relations with the United States will become even more contentious now, as Iran's support for Hamas and Hezbollah and Supreme Leader Khamenei's "game of high-stakes political brinksmanship" with the recent elections will be viewed increasingly as suspicious.[146] Much of Iran's future is dependent largely on its regional politics, particularly on how Iran handles the recent elections and its nuclear ambitions. Among several possibilities that could take place within Iran is that of civil strife, which is likely to take place over the next few years.

CHAPTER 5

Nuclear Dynamics: Potential Threats and Consequences

Our dear Imam [Khomeini] said that the occupying regime must be wiped off the map and this was a very wise statement. We cannot compromise over the issue of Palestine. Is it possible to create a new front in the heart of an old front? This would be a defeat and whoever accepts the legitimacy of this regime [Israel] has in fact, signed the defeat of the Islamic world.[1]

—Mahmoud Ahmadinejad, October 30, 2005

As soon as the green light is given, it will be one mission, one strike and the Iranian nuclear project will be demolished.[2]

—Anonymous Israeli official, January 7, 2007

In his 2006 National Security Strategy, President George W. Bush wrote,

We may face no greater challenge from a single country than from Iran. For almost 20 years, the Iranian regime hid many of its key nuclear efforts from the international community. Yet the regime continues to claim that it does not seek to develop nuclear weapons. The Iranian regime's true intentions are clearly revealed by the regime's refusal to negotiate in good faith; its refusal to come into compliance with its international obligations by providing the IAEA access to nuclear sites and resolving troubling questions; and the aggressive statements of its President calling for Israel to "be wiped off the face of the earth."[3]

Five years later, not much has changed. Despite a shift in policy toward Iran, brought about by the Obama administration, and despite continuing condemnation from world leaders, there are no indications that Iran's quest for nuclear weapons will end anytime soon. In fact, with each rhetorical admonition, with each new threat of sanctions, and with each new diplomatic tactic to dissuade Iran from continuing down this current, dangerous course, the stakes are constantly raised.

While history provides some explanation of the existing hostility between the two states, there is also a different perspective perhaps less explored by the scholars who look at Middle East politics. The question is to what extent restrained relations between the United States and Iran are shaped because of Iran's hostile approach to Israel. In other words, if Iran had better relations with Israel, would its relations with the United States be as restrained as they are today? Can Iran create closer ties with United States simply by overcoming the obstacles of its relations with Israel? What factors affect U.S.-Iranian relations, and in what ways might Israeli-U.S. relations negatively affect Iranian-U.S. relations? On many occasions, Iranian leaders have referred to the stance of the United States toward Iran as appeasing Israel. In March 2009, Ayatollah Khamenei said, "Even the new president of America, who has come to power with slogans about changing Bush's policies, is defending state terrorism by talking about unconditional commitment to Israel's security."[4]

Among other factors, the Iranian nuclear program is perhaps the more important one. However, the origins of animosity between Israel and Iran go back to the early days of the Islamic Revolution when Ayatollah Khomeini's slogans, such as "Israel must be annihilated" or, during Iraq-Iran War, "The road to Jerusalem passes through Karbala" (in Iraq, where the shrine of the first Shia imam Ali is located), shaped Israel's perception of the threat from Iran. When the U.S.-led coalition attacked Iraq, Israel openly hoped that it might also consider Iran as its next target. When rumors about Iran's attempt to achieve a nuclear capability spread, this also triggered a war of words between Iran and Israel. So far, this war has not gone beyond words and fierce saber rattling, but Iran does feel a real threat from Israel and has been trying (1) to minimize the risk of war with Israel and (2) to deter it from any preemptive attack on Iran's nuclear facilities. The declared Israeli strategy of threatening to bomb Iran's nuclear installations—regardless of what the strategy actually applied would be—has made its impact. Iran finds itself within the range of Israeli missiles and air attacks and is convinced that Israel would not hesitate to attack Iran's nuclear sites in the same way that it attacked the Osirak reactor in Iraq in 1981. It may also attempt to pressure the U.S. administration to destroy Iran's nuclear facilities.

The most recent planned delivery of U.S.-manufactured "smart bombs" to Israel increases the already existing concerns about an air raid on Iran's nuclear facilities. As a result, from the very beginning, Iran's entire new facilities were kept completely secret. Wherever secrecy was not possible and the installations were very visible—as at Bushehr—Iran took care to maintain good relations with the United Nations and the International

Atomic Energy Agency (IAEA) on the continuation of work on the nuclear reactors. In fact, in Bushehr everything was transparent, and the IAEA had full access to the sites. It could easily contact the personnel involved in the project, and Iran would generally cooperate with the IAEA.

Iran's nuclear ambitions are one of the greatest and most serious causes of international concern. Its efforts to develop such a program date back to the 1950s and, thanks to U.S. guidance, made great stride until the 1970s.[5] The clandestine revival of the program was revamped in the early 1990s. Russia was the last country that Iran approached after being rejected by two dozen of other countries. Iran's nuclear program, with the help of Russia, has since been a concern of many international players. Suspicions of Iran's nuclear program drew even more attention in 2002 and 2003 when Iran reportedly began researching fuel enrichment, though it claims this is for "clean energy for environmental, agricultural and technological purposes." Iran has admitted to keeping its nuclear program a secret for over 20 years and has also sought help for nuclear technology from China, Pakistan, and North Korea.[6]

The United States and Israel have been the particularly concerned with Iran's nuclear development because of the potential threat that Iran could pose to Israel. In 2007, the United States revealed that Iran had halted its nuclear weapons program, but several sources later revealed that Iran continued to make progress in its ability to enrich uranium, though it is unknown how close Iran is to acquiring nuclear power. There have been reported high levels of low-enriched uranium,[7] but the main source of concern should be the levels of highly enriched uranium, which has a uranium content above 20 percent, or weapons-grade uranium, which has a uranium content of over 90 percent.[8]

There is no doubt that Iran possesses the capability of obtaining more nuclear weapons, but of even greater concern is Iran's potential to directly or indirectly put nuclear weapons in the hands of terrorists. The European Union has tried several diplomatic solutions to resolve this issue but has failed to come to an agreeable alternative. As of 2008, inspectors had not found any indication of Iran's using its nuclear program for the development of nuclear weapons, but international skepticism has remained.[9] In early 2010, the IAEA released a detailed report that confirmed Western fears that Iran has the "potential for producing a nuclear weapon, including further fuel enrichment and plans for developing a missile-ready warhead." The National Intelligence Estimate asserts that Iran is likely to have enough highly enriched uranium to produce a nuclear weapon by 2010–2015.

Regarding the immediate threat, however, sources say that even if Iran had the materials to make a nuclear weapon, it is unclear whether it would know how to develop one, and, even if it did, further technical work would ultimately tip off inspectors.[10] Though nuclear intentions cannot be proved, it is likely that Tehran is keeping the option open to develop nuclear weapons sometime in the near future.[11] The United States has threatened to bomb Iran's nuclear sites and has tried to sway the international community to demand that Iran stop its uranium enrichment, but international opinion is divided, according to one scholar; both China and Russia are pursuing different regional interests than the United States and Europe, and though Europe is currently backing the United States, it has too much invested in Iran to continue to support the U.S. view on Iran's nuclear power. Dr. Mahmoud Reza Amini, a strong supporter of Iran's nuclear program, believes that there must be a secret intent for the United States and Russia to continue to pressure states to halt their development in nuclear energy for civilian purposes because these countries have vowed to reduce their own developments and arsenals but still have enough bombs to threaten the existence of any nation in the world. Amini adds, "Nuclear negotiations and nuclear discourse is not based on reduction of nuclear warheads, but aims to reengineer them and is reminiscent of the use of such weapons by big powers." Despite what the international community believes Iran intends to do with its nuclear program, Amini contends that Iran's religious principles prohibit nuclear weapons (which was the motto of a recent nuclear conference in Tehran: "nuclear energy for all, nuclear weapons for none"). In the eyes of the Iranians who support Iran's right to nuclear energy, Iran will continue to be a nation victimized by hegemonic political and economic pressures until attention can be drawn away from existing nuclear discourse.

While much focus is commonly directed at Iran's nuclear program, it is also useful to examine Israel's nuclear ambitions, particularly with regard to how a potential standoff between Israel and Iran would affect the Middle East security and the triangular relationship between Israel, Iran, and the United States. What would happen if Israel decided to strike Iran? How would the United States react? What if Iran, on the other hand, decided to strike Israel?

As Sam Gardiner mentions in "The Israeli Threat: An Analysis of the Consequences of an Israeli Strike on Iranian Nuclear Facilities," Washington is "other-focused."[12] Washington is focused on health care, on jobs, on the economy, on Iraq, on Afghanistan, and on Pakistan. President Obama and his administration talk very little about the possibility of an Israel-Iran conflict. Even so, both Israel and Iran are discussing the possibility of an eventual war—and they are doing so frequently. Iranians appear to be concerned about the real possibility of an Israeli strike on their nuclear facilities. In November 2009, Iran launched a five-day air defense exercise. On the first day, a general in the Revolutionary Guard said, "Even if Israeli warplanes evade Iranian defenses, Iran will launch surface-to-surface missiles to destroy Israeli air force bases."[13] His message could not have been any clearer.

Not only would Iran launch surface-to-air missiles to destroy Israeli forces, it would also call on its proxy group Hezbollah. Since the creation of Israel, several proxy groups in the region have denied recognition of Israel's sovereignty, and thus a peaceful agreement between the two groups has yet to be agreed on; a new conflict has arose over the past two decades between Israel and the proxy groups Hezbollah and Hamas, both of which backed by Iran. Conflicts over the past decade show that proxy groups are playing a greater role in the Israel-Hamas-Hezbollah situation. Israel has been continuously at war with Palestinian militants, including Hamas in the Gaza Strip and with the proxy group Hezbollah in Lebanon, but there are secondary players (Iran and Syria) that have had a significant impact and influence for these groups by providing them with arms, training, and financial support. Additionally, though the 2006 UN resolution called on Hezbollah to disarm, its leaders indicate that they have no intentions of doing so.[14] Thus, in many ways, Hezbollah is a more serious threat now than it was four years ago, and Benjamin Netanyahu agrees. The Israeli prime minister said that he once considered Hezbollah a militia group but now views it as the army of Lebanon.[15]

According to some within the Israeli government, Israel has been planning to strike Iran for a long time, but there has been no triggering incident that would prompt Israel to manifest such plans. What would prompt an Israeli strike? First, Israel would have to come to the realization that it is responsible for its own security. Under the guardian-like wing of the United States, Israel is somewhat blocked. Attacking Iran unilaterally without U.S. consent would alienate relations between the two longtime allies, delegitimizing Israeli political legitimacy and indirectly strengthening Iran's regime security. Iran may continue to defy the international community and ignore warnings about enriching uranium. If the United States is unwilling to act and Israeli officials believe that they can no longer tolerate what they view as an increased threat, the possibility of an Israeli strike may become more realistic.[16]

Another possibility is intercepted intelligence indicating that Iran's efforts to build a nuclear weapon (and perhaps direct it toward Israel) is moving along at a more rapid pace than initial reports or speculations have suggested:

Israel might receive a report that suggests Iran is very close to building a nuclear weapon, closer than everyone thought. It could receive intelligence on a third, secret nuclear enrichment facility operating more sophisticated centrifuges than at the Natanz facility. A trigger could be an event. According to press reports, the International Atomic Energy Agency has evidence that Iran has experimented with sophisticated nuclear warhead design. Nations' first uranium-based nuclear weapons are most often the so-called gun-type design; a single shot into the uranium pit produces the nuclear detonation. According to some reports, Iran has experimented with two-point implosion devices, a technique for detonating a uranium device from two directions that would produce a smaller warhead that could be put on its medium-range missiles.[17]

The question then remains: what would an Israeli strike look like? Israel says that an attack on Iran may resemble the type of attack they deployed against Egypt in 1967—more than just air strikes. It would likely include Shaldag commando teams, an array of sea-launched missiles, and even explosive-carrying dogs that would penetrate the underground nuclear facilities.[18] A 2008 *New York Times* article titled "U.S. Says Exercise by Israel Seems Directed at Iran" foretold of plans for a potential attack. Israel conducted an open exercise using 100 aircraft (F15 and F16 fighter jets) in a round-trip mission to Greece. If there was any question that the exercise was a warning, Shaul Mofaz, a former Israeli defense minister who is now a deputy prime minister, made the speculation clear. He warned that Israel may have no choice but to attack. "If Iran continues with its program for developing nuclear weapons, we will attack," Mofaz said.[19] "Attacking Iran, in order to stop its nuclear plans, will be unavoidable."[20]

The costs and uncertainties of a military strike are enormous. Air strikes are unlikely to succeed in destroying Iran's nuclear facilities, as experts have estimated the number of nuclear sites to be far more than the 18 the regime claims, with many buried deep underground. Furthermore, if military action in the form of a preemptive strike is unsuccessful, it could incite Iran to double or triple efforts to build and/or purchase nuclear bombs. In addition, there is always collateral damage in the loss of innocent civilians when any type of military action is undertaken. The civilian losses could be in the thousands, and this could incite the people of Iran and terrorist organizations to support Iran and undermine the ultimate goal of the United States. Nonetheless, as recently as November 2010, the former (and somewhat controversial) U.S. ambassador to the United Nations, John Bolton, called on a unilateral preemptive strike on Iran:

The most likely outcome with respect to Iran is that it gets nuclear weapons and very, very soon. Given that diplomacy has failed, given that sanctions have failed, the only alternative to an Iran with nuclear weapons is a limited military strike against the nuclear weapons program. A preemptive military strike against Iran's nuclear program would not cause chaos in the Middle East because the Arab states don't want Iran to have nuclear weapons any more than Israel does.[21]

A unilateral strike against Iran would only further damage Israel's standing in the Middle East at a time when its government is seeking to establish more political legitimacy. As Israel's closest ally, the United States must not lack the vision to search for the resources available in order to facilitate the best possible solution for Israeli and U.S. national security.

And, as a maintainer of world peace (in addition to having vast economic and political interests in the Middle East), the United States should also seek to maintain regional stability.

To do so, the United States must jump on an aggressive learning track regarding Iran, the citizens, the ethnic makeup of the country, the economy, and the education of the people and at the same time educate Iranians about the values of the United States, not the all-too-familiar propaganda that is transmitted from many within the government. Sun Tzu, the ancient Chinese military general and philosopher, has a famous saying: keep your friends close and your enemies closer. This could not be more true regarding the conundrum at hand. Most scholars would argue that both Iran and the United States would benefit from a greater understanding of each others' motives and interests. As the United States seeks to engage the Iranian regime in direct negotiations, it must also seek to engage the Iranian people directly. The United States must respect Iranian history and culture, respect the Iranian people, and have a desire to forge a mutually beneficial relationship. The United States must also translate the positives of the new relationship to the Iranian people in terms of bringing badly needed economic development, foreign investment, increased employment, new educational prospects at home and abroad, and more generally an end to Iran's international isolation. In large measure, Iran's leaders seek nuclear weapons to deter a U.S. attack, so let us display in many ways how this is simply a red herring.

It is also beneficial for the United States to continue to foster and spread democracy wherever in the world it presents itself, including Iran. "It is the policy of the United States to seek and support the growth of democratic movements and institutions in every nation and culture, with the ultimate goal of ending tyranny in our world," President Bush said in his inaugural address after his swearing-in ceremony. More than two years into the Obama administration, it appears that democracy-spreading rhetoric has waned substantially. In a February 2009 *New York Times* article, Peter Baker addressed the decreased emphasis on democracy promotion:

Four years after President George W. Bush declared it the mission of America to spread democracy with the goal of "ending tyranny in our world," his successor's team has not picked up the mantle. Since taking office, neither Mr. Obama nor his advisers have made much mention of democracy-building as a goal. While not directly repudiating Mr. Bush's grand, even grandiose vision, Mr. Obama appears poised to return to a more traditional American policy of dealing with the world as it is rather than as it might be.[22]

In contrast to most Muslim countries in the Middle East, Iran has a viable, indigenous democratic movement. Also setting it apart, the United States is, for the most part, admired politically and culturally by many elements of Iran's democratic movement and by the Iranian population.

The United States can utilize its leadership and seek international cooperation through the building of international institutions and treaties. The Nuclear Non-Proliferation Treaty (NPT) is the most widely accepted arms control agreement with more than 180 countries participating. Preventing and countering the proliferation of nuclear weapons is one of the highest security priorities of the United States, and the NPT remains one of the key elements of U.S. nonproliferation strategy (in which the United States still participates). Even though it is difficult to sometimes enforce compliance because countries like Iran thumb their nose at the agreement, the global community is the only game in town and is worth our continued support, participation, and involvement. In addition to the NPT, the United States will strengthen the IAEA by ratifying the IAEA Additional Protocol and assertively requesting all nations to implement the full-scope safeguards of the agency. Every significant global institution created after World War II was established with U.S. leadership and ideology, including the United Nations, NATO, the World Bank, and the International Monetary Fund, which remain at the forefront of democratic and therefore American ideals. The United States should continue to utilize these international institutions to create peace and stability and to identify common ground for cooperation between Israel and Iran.

As is discussed in more detail in the coming chapters, Iran and Israel need each other, at least in terms of the rhetorical narratives they employ. For Israel, Iran is a threatening enemy that justifies its ambitions for a position of power in the Middle East and gives Israel a reason to maintain its own nuclear program. For Iran, Israel threatens its regime security. An ally of the United States, Iran has made it implicitly clear that, if produced, its nuclear weapons may in fact be used against Israel, for if not against Israel, then against whom? In other words, both of these actors balance their political and military posturing off each other and justify their own maneuvering on the basis of what the other is doing. Therefore, would Iran want to completely "wipe Israel off the map"? If so, who would it turn to next to project vast displays of power and saber rattling? Likewise, would Israel truly want to see Iran's nuclear weapons program ravaged to the point that it could no longer pose a threat? Israel's political legitimacy would be challenged by such a move; the absence of a strong enemy would make it nearly impossible for the Israeli government to advance its political ambitions in the Middle East.

In the event that Israel desired to strike Iran unilaterally, it may employ the same tactic that the United States used in the Gulf War against Serbia in the Persian Gulf: carbon fibers. Dropping carbon fibers onto power lines would damage Iran's electrical grid to the point that nuclear deployment would be impossible. The Natanz facility is flanked by three

aboveground power lines in an open desert terrain. Even the new enrichment facility near Qom has power lines that line the access sites.[23]

This method may not eliminate the nuclear infrastructure of Iran, but it
would deter a nuclear strike. After all, wiping out the nuclear threat that
Israel uses to establish political legitimacy would leave it with no strong
enemy to position itself against. If Israel could deter the deployment of
nuclear weapons yet leave the Iranian facilities intact, it would still be in
a position to negotiate its political legitimacy. Israel could still suggest that
the threat of Iran loomed, its nuclear facilities were not demolished, and
especially that Hezbollah and Hamas—proxy groups funded and supported by Iran—were actively plotting against it.

For Hamas, Israeli leaders contend that they will not reach a peaceful
agreement without proxy groups recognizing Israel's sovereignty; however, "Hamas would never accept Israel's existence because 'peace with
Israel would undermine the very bases of their existence' and thus amount
to 'political suicide.'[24] Even so, Israel and the United States continue to try
to break down these proxy groups, but the end does not appear to be near.
Hamas is not a one-track organization that lives by a monolithic vision
with fundamentalist interests as many people assume; rather, it is an
organization that has demonstrated a willingness to base its policies on
cost-benefit calculations to make a political understanding with Israel.[25]
According to Khaled Hroub, it would be nearly impossible to destroy
Hamas because it is so deeply rooted, and even if it were to be destroyed,
it would still continue to reproduce in some percentage of the Palestinian
population. As Hamas has been dubbed "the most powerful Palestinian
opposition force," this likelihood of reproduction would continue to exist
for Hamas until some of the "bare minimum of Palestinian rights" is
achieved.[26] Complete eradication of a group with such strong prevalence
and power, with countries such as Iran providing support and backing it,
would be nearly impossible for Israel. Several peace-building theorists have
agreed that the complete annihilation of Hamas is impractical; rather, a
more strategic modification of the demands of these proxy groups may be
the key to achieving a peaceful settlement. Hamas leader Musa Abu
Marzuk has stated that Hamas wishes that national unity talks succeed,
but if the pact compromises the rights of Palestinians and if there are conditions against Palestinians principles, they will not accept. Until a peaceful
settlement is reached, Hamas continues to grow its base in Gaza and
threaten the secular Palestinian Authority in the West Bank. Although less
direct, Hamas also continues to threaten Jordan and Egypt, where, as the
2011 revolutions have shown, a destabilized population is feared.[27] More
important, Hamas and Iran will continue to render any "traditional
approaches to the Arab-Israeli conflict obsolete."[28]

As for Hezbollah, "Death to America was, is, and will stay our slogan,"
proclaims the group's secretary-general, Hassan Nasrallah.[29] While Iran

has steadily been heading toward a confrontation with Israel, Iran will likely continue aiding Hezbollah to ensure that a strategic response would result if Israel were to take action.[30] While at the same time Israel is concerned primarily with Palestinian terror, it is also preparing its military for second-strike capability against Iran if the need should arise. If U.S. forces attempt to break down Hezbollah or its state sponsors, Hezbollah could potentially activate one of its cells in Asia, Europe, Latin America, or even the United States itself and could actually increase regional appeal if the United States is unable to sustain an effective counterinsurgency campaign.[31]

President Ahmadinejad has stated that Iran will continue support for Hamas's resistance to Israel because the group's success is always a source of great pride for all Muslims.[32] Until the United States or a combination of nations steps in to defeat Hamas and Hezbollah either directly or indirectly, it is likely that the two groups will continue along the same path.

Historically, instructive examples may provide some clues about the current nuclear issues facing the Middle East, particularly Iran and Israel. Most proponents of preventive policy toward Iran point out Israel's strike on Iraq's nuclear facility at Osirak in 1981. Indeed, there is little to debate in that Israel was successful in its endeavor, as is stated by Mueller and colleagues:

> The Osirak attack was a complete military success, and achieved its goal of wrecking the existing Iraqi nuclear program, requiring its facilities to be built from scratch. The domestic political response to the success was predictably favorable, and following the raid Likud won the 1981 general election. . . . International reaction was condemnatory. . . but Washington's condemnation was far milder than the attack's proponents had feared . . . . In subsequent years, the attack has come to be viewed more favorably in many quarters.[33]

The only problem is that the situation in 2007 is not parallel to the situation in 1981. The Iranian nuclear complex is not composed of a single facility but instead is dispersed throughout the nation. Even declassified sources reveal that Iran has dozens of sites that would need to be neutralized in order to achieve the same level of success. Whereas the Israeli strike force was composed of 14 aircraft that flew only one mission, the United States would have to lead an exponentially larger force into the region and would have to do so for an extended period of time. Furthermore, there are those within the military who believe that in order to truly dismantle Iran's nuclear pursuits or even delay them significantly (beyond a decade), Iran's infrastructure would have to be dismantled, meaning that government buildings, oil fields, and oil pipelines would all have to be destroyed.

Furthermore, Iran's nuclear complex is well built. Many of its sites, like the Tehran Nuclear Research Center, the Esfahan Nuclear Research Center, and the Natanz Fuel Enrichment Facility, have been "hardened" or are constructed underground. At the moment, conventional weapons may be able to "punch holes" in various facilities but could not dismantle them, and while future generations of conventional bunker busters may be able to collapse the buildings from within, such technology has not yet been developed. The only other conventional option would be to hermetically seal the sites with missiles and use a massive ordinance air blast to kill everyone inside, but this violates the Geneva Convention because it targets "nonmilitary" people rather than the facility itself.

Therefore, the theory that is being proposed by the Pentagon is to use nuclear earth penetrators (NEPs), such as the B61-11, which was developed by the Clinton administration and was used to threaten Libya. In theory, the B61-11 would be able to penetrate the earth above a facility, and because of its nuclear warhead, it would be able to destroy or radiate the entire facility, making it useless some time.

The problem with the NEP theory and the new use theorists behind it is that it is hard to explain how one avoids a nuclear war by starting one. Although the Pentagon has tried to justify its strategy by saying that NEPs are "safe" for citizens because they would detonate so far underground that radiation would not loom aboveground, the fact is that such a justification depends on the NEP hitting its target directly and not malfunctioning. It should also be noted that civilians would be heavily affected by radiation in their groundwater, and this seems especially dubious given the fact that nuclear facilities must be constructed near water supplies even if they are underground.

The "mininuke" theory also must take into account that several Iranian facilities are located in urban, cultural centers. There is a special animosity that is likely to occur among Iranians and the international community if nuclear weapons are used in a world cultural site. Even if such weapons do not produce physical radioactive fallout, they are likely to breed a special form of psychological animosity based on the nuances of the violation. This should be taken seriously because, while there is still a battle within the Muslim community about whether the answer to their problems is to simply have the United States out of the Middle East or whether the United States must be destroyed, such an action is likely to grant the few apocalyptic extremists widespread justification for using a weapon of mass destruction on the United States and/or Israel.

Furthermore, just as the Iraqis became more clandestine after Osirak, Iran's nuclear program is likely to become more closely allied with terrorist networks and is likely to completely disappear from IAEA observation, and Iran is still likely to get "the bomb" within the foreseeable future. This is a traditional worry for strategists in that they must weigh the advantages gained against the possibility that the opponent will attack. The problem is that—with the complexity of Iran's nuclear facility, the oil that Iran has at its disposal, and the number of Iranian engineers being educated around the world and the connections they have with Russia and MINATOM—they are still likely to be able to manufacture a "nuclear weapon." The ironic part is that using military force, especially because efficacy will be based on the use of NEPs, is likely to give Iran justification to use it.

Therefore, in looking at the guidelines put forth by foreign relations experts Lee Feinstein and Anne-Marie Slaughter,which suggest that the international community has a duty to prevent security disasters by pre-emptively thwarting their development, it seems that Iran simply does not meet the requirements for being a rational military target despite the fact that it is a proliferation concern. The military operations would have to be large (along the lines of Kosovo), and the length of direct engage-ment could be short, but after dealing with Iranian "swarm tactics" and heightened insurgency in Iraq, it could be considered a long time frame, the outcome is uncertain, there are considerable risks of major violations of the Geneva Convention and mass civilian casualties, and the political "fallout" would be enormous. Furthermore, it would remain likely that Iran would get a weapon of mass destruction in the near future, and because the United States had postured so firmly against such weapons, the world could only assume that it would be a huge political victory for Iran and a huge political defeat for U.S. nonproliferation policy. Worst of all, Iran would have justification to use weapons of mass destruction "preventively" against the risk of U.S. attack. Thus, a preventive strike on Iran suffers as a policy decision because it would be hard to gain legiti-macy for it and because it would be far from definite in succeeding. The advantages gained do not greatly outweigh the risks perceived, and it seems that it could make the situation worse rather than better. These forces work together to produce a far wider field of failure than of success; furthermore, with a field of failure that broad, it can be surmised that the chance of a catastrophe exists and that, as such, military preventive action is an extremely unwise decision. Simply put, unless the United States is willing to gamble everything it has on this question and is willing to com-pletely separate itself from the world, it would be prudent to employ another nonproliferation policy. That brings us to the next and perhaps most discussed course of action regarding nuclear proliferation: the diplomatic track.

The most well established alternative nonproliferation course of action to military action is diplomatic action. Diplomacy works through a series of bargaining steps in which "carrots and sticks," usually in the form of economic incentives and sanctions, are used to achieve success. The strength of diplomacy resides in the fact that it engages "the Other."

Indeed, nonproliferation has been most successful through diplomacy, and proponents of diplomatic action in nonproliferation can look to the victories achieved by the United States and the Soviet Union with each other, Italy with Libya, Europe with Sweden, and West Germany with East Germany. Proponents need to be conscious, however, that there have been several failed episodes of nonproliferation diplomacy, including that with North Korea.

In the case of Iran, reaching a favorable conclusion diplomatically will be difficult because it has a commodity that everyone wants: oil. Therefore, as has been the case, nations like China have been especially reluctant to get "on board" with strict sanctions. Putting rhetoric aside, Iran feels that there is a vast sea in which to go fishing should someone take away its goldfish bowl, and therefore economic leverage may not be the same as it was in the past. Israel is different in this regard. Relying on the long-term support and friendship of the United States, Israeli leaders know that, no matter how dangerous the threat of Iran may be, engaging in a direct attack would weaken relations with the United States and would jeopardize the country's political legitimacy.

Moreover, diplomatic pressure has meant that the United States has had to lean on some its newer alliances, as it has with Armenia. The United States should be especially aware of this situation, as these tactics may backfire by collapsing the still-fragile new democracies in Central Asia and may further frustrate the developing world from wanting to work with the United States because of its many political and cultural demands in addition to its demands being "bad for business."

Of course, the other very real problem with diplomacy is that while diplomacy is being waged, Iran is conducting it HEU operations. Recently, Iran has admitted that in Natanz the construction of a cascade of several thousand centrifuges has been completed and that uranium has been refined, albeit at grade "much beneath" that required for weapons. Therefore, proponents of diplomacy need to realize that while discussions are being scheduled, delayed, and held, the problem is growing and that in this situation there is a real possibility that Iran is simply stalling the process. While the European Union's foreign policy chief Javier Solana can report only that "nothing concrete" has been accomplished in his dialogue with Larijani and while IAEA diplomats complain in Vienna that in their meeting with Javad Vaidi "nothing concrete" was even discussed, Iran is simply buying time to refine better uranium. For Germans and other Europeans who want to flaunt the success of Ostpolitik in the Cold War, it is important for them to realize that the world does not have 30 years to wait on this one.

Diplomacy is also difficult because in many ways it is only an illusion of order in that, by its very nature, diplomacy is an arrangement between two or more parties, and this arrangement supplants the idea that laws should set guidelines and principles. In other words, diplomacy in nonproliferation may solve a specific problem, but at best it will only indicate solutions to future problems. In the case of Iran and nonproliferation, this factor is especially acute because Iran, more than North Korea, sits at the nexus of these problems, and therefore it is with Iran that fundamental decisions must be made about the future of nonproliferation policy.

The fact is that nonproliferation policy has been successful in the past, but nearly half the world's nuclear powers now sit outside the international system, and while diplomacy may work for some of these situations, it creates no real solutions. Furthermore, diplomacy does not address the fact that those that have ratified the various nonproliferation protocols are proving reluctant to enforce them. In summarizing the current state of the 1970 NPT, the Italian foreign minister, Massimo D'Alema, stated that the NPT, while having obtained important results, is now faced with serious risks. According to him, it should be strengthened, or it risks being eroded.

Diplomacy with Iran and Israel should certainly be viewed as the recommended course of action for the time being, but a permanent system must be devised soon, and Iran provides an excellent opportunity for a new system to be introduced. Too much proliferation exists outside the NPT, Israel has knowingly defied the system for several decades, and the lesson of India and Pakistan, which are being economically enticed into the network, is to "build the bomb." This is where Graham Allison's strategy of the "three nos" (no loose nukes, no nascent nukes, and no new nuclear states) fails. As they have demonstrated, the European Union and other major players may view proliferation as a concern but are simply not worried enough to enforce it, and, contrary to Allison's beliefs, the United States does not have the political power to make them.

Iran and the United States have a 30-year-long history of contention and conflict. Under the Bush administration, the conflict escalated, even approaching a state of war. This is not set in stone, and under the current Obama administration, there seems to be interest in changing the approach. But is Iran ready to move forward and break its three decades of international isolation? What are the challenges and obstacles, and to what extent are they surmountable? One can argue there are three major points of contention that define the relationship between the United States and Iran while also being a context where cooperation could be possible.

First, in this list is the U.S. accusation of Iran being a state supporter of terrorism. Given the current war against extremism and terror, this accusation is problematic. American policymakers should decide whether the United States is going to fight with Iran because it practically supports terrorism or whether it is just an instrument of Iranian policy for bargaining and negotiating the terms and conditions of a better relation. In other words, the United States might want to look at the relation from a different perspective if Iran is ready to give concessions. In particular, the United States accuses Iran of providing support to Hezbollah, Hamas, and al-Qaeda, as has been briefly discussed in this chapter. Iran was first designated a state supporter of terrorism in 1984 and has remained on the State Department list since then.[34] The State Department has declared Iran the most active state supporter of terrorism in 2006.[35]

Next, the United States believes that Iran has been actively supporting insurgency activities in Iraq and to some extent in Afghanistan to undermine the U.S. War on Terror. Iran has been accused of providing weapons such as advanced armor-piercing roadside bombs and improvised explosive devices, training, financing, and, in some cases, fighters to facilitate the insurgency and influence the future of the Iraqi state.[36] However, in November 2007, then Vice President Dick Cheney argued that a U.S. withdrawal from Iraq could allow "competing factions" (in which he specifically included Iran) to "unloose an all-out war, with violence unlikely to be contained within the borders of Iraq [resulting in] carnage [that would] further destabilize the Middle East."[37] Iran denied that it has played such a role.[38] Theoretically from the Iranian point of view, both the United States and Iran have strategic interests that necessitate regional cooperation. "Iran can help in building stability in Iraq and Afghanistan," and, as seen during the "Baghdad negotiations," there are certain "permanent mechanisms for dialogue" that can guarantee mutual interest."[39]

However, the mystery of Iran's material support for Taliban poses problems for that statement. According to BBC News, "Taliban members said they had received Iranian-made arms from elements in the Iranian state and from smugglers." Additionally, "Taliban commander and other sources in the south" of Afghanistan confirmed that Iranian weapons are being delivered to Taliban through both "smugglers for profit" and "elements of the Iranian state donating arms." Even the British ambassador in Kabul, Sir Sherard Cowper-Coles, made the same allegation in the following statement:

We've seen a limited supply of weapons by a group within the Iranian state, not necessarily with the knowledge of all other agencies of the Iranian state, sending some very dangerous weapons to the Taliban in the south. It's a very dangerous game for Iran, a Shia state, to be supplying Sunni extremists, like the Taliban.[40]

The problem with this statement and the media report is that they are based on the confirmation of the Afghani warlord who is in fact fighting with British or U.S. troops. There is no doubt that Iran has an interest in increasing the cost of war for the foreign troops in order to avoid the temptation to attack Iran, but how can one depend on the information acquired from the members of an insurgent groups directly fighting against you?

In May 2009, U.S. Defense Secretary Robert Gates described the alarming situation in Afghanistan and predicted that the U.S. public's support for the conflict may decline if no significant progress is seen soon. By expressing particular concern that "Tehran might step up its shipment of explosively formed penetrators, powerful roadside bombs capable of punching through even the strongest armor," he blamed Iran for "harming" U.S. interest in Afghanistan by sending weapons to the Taliban and other armed groups."

As for nuclear controversy, at least since 2003, Iran has persistently claimed that it is seeking enrichment technologies only to help fulfill and diversify its energy production capabilities. The IAEA has visited Iran's heavy-water reactor at Arak, confirmed that materials were not being diverted, and declared that Iran has been relatively truthful about its nuclear-relevant activities.[41] The United States (and many others in the international community) argue that the technologies desired by Iran are "dual-use" technologies and would give it a nuclear weapon capability "even if the intention is not to develop a nuclear arsenal at this stage."[42] Other technologies are available that could provide for power generation without fostering a weapons program. Among the potential solutions proposed are the building of a light-water reactor rather than a heavy-water reactor, but Iran refuses the provision of nuclear fuel by other states, persistently claiming that it has a right to produce nuclear fuel locally and says that this right has been given to it by the virtue of the NPT, which it signed in 1968. In fact, under obligation of full cooperation, article IV of the NPT reaffirms the "inalienable right of all NPT parties to develop research, production, and use of nuclear energy for peaceful purposes, without discrimination and in conformity with Articles I and II of this Treaty."[43]

At times, there has been mixed messages from Iran about its nuclear weapons aspirations. On the one hand, there are pronouncements from Iran's religious community that "Islam bans shedding blood of nations; on the same ground, production of a nuclear bomb and even thinking on its production are forbidden from Islamic point of view."[44] Similar statements have been issued by Ayatollah Khamenei, the supreme leader of the Islamic Revolution.[45] Even stronger statements have come from Ayatollah Sanei, who is considered a high-ranking ayatollah opposing Khomeini. His statement goes beyond weapons of mass destruction, as it also strongly prohibits suicide bombings.[46] However, in other instances, the supreme leader has stated that Iran would never give up its enrichment plans at any price.[47] Furthermore, President Ahmadinejad has made statements that it is the sovereign right of nations to acquire nuclear weapons as well as threatening Israel with annihilation.[48] Despite the most recent intelligence assessments about Iran's actual capability,[49] these kinds of seemingly contradictory statements from key members of Iran's government tend to foster distrust in the international community.

It appears that the nuclear issue provides the best context for a dialogue, and President Obama and the State Department are willing to engage Iran in a direct and unconditional dialogue, even despite recent sanctions and harsh rhetoric. The unexpected release of the five Iranian detainees "at the request of the government of Iraq," however justified as part of U.S. compliance with the "security agreement between United States and Iraq,"[50] has definitely been a major step forward. Unfortunately, the events following the disputed presidential election in Iran and the arrest of the three U.S. hikers at the border between Iraq and the Iranian Kurdish areas have complicated the situation. Iran confirmed the detention only 12 days after they were detained and were sent to Tehran from the mountainous areas of the Iran-Iraq border.[51]

Iran's poor human rights record is in fact another item that could be added to the list, and an emphasis on this record used was in both President Clinton's and President Bush's agendas, but it seems that, under current international circumstances, it is having less importance for the Obama administration. Several people with dual nationalities have been detained and taken to trial since the Iranian presidential election in July 2009, but no major action has been seen from the U.S. side. The list of detainees includes Iranian Canadian journalist, Maziar Bahari (released recently) and Iranian American scholar Kian Tajbakhsh and French student Clotilde Reiss, who was a language teacher in Iran. Several detainees have been murdered, tortured and mutilated, raped, and forced to confess crimes they have not committed. The entire process is against the accepted norms of international human rights, but so far, unlike the European Union, the U.S. administration has been relatively silent.

The harshest reaction from Secretary of State Hillary Clinton in the face of mistreatment and bulk trial of the detainees was that the trial "demonstrates that . . . this Iranian leadership is afraid of their own people, and afraid of the truth and the facts coming out."[52] Despite the ongoing military clampdown of the opposition in Iran, the question of human rights has dissipated in relation to other important regional issues. It is also possible that public opinion is so sensitive to the political outcome of the current turmoil in Iran that its immediate civil or human right issues have been neglected.

American dissatisfaction is not limited to Iran's conduct of domestic policies. Iran is stubborn when it comes to its nuclear policy as well. All suggestions to swap Iran's low-enriched uranium with nuclear reactor usable fuel has come to a stalemate, and the involved parties seem to be divided on how to deal with Iran. A recent nuclear summit and pressures on China and to some extent to Russia have proved to be either ineffective or rejected by members of UN Security Council. Diverging interests have made it almost impossible to confront Iran through military or economic means.

In the absence of support for UN sanctions on Tehran's nuclear program and under great pressure from Israel—including threats of unilateral strikes—Hillary Clinton fears that "ignoring the threat posed by Iran will put the world in a more precarious position within six months to a year."[53] This statement clearly shows that the United States is concerned that a unilateral strike by Israel could trigger yet another regional conflict in a region already stricken by two wars.

If President Obama decides to stay the course for a dialogue with the Islamic Republic and change of approach toward Iranian government after 30 years of confrontation, he will have to face serious criticism from both Americans and Iranians, first because many Iranians strongly oppose Ahmadinejad's legitimacy as the president of Iran given the accusations of fraud and the turmoil following the election. Khamenei's authority has also been damaged. Negotiations and a change of approach by the United States toward Iran should not make the regime stronger and more persistent in suppressing its domestic dissidents.

Second, most European leaders have openly criticized Ahmadinejad and have announced that they are not going to congratulate him for *winning* the election. This approach has even forced the White House to change its language and stance on the issue. In the meantime, while it seems like Secretary of State Clinton is still hopeful of getting a response from Iran on the U.S. initiatives, several factors are making it more and more difficult. Clinton was quoted by BBC as saying,

We've certainly reached out and made it clear that's what we'd be willing to do, even now, despite our absolute condemnation of what they've done in the [June 12 presidential] election and since, but I don't think they have any capacity to make that kind of decision right now.[54]

Relations with Iran are important for the United States, but they do not have the same level of importance for Iran. The Islamic Republic of Iran seems to be concerned that the establishment of a long-term relations with the United States may practically jeopardize the very existence of the regime and bring about a regime change.[55] Tehran-based analyst Saeed Leylaz believes that "there are lot of radicals who don't want to see ordinary relations between Tehran and Washington. To convince Iran, they should send a very clear message that they are not going to try and destroy the regime." On the other hand, relations with Israel are of extreme importance to the United States and to Israel. For the United States, having a strong ally in the region—and a democratic one nonetheless—is crucial to negotiating and realizing policy goals. For Israel, having the support of the United States is part of what gives the nation an outward sense of political legitimacy.

Despite the fact that Israel has been and will continue to be the enemy of Iran, the relationship between Israel and many Arab states could change, depending on the eventualities of Iran's nuclear buildup. The situation is complex, particularly because of the long-held hostilities of the Arab-Israeli conflict and specifically the Israeli-Palestinian conflict—two ongoing disputes that have rallied Arab nations in opposition to Israel. As Eliot Abrams points out in the *Washington Post*, the usual description of Arab-Israeli relations as antipathetic, hostile, or belligerent is giving way to a more complex picture.[56] He writes,

Following the joint Arab military efforts to prevent the formation of the Jewish State in 1948, and the wars that followed in 1956, 1967 and 1973, this is a bizarre turn of events. Israel is as unpopular in the Arab street as it has been in past decades (which is to say, widely hated), but for Arab rulers focused on the Iranian threat all those Israeli Air Force jets must now appear alluring. The Israeli toughness the Arabs have complained about for over a half century is now their own most likely shield against Iran.[57]

The view that someone, whether the United States or another global actor, should bomb Iran and stop it from its current nuclear path is widely held among Arab leaders, particularly those in the Gulf states. United Arab Emirates ambassador to the United States, Yousef Al Otaiba, spoke of a "cost-benefit analysis" and said that despite the upset to trade that would result and the inevitable "people protesting and rioting and very unhappy that there is an outside force attacking a Muslim country," the balance was clear.[58] He said, "If you are asking me, 'Am I willing to live with that versus living with a nuclear Iran?' my answer is still the same: 'We cannot live with a nuclear Iran.' I am willing to absorb what takes place."[59] What the ambassador meant by "an outside force" was unclear, though many speculated that without specifically mentioning the United States, he intended his remarks as a plea for its aid. Additionally, the adage "the enemy of my enemy is my friend" may be fitting when discussing the relationship between Israel, Iran, and the United States as well. It is possible to see how this scenario would work for Iran in the following example: the enemy of Iran is Israel; the enemy of Israel is the Arab states; thus, Iran may view the Arab states in a more friendly fashion as they negotiate their relationship with Israel. This may be seen best with regard to Palestine—how will Iran approach the ongoing Palestinian-Israeli conflict, especially if, as Abrams points out, potential Israeli air strikes may be seen as a buffer or as a welcome protection to Arab states that do not want to deal with the threat of nuclear Iran? Abrams concludes his article with the following:

Perhaps the enemy of my enemy is not my friend, if he is an Israeli pilot. In that case, all gestures of friendship will be forsaken or carefully hidden; there will be denunciations and UN resolutions, petitions and boycotts, Arab League summits and hurried trips to Washington. But none of that changes an essential fact of life well understood in many Arab capitals this summer: that there is a clear coincidence of interests between the Arab states and Israel today, in the face of the Iranian threat. Given the 60 years of war and cold peace between Israel and the Arabs, this is one of the signal achievements of the regime in Tehran—and could prove to be its undoing.[60]

In fact, what may frighten the Iranian system is a severe decline in the regime's support from the people. Obviously, a regime security guarantee would be what the radicals might be looking for before they accept any commitment to better relations. In addition, Iran does not really seem very enthusiastic about opening up contacts with United States; the outcome of an unrestricted relation could be more harmful to the Islamic Republic of Iran though extremely useful for the people of Iran. There is no need to emphasize that the clerical leadership has not missed any single opportunity to talk against relations with the United States.

Though intrusive sanctions, U.S. support for Israel, the war with Iraq or Afghanistan, and the U.S. military presence in the Persian Gulf have been the usual context in which reject better relations, there is one more reason that the clerical leadership does not want to reestablish its ties with the United States, namely, the more fundamentally antagonistic conflict between the nature of the two political systems. The fear of regime security cannot be overcome. International community needs a strong and cohesive nonproliferation policy, but it needs to be based on things that the major governments of the world are willing to enforce and that the developing nations of the world, which want to pursue the quickest way to "status" (nuclear weapons), will be willing to follow. This new nonproliferation policy system needs to decide what the biggest risk of proliferation is and decide how to frame this risk in a way that is enforceable, and this system must be all-inclusive and not allow for any party to sit outside the system. It is only in this way that future proliferation problems can be solved and nonproliferation cohesively addressed.

CHAPTER 6

Recent Conflicts

In the aftermath of the 2006 Hezbollah War, we can look at the conflict and the events that shaped it to arrive at a number of critical conclusions about the gains and losses of each side. When considering Iran and Israel, the Arab-Israeli conflict, and the future of political legitimacy in the region, we must not become trapped by status quo assumptions of the past. One of the most common of these assumptions is that this conflict, like those of the past, was a zero-sum game. The 2006 Hezbollah War shatters that idea in fact. It has been common to assume that Israel's loss is always the other side's gain—in other words, as long as Israel suffers some form of defeat, the Arabs win and vice versa. Yet, while perceptions of Israel's military invincibility were certainly tarnished and Hezbollah proved to be a force to be reckoned with, both sides gained something from the conflict.[1] In August 2006, Margaret Warner, senior correspondent of the Public Broadcasting Service, interviewed military and foreign affairs analyst Mark Perry of Conflicts Forum. In the interview, Warner brought up the very idea of the zero-sum game and suggested that both Hezbollah leader Sayyid Hassan Nasrallah and Israeli Prime Minister Ehud Olmert were claiming victory. The following portion of that interview clarifies this issue:

WARNER: If you listen to both Olmert and Nasrallah, they both seem to be claiming that they're gaining with every day. Can both be right?

PERRY: No, one has to be right and one wrong. These are, as you point out, two very different narratives. Let's take a look at Hezbollah. They're still able to field an army. They still have command and control. They still have their communications systems in place. They're still able, in southern Lebanon, in those villages of southern Lebanon, where the IDF went even a week ago; they're still fighting in those villages. And as we saw today, they're able to launch rockets at Israel.

So, if there is a degradation of Hezbollah capabilities, it's certainly not shown on the field of battle, and that's where it's important to see it.[2]

WARNER: So you would say—your assessment is that Hezbollah is winning?

PERRY: They're holding their own, and they don't need to win to win. They need to survive to win. And if you're in the Arab world right now, there's not anyone in that world who isn't thinking about 1967, when Jordan, Syria and Egypt fought for six days and were thoroughly defeated. We're now in day 24; that's 18 days better. It's quite an accomplishment.[3]

It should also be noted that three weeks into the conflict, Hezbollah was in a much weaker position than Israel. While they proved to be a contender in the fight, media outlets were concerned primarily with covering Israeli soldiers' deaths, while little coverage of Hezbollah's losses ever made it to the airwaves. Hezbollah entered the conflict in a weaker position militarily and left the conflict in the same position. Israel's decadelong quest to pacify its northern border saw great gains throughout the conflict. Additionally, Israeli offensives seemed to weaken public support for Lebanon's ruling coalition, which claimed to have U.S. backing. Israel, supported by the United States in this conflict, undermined the Lebanese coalition's credibility, further fanning the flames of anti-U.S. sentiment in the region. Hezbollah won in the game of expectations. That is, when comparing Hezbollah and Israel, Israel fell short of its military expectations, while Hezbollah far exceeded what the public thought it was capable of producing. Winning a political victory at home, Hezbollah upstaged Olmert and his administration's war plans as the guerilla tactics proved to be more than the Israeli armed forces were capable of handling, let alone thwarting. Ultimately, the gains minimize the effects of each side's losses, and, further, they signal a shift in the dynamics of the conflict to a period of more balance and equilibrium.[4]

While Iran and Syria may point to instances of Hezbollah's success and claim victory, such expressions are hardly legitimate. It is more likely, rather, that Hezbollah alone will accrue political payoffs, not Hezbollah as a proxy group, the host and financial backers of which may be rewarded on successful military endeavors. This success is based on a number of different factors.[5] First, unlike their supporters, Hezbollah itself has no national boundaries or geographic limitations. While it operates primarily out of Lebanon, it is not bound to the country of Lebanon itself and may employ subgroups elsewhere in the world. This elasticity allows it to be successful in a multitude of settings. The lack of defined parameters (borders, constitution, and national boundary lines) makes it nearly impossible to defeat Hezbollah with military force, as Israel witnessed during this 2006 conflict. The politics of war has changed, and Israel, during the 2006 Hezbollah War, fought an "old war" using traditional methods while Hezbollah changed the rules of the game. Next,

Hezbollah does not operate under a systemic political structure. Though Nasrallah acts as the group's leader, the members of Hezbollah "carry no cards and bear no specific responsibilities." Therefore, unlike Iran and Syria, the populations of which demand that their government conduct affairs in certain manners, Hezbollah does not answer to anyone. There are no politicians seeking election or reelection, and the future of the group depends on the success of the next conflict at hand and the continued backing of Shia states.[6]

Many questions have been raised regarding the definitions of victory and assessments of gains and losses. Militarily, Hezbollah's rockets began to reach increasingly farther into Israel the longer the summer conflict lasted. Additionally, Hezbollah increased its rocket launches as well with more and more rockets being launched over time. According to Gal Luft at the Institute for the Analysis of Global Security, this is exactly what Hezbollah wanted to show. Understanding that it was perceived as the underdog, Hezbollah's offensive achieved an often-overlooked objective; that is, by showing that the rockets could not be stopped and, further, that they had the capability to maintain a presence even through a residual rocket, they changed the rules of the game. Thus, if victory according to Israel is to stop rocket fire, the chances of that being accomplished are slim to none. Yet, if victory is defined as changing the game on the ground, the possibility increases.[7]

There is no question that Israelis largely supported the 2006 conflict. They viewed it as legitimate response to an attack on Israeli soil and believed that such a response was long overdue, as they had been subject to rocket attacks in northern Israel for years. However, though the initial public support was nearly universal, as the conflict continued and Hezbollah retained its arms and refused to release Israeli soldiers, the media began to critically question the manner in which the war was being operated and managed. This signaled disaster for Olmert. Because Hezbollah was able to withstand an immense amount of Israeli rocket attacks and fought using guerilla tactics, the everyday observer did not see a degradation of their military capabilities.[8] Military expert Anthony Cordesman, author of "Lessons of the 2006 Israeli-Hezbollah War," said the following in his assessment of the conflict:

According to one US official who observed the war closely, the IDF's [Israel Defense Forces's] air offensive degraded "perhaps only 7%" of the total military resource assets available to Hezbollah's fighters in the first three days of fighting and added that, in his opinion, Israeli air attacks on the Hezbollah leadership were "absolutely futile."[9]

This lack of observable degradation of Hezbollah was compounded by what appeared to be an utter failure of Israeli strategy. Israel's military fell short of expectations. While the White House, which fully supported Israel, publicly acknowledged that the Israeli strategy was severely damaging Hezbollah forces, the reality on the ground proved just the opposite. Having bypassed military intelligence that suggested the need for a substantial number of additional Israeli ground forces, Halutz and the IDF relied heavily on air strikes. Launching a substantial air campaign that targeted and demolished Hezbollah rockets, command centers, and local infrastructure, Halutz and Olmert declared the mission accomplished.[10] Yet Israel's attacks on Hezbollah had merely awakened the sleeping lion. The IDF strategy proved to be a miscalculation, as a more comprehensive plan was needed to to thwart the massive Hezbollah offensive: 100 civilian-targeted rockets per day with over 4,000 fired by the end of the 34-day war. Israel's objective was to diminish Hezbollah's ability to fight across the border. Containing this guerilla-based, movable group was half the battle. This demotion of military objectives masked in political and diplomatic objectives is evident in Israel's hesitancy to begin a major on-the-ground offense until the very end of the war. Widely criticized by media outlets within Israel, the policy was based on the understanding that military objectives would not be won until Hezbollah faced an arms embargo or other restraints. In addition, a sustainable ground war against Hezbollah's powerful guerrilla warfare would have cost Israel more than it was ready to incur, both in money and in casualties. Moreover, Israel fell short on another measure—basic necessities of troops. The Israeli army went to battle without an adequate supply of food, water, and other basic supplies as a result of cuts in defense spending.[11]

As we continue to examine the strategic outcomes of the Hezbollah conflict, a few other considerations must be made. First, the Israeli campaign was designed primarily to frighten tourists. In other words, as Gary Gambill of the *Mideast Monitor* puts it, to "raise the costs of Hezbollah's adventurism to such a degree that deliberate provocations will not be politically tenable for the foreseeable future."[12] Israel's campaign certainly enhanced the preclusion of Hezbollah. Nasrallah presented his hypothesis of Israel being a "spider web" on a number of occasions. By this, he simply meant that the technological advancements and progress of Israel masked a weaker society that was largely unwilling to make the necessary sacrifices for national security interests. Thus, Hezbollah leaders who proclaim that their efforts have dented Israeli infrastructure may not be completely accurate. Surely, the attacks on Israel were large and unexpected and produced casualties unlike many other Israeli conflicts. For this reason, many Israelis were eager for a rematch and wanted to restore some of the dignity lost in this battle.[13]

Diplomatically, it is certainly necessary to discuss UN Security Council Resolution 1701. Unanimously approved on August 11, 2006, the resolution demanded full cessation of hostilities, Israeli withdrawal from Lebanon, disarmament of Hezbollah forces, and the full control of Lebanon by the Lebanese government. Interestingly, the resolution called for an end to Israeli "offensive" operations, meaning that Israel had room for interpretation, as it could classify attacks on Hezbollah as "defensive" in nature if given the opportunity. It also sought to limit Hezbollah's military potential by protecting the eastern border of Lebanon, thereby decreasing arms flow and hindering the potential involvement and/or ambitions of Iran.[14]

In addition, the resolution had other diplomatic objectives. It called for 15,000 peacekeeping forces of the UN Interim Force in Lebanon (UNIFIL) to secure the border in southern Lebanon. Hezbollah, which operated in a guerilla warfare fashion, would have a more difficult time rebuilding its bunkers, bridges, and underground tunnels and hideouts with these troops guarding the area. While Hezbollah may have been able to store its rockets and ammunition, it will not be allowed to deploy them fully, as UNIFIL's watchful eyes would prevent such things from taking place.[15]

Politically, there are a number of things to consider. First, the surprising capabilities of Hezbollah damaged the Israeli government. Following the last war that Israel lost in 1973, then–Prime Minister Menachem Begin agreed to accept a peace deal with Egypt's president, Anwar Sadat. The deal was simple and modest. Both parties were allies of the United States. No such advancement took place after the Israel-Hezbollah War.

Some Israeli's believes that Israel lost its ability to prevent Hezbollah from acting and that, as a result, Israel must now seek a way to restore those abilities. The discussion of another war has loomed for some time, and many in Washington and other political circles see that such a war is only a matter of time. Israel's army must be restructured if such a war is to take place in order to deal with the perseverance and stamina of Hezbollah guerillas. Some have even gone so far as to compare what Israel needs to do with what the United States needed following Vietnam.

For Lebanon, the most obvious political difficulty is the possibility that Hezbollah's objections to any political move may mean that Shia leaders will become disgruntled and leave their posts. Therefore, Nasrallah has been placed in a sticky situation, as he must carefully determine whether he has the ability to find replacement Shia leaders if those current leaders leave and also work to maintain some adherence to his objectives with some degree of legitimacy. During the conflict, Nasrallah believed that Hezbollah could take advantage of operating out of residential areas and other on-the-ground facilities, including a hospital. As Israel attacked those facilities, the residual or collateral damage would present a negative image and give Hezbollah a boost in public opinion.[16] Additionally, Israel miscalculated in thinking that the hijacking of a public news channel and spreading pictures of corpses while saying that Nasrallah was hiding the number of casualties would have any effect. In fact, Hezbollah's public support had less to do with military conflict and battle records and more with the Israeli-Palestinian conflict.

As Gary Gambill recounts, in "Implications of the Israel-Hezbollah War," Israel's strategy to sow discord among Shia was not helped when Israel bombed the residence of Sayyed Muhammad Hussein Fadlallah, one of Lebanon's most respected clerics. Gambill says,

If anyone in the Shiite community had the stature and motivation to depart from Nasrallah's script and voice a more nuanced interpretation of the war with Israel, it was Fadlallah. Although several secular Shiite intellectuals criticized Hezbollah during and after the fighting in articles run by elite-owned newspapers and one Shiite cleric later challenged Hezbollah's claim to have won a great victory, dissent against Hezbollah remained surprisingly marginal within the Shiite community, in spite of its immense suffering.[17]

For Olmert, the handling on the war spelled disaster for his political future. As the public grew more and more weary over the methodology and implementation of war tactics and strategies, calls for his resignation rang loud and clear. Many perceived the 34-day war against Hezbollah as an utter failure and blamed Olmert for not having organized and planned in a manner that would lead to the best results. Various polls published in Israeli newspapers toward the end of the conflict indicated that two-thirds of Israelis wanted Olmert to resign immediately. The surveys suggested that Benjamin Netanyahu of the opposition Likud Party would win if new elections were held, which we now know to be true.

After these reports were issued, Olmert struggled to maintain his coalition. One minister from the Labor Party, Olmert's coalition partner, resigned, and there were numerous indications of eroding support within Kadima. In his resignation speech, Olmert said the following:

In the security arena, we strengthened the Israel Defense Forces: We continued to build up its might and greatly increased its resources. There is calm in the north and it is not under any immediate threat. Israel's deterrent capability has improved beyond recognition. We also learned our lessons and rectified our mistakes. The self-examination processes are essential mechanisms to a healthy society—I am proud of them.[18]

Israel may have achieved certain diplomatic ends, but the implications of miscalculation put Israel in a difficult place. Because Olmert and Peretz had limited backgrounds in military affairs, they were forced to rely on Dan Halutz. According to Captain Daniel Helmer, a Rhodes Scholar and author of "Not Quite Counterinsurgency: A Cautionary Tale for US Forces Based on Israel's Operation Change of Direction," Halutz was a general who was completely unprepared for a full-scale ground war with Hezbollah.[19] In an attempt to drive Hezbollah forces out of southern Lebanon, Halutz convinced Olmert and Peretz that Israel should retaliate with air strikes against Hezbollah and the Lebanese central government. By attacking symbolic targets and political leadership, Halutz believed that Hezbollah would abandon its war strategy and retreat under pressure from the Lebanese government. However, this proved to be difficult, as Hezbollah countered with a campaign of assault that caught Israeli forces and commanders off guard, suggesting that the Lebanese government was too weak to thwart Hezbollah.[20] Having bypassed military intelligence that suggested the need for Israeli ground forces in more substantial numbers, Halutz and the IDF relied heavily on air strikes. Launching a substantial air campaign that targeted and demolished Hezbollah rockets, command centers, and local infrastructure, Halutz and Olmert declared the mission accomplished. Yet Israel's attacks on Hezbollah had merely awakened the sleeping lion.

Nasrallah began the campaign by suggesting that Hezbollah desired to act out of sympathy for the Palestinians. Yet the 2006 Hezbollah War put the question of Palestine on the back burner to the point that Israel's military imprisoned Hamas officials in the Gaza Strip, questioning and arresting terror suspects. Toward the end of the war, Nasrallah's resistance had taken a toll on Olmert, the only politician in Israel who made a withdrawal from the West Bank a mandated promise for the coming years.

David Makovsky and Jeffrey White, authors of "Lessons and Implications of the Israel-Hizbollah War: A Preliminary Assessment," say,

Palestinians have Nasrallah to thank for the likelihood that Israeli control of the West Bank will be even more prolonged. Even if Iran opposed the timing of war as a premature exposure of its deterrent, there should be close U.S.-Israeli consultations to discuss how to deal with Iran and its determination to obtain a nuclear capability. Israel may also find that the leaders of Sunni states that share similar fears are receptive to deepening quiet ties in ways that do not require Israel to insert itself into the Sunni-Shiite divide in the Middle East.[21]

The United States may have the ability to facilitate such ties and play a role in their progress. Such progress would come, however, if apprehensions of Iran's rise to power in the region and world would lead Saudi Arabia to make efforts toward dialogue with Israel. As Makovsky and White point out, "The probability is low, but Riyadh needs to weigh the contained risk of its usual inaction with the risks that Israeli-Arab deterioration plays into Tehran's hands."[22] Additionally, another major implication of the war is the boost that Hezbollah saw in its approval ratings and status on the world stage. While Hezbollah certainly suffered its fair share of setbacks, the war single-handedly boosted its appeal. This new appeal eroded much of the strength of its adversaries. Nasrallah, thus, had more political leverage and capabilities than he had ever had before.

Fouad Siniora ordered a deployment of Lebanese military forces after arriving at an agreement with Nasrallah in which Hezbollah was allowed to retain its weapons as long as they were out of the public view. This raised the issue of status quo ante in which the weapons would remain, no one would raise questions concerning them, and no major new initiatives would be brought to the table, therefore creating a stalemate of sorts. As it is not likely (or possible) that Israel would disrupt any resupply of Hezbollah without a massive, unprecedented air and ground campaign that reaches across multiple Middle Eastern borders, Resolution 1701 may not be enforced as it was planned. Such enforcement would necessitate the full and complete cooperation of the Syrian and Lebanese governments, and the likelihood of that occurring in the immediate to near future is slim. The sudden proliferation of calls for negotiations with Assad among U.S. pundits is a pretty good indicator of how dimly prospects for the former are viewed in Washington.[23]

The conflict has been considered by many to be a proxy war fought by Hezbollah and Israel with the support of Iran and the United States. In fact, Hezbollah is considered to have close ties with Iran and has even been dubbed an extension of Iran. Therefore, by defeating Hezbollah, a clear and strong message would be sent to Iranian leaders in Tehran. Though Iran was not the explicit focus of the 2006 war, world leaders and U.S. foreign policymakers in particular understood the centrality of Iran with regard to U.S. foreign policy engagements. Hence, the 2006 Hezbollah War gave the United States a way to indirectly challenge Iran through Israel without engaging Iran directly. To highlight this point, it is necessary to consider the words of President George W. Bush at the 2006 G8 Summit. Bush said that the attendees of the summit

were able to reach a very strong consensus that the world must the root causes of the current instability. And the root cause of that current instability is terrorism and terrorist attacks on a democratic country. And part of those terrorist attacks are inspired by nation states, like Syria and Iran. And in order to deal with this crisis, the world must deal with Hezbollah, with Syria, and continue to work to isolate Iran.[24]

Jeremy Pressman of Brandeis University's Crown Center for Middle East Studies suggests that the more the conflict resembles a military defeat for Hezbollah and the more Hezbollah loses its control and power within the confines of the Lebanese government, the greater the defeat is for Iran. Iran's standing in the world, under these circumstances, would suffer greatly. Additionally, Pressman probes the possibility of Syria backing away from the scene—calming the narrative of an Iranian alliance. In this case, it would appear that Iran would also suffer a blow, as it would be, of course, further isolated. By contrast, the stronger Hezbollah appears, the better Iran appears, and given the history of the military conflict, the detailed descriptions of on-the-ground combat, and depictions of various strategies, Hezbollah seemed poised to take on an appearance of strength and agility. Momentum was tipping toward Iran as a result of Hezbollah's massive assaults and surprising performance.[25] Perhaps Iran realized this. In efforts to increase the tide, the Iranian government launched a propaganda campaign that sought support for public agendas by having schoolchildren write their thoughts about the ongoing conflict, thus portraying themselves as victims. It should certainly be made clear that Iran provided no support to Hezbollah beyond moral and spiritual support, though there was universal agreement that the two were aligned. The campaign that begin in Tehran was seen a way to rouse the Muslim world and radicalize the response to the war. It was clear from the reponses within the Iranian government to various aspects of the conflict that Iran would not back down from its nuclear ambitions or its posturing on the political stage. Many world leaders believed that the outcome of this conflict would serve to make Iran less confrontational. After all, if Hezbollah was severely routed in warfare, Iran would lose a degree of its credibility. The August 31, 2006, deadline to suspend its uranium enrichment passed, and the following month, as Iranian President Mahmoud Ahmadinejad traveled to the United Nations, his anti-Americanism and, perhaps more critically, his anti-Israelism were more prominent than ever. Syria also took advantage of the end of the conflict with similar rhetoric that linked both Iran and Syria in further isolation. Bashar Al-Assad, president of the Syrian Arab Republic, said of the resistance,

Why this resistance is essential, let us just think of the direct achievements of the latest battles on the ground. The greatest achievement of those battles is that they came as a national response to the cowardly propositions that have been circulated through our region especially after the Iraq invasion. What made them more glorious is the reaction of the Arab people in general, which was marked by being a purely pan-Arab response to the abominable, seditious propositions that we have heard recently and to those who stand behind them.[26]

It is clear at this point that Iran's and Syria's global ambitions after the end of conlfict did not change completely. Iran still insited on pursuing nuclear options as it touted victory through the proxy war. Syria joined in this discourse, denouncing blind support of Israel by the United States and the global community and calling on Arab countries in the region to rally in support. Emily Landau of the Carnegie Endowment for International Peace suggests, interestingly, that though Iran may not have changed its approach after the war, the context in which Iran's involvement in the Middle East is considered has indeed changed.[27] Fault lines that created the greater conlflict initially were centered around the age-old Arab-Isralei conflict but more recently and specifically have been situated around the Israeli-Palestinian conflict. But this war, with respect to Iran's gains as a result of Hezbollah's unexpected success, has altered the context in which Iran is considered. Concentration has now shifted to radical forces in the region other than those groups that operate within the frameworks of the Arab-Israeli conflict. The growing distinctions among radical groups has drastically changed the map. With the eyes of the world on Hezbollah and thus Iran, the nuclear ambitions of the Iranian government have become a centerpiece of discussion on the greater Middle East—moreso than they were before the 2006 conflict escalated. Landau notes that much of this context could be seen in the very beginning of the war. Hezbollah was targeted with criticism, leveled by Saudi Arabia, Jordan, and especially Egypt. This was largely a result of suspicions that close ties to Iran would lead to new possibilities for Iran's hegemonic ambitions. These notions of hegemony, once theoretical and uncertain, were becoming more realistic and were clearly evidenced in the rhetoric of Ahmadinejad, who on more than one occasion expressed interest in eliminating Israel by "wiping them off of the map."[28]

Considering this, it will more than likely take a few years, even from this point, to fully understand all the ramifications of the war between Israel and Hezbollah. Certainly, it appears that Israel and Hezbollah, with Syria, Iran, Lebanon, and the Palestinians alike, will each share their positive and negative consequences. Hezbollah may have been bruised in the battle, but it certainly was not defeated. More than likely, Hezbollah has found that their ability to move and operate freely has declined. Israel came out of the conflict with one major win, namely, that Lebanon will more than likely replace Hezbollah in the north, making Israel far safer than it was before. In addition, Syria and Iran appear proud of their proxy's (Hezbollah's) ability to withstand such a powerful member of the region. Finally, both countries may understand that the ramifications of the war include pitfalls that will need to be addressed in the future. Syria must deal with the fact that there is always the possibility of a more independent and sovereign Lebanon. American and Israeli worries about an Iranian nuclear program have intensified, increasing the possibility that if diplomacy fails in an attempt to stop Iran from further developing its nuclear arsenal, a strike on nuclear facilities may be imminent and the only option for maintaining that balance in the Middle East. For this reason, any claims of the Iranian or even Syrian government of being strengthened as a result of a good performance by one of its proxies must be qualified further. There is no indication at this point that the results of the 2006 Hezbollah conflict have any bearing on Iran's position on the world stage.

Thus, in considering Iran, the results are somewhat mixed. The widespread UNIFIL deployment will impede Iran's efforts to provoke anti-Israeli violence from within Lebanon as Tehran faces the global community's efforts to prevent the expansion of a nuclear program. Though Iran gained some possible diplomatic leverage in the war, most scholars agree that Iran's assertion of gaining strength through Hezbollah is not completely accurate. Additionally, the determination of the United States to shut down Iran's nuclear program has, if anything, been increased by the crisis. Anti-Israeli sentiment in the Arab world can benefit Iran, though the destruction of Lebanon during the war prevents feelings of aggression from becoming pronounced in actual acts of terror or violence. Skyrocketing popular support for Hezbollah could also discourage Arab governments from supporting U.S. policy in the region as well.

Immediately following the aftermath of the war in 2006, Hezbollah retreated from the public eye. While there was little or no physical presence of the group in the months that followed, many believed it to be recuperating monetarily and militarily. Seven months later, in October 2006, President Ahmadinejad, in some of his more hostile words since the summer war, said that Israel would soon disappear. Speaking before a rally in support of Palestinians, Ahmadinejad's words resounded among the audience: "Efforts to stabilize this fake [Israeli] regime, by the grace of God, have completely failed. You should believe that this regime is disappearing."[29] The United Nations reported less than one year after those remarks that Hezbollah had increased its military in size, capability, and influence comparable to the period before the July 2006 conflict began. The buildup of Hezbollah, aligned with Iran's claims of being capable of producing a nuclear weapon within the year, raised many eyebrows in the international community. And, though many Iranian officials denied having supplied Hezbollah with weapons for the 2006 conflict as well as denying the monetary and military buildup of Hezbollah one year later, such claims should be viewed with skepticism. In fact, in August 2006, Ali Akbar Mohtshamipour, a former ambassador to Lebanon who also held the title of secretary-general of the Intifada Conference, told an Iran-based newspaper that Iran had indeed transferred Zelzal-2 missiles to the Shi'ite militia and also suggested that Iran offered its blessings in using them against Israel during the war.[30] Additionally, *Jane's Defense Weekly*, a military specialist magazine, reported in early August 2006 that Iran would supply Hezbollah with surface-to-air missiles to be used in the campaign against Israel. Robin Hughes, the magazine's Middle East editor, said, "The details coming from the meeting reveal that they are about ensuring a constant supply of weapons to support Islamic Resistance operations against Israel."[31] As reports like these began to surface, the international community paid closer attention to Iran. Talks of nuclear programs only heated this already intense dialogue. While Israel undoubtedly felt threatened by Hezbollah and its connection to Iran, the nuclear factor also played into the situation. Israel admitted in very clear terms that it would not stand by idly and allow Iran to possess nuclear weapons. While these sentiments are certainly backed by the United States and Europe, Israel itself had few options to derail such things from happening. Estimations suggest that Iran has between 12 and 20 uranium enrichment sites, and Israel, though it proved its strength to some degree in fighting Hezbollah, cannot strike all of Iran's nuclear sites. Israel, on the other hand, is likely to recall the 1981 effort when Israeli air forces crippled the Iraqi nuclear program. That being said, it is likely that Iranians have studied the events of 1981 and have protected their prized Natanz facility, the heart of Iran's nuclear program with some 5,000 centrifuges operating.[32] The location of the site, in addition to the fact that it is located in an underground, hardened structure, presents real problems for Israel's claim. Because Israel and Iran do not share a common border, the Israeli air force would be required to fly into and over hostile territory before attempting a strike on the site. This is a highly unlikely move on the part of Israel. First, before such attempts can even be discussed, Israel would have to ensure that its air force was capable of completing such a mission. Refueling is an important issue. Certainly, Israel's air force is capable in terms of size, but Israel has been concerned so long with only the surrounding Arab countries that its long-term strategies for flyovers or invasion may need some adjustment. The possibility that seems most viable for Israel's current military is to refuel at U.S. air bases in Iraq. While such a move would be possible, it would require the cooperation and consent of the U.S. military. Such a commitment would be dangerous unless the United States were ready to go to war with Iran itself.

While air strikes such as these remain unlikely despite various discourses that have arisen suggesting their likelihood, the 2006 conflict in Lebanon did cause Israel to pause and regroup, much like Hezbollah did. In a statement to the *Sunday Times* of Britain, an Israeli general, speaking on condition of anonymity, said, "The challenge from Iran and Syria is now top of the Israeli defense agenda, higher than the Palestinian one."[33] Israeli Deputy Defense Minister Ephraim Sneh echoed this tone, insisting on the possibility of strikes against Iran: "I am not advocating an Israeli pre-emptive military action against Iran and I am aware of its possible repercussions. I consider it a last resort. But even the last resort is sometimes the only resort."[34] Certainly, this statement reflects the serious nature of Israel's strategy reconfiguration and the possibility of war. The conflict between Palestine and Israel had long occupied a central place in public discourse. The Israeli general went on to say,

In the past we prepared for a possible military strike against Iran's nuclear facilities, but Iran's growing confidence after the war in Lebanon means we have to prepare for a full-scale war, in which Syria will be an important player.[35]

Iran's growing confidence over the ineffectiveness of the IDF raised the prospects of an eventual attack. And with Syria having come into the picture more prominently, many Israelis may have been concerned with the 1937 Golan Heights event, where the Syrian army captured an Israeli stronghold. Israeli analysts believed that Syria may be positioning itself to capture the post again; thus, its alignment with Iran posed a threat for a number of reasons. Analysts at the time indicated that Israel and Syria were very capable of using missiles able to cover most of Israel, including the city of Tel Aviv. As evidence of this became clear, the United States carefully monitored the situation. Even so, any action on behalf of the United States would likely produce more chaos in the region than intended. Just as it would be dangerous to use U.S. bases in Iraq for refueling, it also would be dangerous for the United States to send warnings to Iran, indicating the possibility of a U.S. strike. Ali Akbar Mohtashamipour, the Iranian founder of Hezbollah, said during the 2006 war that an attack by the United States would warrant an Iranian attack on Tel Aviv.[36] Thus, while many Washington experts agreed that air strikes against Iranian nuclear sites would be a straightforward task, it would risk an Iranian eruption in Israel. Further, with Syria spiraling into chaos, U.S.-led attacks on Iran would likely anger sleeping insurgent groups of radical fundamentalists waiting for a reason to cause further instability in the Middle East.

Seymour Hersh, a veteran U.S. journalist known for his reporting on military affairs, particularly investigative reporting, suggested that though a U.S. military strike would further complicate matters in the region, such things were indeed being explored by the Bush administration. In an August 21 article in *The New Yorker*, Hersh reported,

The Bush Administration, however, was closely involved in the planning of Israel's retaliatory attacks. President Bush and Vice-President Dick Cheney were convinced, current and former intelligence and diplomatic officials told me, that a successful Israeli Air Force bombing campaign against Hezbollah's heavily fortified underground-missile and command-and-control complexes in Lebanon could ease Israel's security concerns and also serve as a prelude to a potential American preemptive attack to destroy Iran's nuclear installations, some of which are also buried deep underground.[37]

Based on this assessment, the United States would treat Hezbollah much like Iran treated Hezbollah—a symbolic group caught in the middle of a larger, looming narrative, namely, the United States versus Iran. Iran's use of Hezbollah in Israel pitted Iran not only against Israel itself but also against the United States, Israel's closest ally. And an Israeli air campaign, though difficult to carry out, was seen by Israelis and U.S. political leaders as viable for a number of reasons. First, by conducting air strikes on Hezbollah, Israel believed that the Lebanese government could potentially be strengthened. A stronger Lebanese government would mean that it could assert itself more strongly in the south—an area of the country controlled by Hezbollah. Next, by such measures, a stronger Lebanese government in the southern Hezbollah strongholds would mean that Hezbollah's weapons would likely be reduced and that missiles that could be used against the United States or Iran in the event of a strike would be eradicated. Hersh also suggested that while the United States remained very firm about resolving the conflict in a diplomatic manner, talks between Israel and the U.S. Air Force had been going on for some time, with both sides weighing options for a move in the direction of war. Hersh said,

The United States and Israel have shared intelligence and enjoyed close military cooperation for decades, but early this spring, according to a former senior intelligence official, high-level planners from the U.S. Air Force—under pressure from the White House to develop a war plan for a decisive strike against Iran's nuclear facilities—began consulting with their counterparts in the Israeli Air Force.[38]

The possibility of Israel striking Iran also meant that the United States could claim defeat of a major terrorist-labeled organization and not have to participate fully. Much like Lebanon used Hezbollah to carry out attacks, so too could the United States use Israel. Involved in wars in both Afghanistan and Iraq, the U.S. military would become stretched, and by providing the Israeli government with other tools to implement the striking of nuclear facilities, the United States would be once removed from the immediacy of the situation. Alternatively, if such a thing were to occur and the results proved to be catastrophic, the United States could claim that it had no direct involvement even though it would lend support to Israel. Israel undoubtedly has been concerned and even agitated with the way the United States has handled the situation in Iraq. And Iran has used the 2003 invasion to justify its claims of U.S. weakness—of a government and a military that are overextended on two fronts and a government that has taken its eyes off Israel. For this reason, Israel may have felt particularly vulnerable and, understanding that such U.S. overextension would reduce the likelihood of immediate action against Iran, felt compelled to purse these options of striking nuclear facilities in Iran with or without U.S. assistance. The rhetoric back and forth on both sides about the possibility of war between Iran and Israel, regardless of the move that the United States projected itself to make, heightened to a level where most people believed that the question was not a matter of *if* but rather *when*. In fact, in 2007, military and foreign policy analysts were nearly certain that such a thing would take place. Giora Eiland, head of the Israeli National Security Council, said in 2007,

> Imagine a situation of escalation in the North where Hezbollah is firing barrages of Katyusha rockets on the Galilee and causing human and property damage. Israel is trying to stop the force and is incapable of doing so through routine means—applying military and political pressure. Should we escalate our response? Deciding in an age where Iran has nuclear weapons we will have to weigh considerations other than those directing us today.[39]

David Samuels, foreign affairs reporter for *Slate* magazine, noted that a potential bombing of Iranian nuclear facilities by Israel would give Israel a restored sense of legitimacy as a military power, much of which was trampled on during the 2006 Hezbollah War:

> The fact that this approach may be the international-relations equivalent of keeping your boyfriend by shooting the other cute girl he likes in the head is an indicator of the difference between high-school romance and alliances between states—and hardly an argument for why it won't work. Shorn of its nuclear program and unable to retaliate against Israel through conventional military means, Iran would be shown to be a paper tiger—to the not-so-secret delight of America's Sunni Arab allies in the Gulf.[40]

It is useful to consider the political and military climate of the United States after Iraq and the steps that Israel and Iran may take toward one another. With over 47,000 U.S. troops in Iraq, the standoff between Israel and Iran seems to be the only viable option. And while Israel has certainly been vocal about the likelihood of an attack on nuclear weapons facilities, it has not discussed in depth the consequences of taking action *without* the United States. In fact, because of U.S. support for Israel—support that is seen by many in the Arab world as blind—whether Israel involves the United States makes little difference. The United States would be guilty by association if there were to be an attack. With troops on the ground in Iraq, the possibility of stepped-up violence and increased threats from Iran would make U.S. forces little more than hostages in a violent area of the world. The real thing to consider is the time frame of the U.S. military occupation of Iraq and the events that would precede a pullout of troops. As the United States becomes less involved in Iraq, the possibility of war with Iran actually increases. When it becomes clear that military actions in the region are in the process of winding down, it is highly likely that the discourse of pursuing disarmament of Iran will include a more active U.S. voice. Senator Lindsey Graham of South Carolina said, "I think an

Israeli attack on Iran is a nightmare for the world, because it will rally the Arab world around Iran and they're not aligned now. It's too much pressure to put on Israel."[41] He continued to suggest that if the time came for actions against Iran, the United States, not Israel, should not only seek to dismantle the nuclear program and its corresponding facilities but to "destroy their ability to make conventional war. They should have no planes that can fly and no ships that can float."[42]

But what interests and objectives did the United States have in the conflict specifically other than the obvious protection and support of Lebanon? First, the United States would benefit by enhancing Israeli security. Yet few achievements were made on that front. While Israel put a dent in Hezbollah, some 20,000 missiles remained, and some reports after the war showed that Hezbollah was rebuilding and appeared to be stronger than ever. Next, the United States had some interest in the advancement of Lebanese democracy. Hezbollah did not appear to have expanded its base within Lebanon, and this was seen as somewhat of a victory. Jeremy Pressman reported,

It may have miscalculated that non-Shiite Lebanese would rally around it in the face of an Israeli assault. It may have been thinking that all Arabs, regardless of religion, Islamic sect, or national interest, would repudiate Israel—a common enough dynamic in the history of the Arab-Israeli conflict. Yet, as Abdel Monem Said Ally noted in an earlier Middle East Brief, the Arab reaction during and after the war was not solely anti-Israel.[43]

The positive efforts to advance a Lebanese democracy were, however, also met with the fact that the war dismantled the infrastructure of Lebanon. The destruction that took place put major hardships on the Lebanese economy. Lebanon made many efforts to overcome the destruction of its own civil war and the damage the country faced as a result of Israeli air raids, and attacks on Hezbollah were reminiscent of that war.

It is also worth considering Israel's air strikes on Syria in September 2007. Israel launched air strikes against Syria, saying that the strikes were meant to target weapons believed to be headed to Hezbollah. Israel aimed for nuclear-related targets, two of which were said to be weapons locations that contained Iranian missiles provided to Hezbollah. Through this attack, Israel was able to move in the direction of asserting itself more vigorously in the region, and, rather than striking Iran directly, it was able to do so metaphorically by striking Iran's close ally. Reports surfaced that the Israeli government, on discovering the weapons collection, went to the U.S. Central Intelligence Agency and asked that the weapons be destroyed by the U.S. military. ABC News first broke the story, saying that after presenting pictures of the sites to the U.S. government and urging action, the Bush administration considered the information and began preparing ways to destroy the site.[44] Targets were drawn up, special raid forces were assembled, and plans for a U.S. strike seemed imminent. Yet the United States pulled out at the latest minute, saying that it was not interested in pursuing the raid. As a result, Israel pursued its plans to eradicate the weapons, and air strikes began. Initially, the United States indicated that the reason for the pullback was that it could not guarantee that the site that Israel claimed had weapons was indeed a legitimate weapons site, and speculative attacks were not in the interest of U.S. military officials.[45] While this may be the case, there are other implications and consequences that likely spurred the United States to avoid such actions, the main reason being the threat of Iran. So much focus had been on the heated discussion between Iran and Israel that seemed to build up toward some form of military action that Syria had not fully come into the equation. Syria's close ties to Iran posed a unique threat to the United States, as actions taken against Syria would be seen as actions taken against Iran. Further complicating the matter was the fact that Iran, in making its case to the U.S. government for a potential attack, suggested that North Korea was aiding Syria in its efforts to amass nuclear weapons. Though the Bush administration treated these concerns as suspect, there was some dialogue in political, military, and foreign affairs circles that indeed North Korea was involved in aiding Syria. In fact, in April 2008, a video surfaced that was taken inside a secret Syrian nuclear facility. This video convinced the Israeli government and some members of the Bush administration that North Korea was involved in helping Syria construct a reactor that was similar to one in North Korea's nuclear arsenal. Officials later said that the video of the site in Syria, called Al Kibar, showed North Koreans inside.[46]

On April 25, 2008, the Bush administration committed itself to believing that indeed North Korea was involved, with Press Secretary Dana Perino saying,

We are convinced, based on a variety of information, that North Korea assisted Syria's covert nuclear activities. We have good reason to believe that the reactor, which was damaged beyond repair on September 6 of last year, was not intended for peaceful purposes.[47]

As a result of this turn of events, it is obvious that the United States viewed any actions directed toward Iran as complicated and potentially disastrous. The logic was simple at the time: Iran had ties to Syria, Iran produced nuclear weapons, Syria had ties to North Korea, and North Korea produced nuclear weapons. Thus, tapping into this three-way network may have sparked a nuclear arms race that mimicked the Cold War or, worse, it may have very well led to attacks on multiple fronts.

With so much focus on Iran, Israel, and Syria as a result of a possible nuclear showdown, less attention was paid to Hezbollah. While Hezbollah's efforts during the 2006 war with Israel were seen as successful, it did suffer losses in military strength and supplies. However, it appeared that by early 2007, Hezbollah had rebuilt and strengthened its military. The United Nations reported that Hezbollah's military strength was at a level similar to the months leading up to the conflict in 2006.[48] Additionally, the report called on Iran and Syria to renew political dialogue. UN Secretary-General Ban Ki-Moon said,

I also expect the unequivocal cooperation of all relevant regional parties who have the ability to support such a process, most notably the Syrian Arab Republic and the Islamic Republic of Iran, which maintain close ties with the party, for the sake of Lebanon's and the wider region's security, stability and welfare.[49]

With this increased strength, it would seem likely that Hezbollah would resurface in a more active role. And, while the group is said to function as an extension of Iran and would be crippled without funding, the possibility of Hezbollah gaining enough momentum to stand on its own, if even momentarily, has caused the international community to take pause and examine the situation. In South America, particularly in the border regions between Brazil, Paraguay, and Argentina, a revived Hezbollah presence was felt. Hezbollah was also said to have established a presence in Colombia and became wrapped up in the drug-trafficking efforts of that country, though they denied such claims. The flurry of Hezbollah activity after the 2006 Hezbollah War marks a drastic shift in the future of military engagements. In fact, Hezbollah may very well be a paradigm—a new model of nonstate actors using nontraditional tactics of warfare and funded by larger, more prominent members of the international community. This shift will mean that Israel and the United States will have to readjust their strategies of contemporary warfare. Prior to the 2003 engagement, both the United States and Israel used military tactics that were largely traditional. The pre-2003 nature of these militaries was specialized—air forces and ground forces trained in particular areas of combat and unprepared for the variety of methods employed by Hezbollah. This shift in the way the 2006 war was fought provided difficulties for the United States in particular. With ongoing conflicts in Iraq and Afghanistan and troops on the ground in the mountainous regions of Pakistan, the U.S. military could not employ new strategies without risking failure in other areas. Though the future is not likely to be one of guerilla-like warfare, guerilla groups that are trained, supplied, and financed by legitimate states indicate that if the United States is serious about combating these groups, a reassessment is needed. There cannot, however, be a trade-off of traditional warfare tactics for guerilla-based tactics. Maximizing performance in one area may lead to failure in another, and the risks are too great for such a thing to take place. Iran and Syria, with the alleged aid of North Korea providing weapons, forced the hand of Israel to play a game of specialized warfare that Israel was not prepared for. The future of the relations between these countries may be based largely on this strategy, as it has proven to be successful. Nonstate actors used in combination with threats of state actors means that militaries will need to be capable of fighting on both fronts. Some may suggest that the streamlined and focused nature of Hezbollah's attacks—the emphasis of holding terrain and concentrating forces in particular regions—worked in favor of Israel. The implication here is that more damage could have been done and Hezbollah's legitimacy could have been heightened if more traditional tactics were implemented. However, it is likely that the differential between the United States and Israel on the one hand and Hezbollah on the other will work in Hezbollah's favor. There were many implications that came from the 2006 war, but the most overlooked yet perhaps the most important one is the way that the game of war has been shifted to favor the smaller group. It has been said of the War on Terror that the United States and its allies have attempted to fight an ideological war with traditional war tactics—something that is impossible. The same thing may also be said about the 2006 war and the future of relations between these actors. The war will prove to be influential to the future of foreign policies, not just of the United States but also of other major actors on the global stage. Nonstate actors will become more common, and the foreign policies of state actors will need to be examined and adjusted to meet these challenges.

CHAPTER 7

Iran and the United States

Obviously, Iran is one of the most serious problems in the Near East. Our two countries and the entire international community are seriously concerned over Iran's permanent non-fulfillment of commitments over its nuclear program, support to terrorist groups. Keeping attempts to affect Iran by the international community through pressure and appeals for dialogue are critically important for changing Iran's strategic course and preventing Iran's obtaining nuclear weapons.[1]

—U.S. Deputy Secretary of State James Steinberg and Israel's Deputy Foreign Minister Danny Ayalon

Today, the relationship between Iran and the United States is more complex than ever. It is one of historical intricacies and contemporary challenges, cautious opportunities, and consequential actions. The relationship hinges on Iran's desire for regime security, political legitimacy, and the ever-so-critical actor operating within the peripheral view of both the United States and Iran: Israel.

Over the course of the past 65 years, relations between Iran and the United States have been at the center of debates within both inner policy circles and the public sphere. And, over time, because of the political ambitions and alliances of various actors in the Middle East, the relationship between Iran and the United States has grown to become triangular.[2] More specifically, the close relations between Israel and the United States and the growing enmity between Israel and Iran have created an atmosphere of extreme political sensitivity. Perhaps a result of a deep-seated ideological rivalry, the conflict between Israel and Iran must not be examined exclusively from a one-dimensional Manichaean perspective. Nor can the relationship between Iran and the United States truly be considered a rivalry between superpowers. Rather, this relationship must be considered in the context of the triangular interactions between Israel,

Iran, and the United States, focusing on geopolitical concerns exclusively. This does mean that the ideologies or worldviews of these global actors can be regarded as unimportant or noninfluential in terms of their foreign relations. However, it is the regime security of Israel and Iran, as well as their desire to convey a real sense of political legitimacy to one another and to the United States, that is the focus of this chapter and the focus of foreign policy measures over the foreseeable future. To begin this discussion, it is necessary to examine and analyze some key events in the history of Iran and the United States in order to better understand the complexities of the contemporary dynamics of this relationship in its current triangular state.

Political relations between Iran and the United States in the 1800s were largely amicable. Even before this period of time, many Americans traveled to Iran, and in 1883 the first U.S. diplomatic envoy was appointed to Iran.[3] Persia's desire to break away from Britain and Russia is said to have been the driving factor behind this friendly dialogue with the United States, and it remained clear that the United States, an upcoming world superpower at that time, was seen as the potential third party that may have influence in the liberation of Iran from Anglo-Soviet domination. Additionally, there was political gain for the United States in the close relationship. Iran shared a border with Russia, the foe of the United States in the Cold War. As the 1940s approached and Shah Mohammed Reza Pahlavi came to power in Iran, the relationship between Iran and the United States heightened to perhaps its closest point in history. Iran became the solid rock and foundation of the United States in the Middle East and an ally against the Soviet Union.[4]

Despite these initial friendly relations, 1953 signaled a sharp change in the relationship between these countries. Mohammed Mosaddeq, the prime minister of Iran, was elected on April 25, 1951, and for two years was very outspoken on a number of controversial issues, including the nationalization of oil. In June 21, 1951, Mosaddeq said,

Our long years of negotiations with foreign countries have yielded no results this far. With the oil revenues we could meet our entire budget and combat poverty, disease, and backwardness among our people. Another important consideration is that by the elimination of the power of the British company, we would also eliminate corruption and intrigue, by means of which the internal affairs of our country have been influenced. Once this tutelage has ceased, Iran will have achieved its economic and political independence.[5]

Growing increasingly frustrated with Mosaddeq's policies and particularly perturbed over the nationalization of Iranian oil, Britain began to posture and make various attempts to regain some leverage in the region. Turning to the United States, British officials sought some alliance in their efforts, and while initial talks produced no such results, the election of President Dwight Eisenhower in 1953 brought about new policy views and attitudes toward Iran.

Eisenhower feared that internal tensions may lead to a governmental breakdown and rise of the Communist Party in Iran, and after months of debating, he agreed to work with Britain in an attempt to remove Mosaddeq from power. During the summer of 1953, Operation Ajax, as it was called, was under way and after two attempts was successful. Mosaddeq was overthrown by the U.S. government, and the shah of Iran assumed power, proclaiming the need to westernize policy and develop more modern models of governance. This irritated hard-line Islamists to say the least, and anti-U.S. tensions began to flare. These tensions set the stage for the 1979 Iranian Revolution and the hostage crisis: two events that, like the 1953 coup, forever changed U.S.-Iranian relations.[6]

The U.S.-backed shah of Iran, Pahlavi, became increasingly unpopular. His regime was considered to be oppressive, brutal, autocratic, corrupt, and overly bent on an alliance with the United States. Perhaps the most outspoken voice of this movement and the face of the Islamic Revolution was Ayatollah Ruhollah Khomeini. Khomeini first became a part of Iran's political scene in 1963 when he led a "White Revolution" but since that time had been in exile. As tensions increased, Khomeini began to inspire support for his objectives. Small episodes of violence began to erupt in Iran, most associated with protests, particularly those of the youth. Yet by the summer of 1978, the protests began to pick up steam and became a part of the regular political stage in Iran. It was clear that indeed a movement was taking place and that the shah needed to do something to control it. By the following month, tens of thousands of protestors stormed the streets of Isfahan and Tehran. In the city of Abadan, a cinema was set on fire, killing some 400 youth. The following day, families numbering upwards of 10,000 join the protests ,shouting, "Burn the shah." A new prime minister, Jafar Sherif-Emami, was installed, and many were hopeful that he would reverse some of the shah's policies. In fact, Sherif-Emami did just that though not at the levels that many of the protestors wanted. However, by late 1978, it appeared as if a viable opposition group had been established and organized, and a possible overthrow of the Shah seemed eminent. As December approached, an estimated 10 million people had joined opposition forces and demanded that the shah be removed from power. Just one month later, on January 16, 1979, the shah stepped down from power and left Iran.[7]

Following these events in 1979, the United States, under the direction of President Jimmy Carter, declined to give the shah any additional support and was insistent that the shah not return to his position of power. However, Carter eventually allowed the shah entry into the United States to seek medical treatment. This led to an increase in anti-U.S. sentiment, and in early November1979, the Muslim Student Followers of the Imam's Line, stormed the U.S. embassy in Tehran and held 52 U.S. diplomats hostage. This event became known as the Iranian hostage crisis. After a long series of negotiations and release attempts, on January 20, 1981, 444 days after the takeover, the U.S. hostages were released into U.S. custody.

The hostage crisis changed the political realm of both the United States and Iran. In fact, most Americans would agree that Jimmy Carter's mishandling of the hostage crisis was the sole event that led to his defeat in 1980 by Ronald Reagan. However, fewer Americans are aware of the impact that the hostage crisis has had beyond electoral politics, both domestically and internationally. The takeover of the U.S. embassy in Iran provided hard-line Islamists the ability to hijack Iran's revolution as well as undermine the temporary government in Iran. Moreover, the crisis allowed the Islamists to hinder any attempts at renewed relations with the United States. This was perhaps the most important goal of the Islamists during that time. While the hard-liners certainly demanded that the shah be reinstated, most analysts agree that their real goal was to thwart any attempts made by the United States or Iran to reexamine the situation and engage in mutual, friendly negotiations that sought to restore some sense of peace to the chaos that had wreaked havoc in the region.[8] Working in their favor was Ayatollah Khomeini. Any attempts made to improve relations between the United States and Iran would be considered intolerable. Khomeini, who called the United States "the Great Satan," felt that such a relationship would be detrimental to the values emphasized by the 1979 revolution—values that were seen as anti-Western and, more specifically, anti-American.[9] As the crisis escalated, President Carter made a decision to abstain from using force. This move, admonished by many of those critical of the Carter administration, forced the conflict to move to the next step as the United States had weakened its bargaining power and, in fact, strengthened the hand of the hard-line Islamist militants. Next, Carter's administration became involved in a series of negotiations with Iran. During these negotiations, the United States made concessions. One such concession was the agreement to establish a UN commission to investigate crimes of the shah and possible U.S. involvement. In each case of negotiation, the Iranians reneged on their end of the promise.

What did these diplomatic events entail? First, to the Iranians, it became quite clear that terrorism works and that the United States at the time was playing the game in a passive manner, not ready to make forceful commitments and deploy its vast military strength in any fashion. This enlightenment of the value of terrorism soon became broadened as the use of terrorism became a major part of Iran's foreign policy. The Iranian Revolutionary Guards were deployed to various Muslim countries and also trained the now-famous and ever-prominent Hezbollah. The abilities of Hezbollah, outlined in the preceding chapter, are largely a result of this initial boost of training.

President Carter's decision to abstain entirely from the use of force is worth critical examination, particularly with respect to the current political climates in Iran and the United States. By refraining from the use of force and, further, by making that decision known, it may be said that the position of the United States was weakened. Speaking on November 16, 2009, Carter said, "My main advisers insisted that I should attack Iran. I could have destroyed Iran with my weaponry. But I felt in the process it was likely the hostages' lives would be lost, and I didn't want to kill 20,000 Iranians. So I didn't attack."[10] Indeed, Carter's weaponry could have landed devastating blows to Iranian infrastructure, but to him the possibility of mass casualties outweighed the likelihood of capturing or killing those responsible for the crisis. Compared with the current political situation, it is helpful to see the differences in the rhetoric of President Carter and President Barack Obama in dealing with Iran. "If countries like Iran are willing to unclench their fist, they will find an extended hand from us," Obama said in an interview broadcast January 27, 2009, on Al Arabiya television.[11] The following day, Iranian President Mahmoud Ahmadinejad urged the United States first to apologize for criminal actions taken toward Iran over the past 60 years. Days later, on February 3, Iran announced that it launched its first satellite into orbit.

Campaigning for president on the need for increased dialogue with Iran and a regrouping of failed strategies of isolationism, Senator Obama was mum on the topic of a U.S. strike on Iran. But as president, he has become more outspoken, saying that he has not taken the option off the table. In essence, the threat of a U.S.-led military strike against Iran's nuclear plants is still very much on the table. Yet also on the table are a vast array of soft-power choices. The Bipartisan Policy Center in Washington, some of whose members advise the president, released this statement in September 2009:

If biting sanctions do not persuade the Islamic Republic to demonstrate sincerity in negotiations and give up its enrichment activities, the White House will have to begin serious consideration of the option of a U.S.-led military strike against Iranian nuclear facilities.[12]

Even so, the likelihood of such a course of action is doubtful for a number of reasons. First, beyond basic diplomatic showmanship, President Obama's willingness to extend a hand will not deter Iran from acquiring and developing nuclear weapons. The ongoing enmity between Israel and Iran has prompted both countries to flex their nuclear muscles regardless of international scrutiny or mediation. For Iran, there is little to gain by becoming a peaceful member of the international community—their credibility of their regime would in many ways be reduced. Iran needs Israel and the United States to remain in a position of vigilance, strength, and legitimacy. Still, whatever strength Iran's regime hopes to convey to its people is matched and abrogated with stark realities: its economy is faltering by the day, particularly with petroleum prices down 70 percent from a high in 2008 and a recession ensuring that prices will not rise for some time. Internally, Iran is split between an ultraconservative and aging leadership hoping to hold on to power and a youngish population dreaming of a better life than the one they currently have.

While it is certainly clear that Obama would prefer a more peaceful solution to Iran's nuclear problem, he has faced pressure from not only think-tank groups that advise him regularly but also from many world allies. Their message: act now. Shortly after appearing the British Prime Minister Gordon Brown and French President Nicholas Sarkozy at the G8 Summit in Philadelphia warning Iran that sanctions will be taken if Iran refuses to open up a newly discovered uranium enrichment facility, Sarkozy appeared disturbed with the approach taken by the United States. He said,

I support America's "extended hand." But what have these proposals for dialogue produced for the international community? Nothing but more enriched uranium and more centrifuges. And last but not least, it has resulted in a statement by Iranian leaders calling for wiping off the map a Member of the United Nations. What are we to do? What conclusions are we to draw? At a certain moment hard facts will force us to make decisions.[13]

At the very least, there is a multitude of discussion within the international community and from within the U.S. government itself that indicates that all options are on the table. In fact, President Obama himself has said just that: "All options are on the table."[14] That being the case, Iran understands very well that the current situation may not be exactly identical to that of 1979. When Carter declared that the United States would categorically refuse from striking Iran, Khomeini and other hard-line Islamists were given the nod to take the "second revolution" to the next level. What could they possibly have feared at the same level that they may have feared U.S.-led air strikes? And while the United States is the principal actor involved in this two-state standoff, comments like those of Sarkozy echo within the governmental circles of Iran. The United States is not alone in its opposition to Iranian nuclear advancements, nor is it alone in leaving the possibility of a strike on the table. This approach—a diplomatically and peacefully charged mission with every option, including military strikes, on the table—fosters a situation in which both parties understand that the actions of the other may precipitate military intervention. Yet the costs and uncertainties of a military strike are enormous. Air strikes are unlikely to succeed in destroying Iran's nuclear facilities, as experts have estimated the number of nuclear sites to be far more than the 18 the regime claims, with many buried deep underground. Furthermore, if military action in the form of a preemptive strike is unsuccessful, it could incite Iran to accelerate efforts to build and/or purchase nuclear bombs. In addition, there is always collateral damage in the loss of innocent civilians when any type of military action is undertaken. The civilian losses could be in the thousands, and this could incite the people of Iran and terrorist organizations to support Iran and undermine the ultimate goal of the United States. A unilateral strike against Iran would only further damage U.S. standing in the world at a time when U.S. prestige internationally is at an all-time low.

As we moved forward in this era, defined by a new threat of Iran, much discussion has been made of dialoguing with Iranian leaders. Particularly during the U.S. presidential election of 2008, stark contrasts were drawn between those leaders who believed that engaged discussions were "appeasement" and others who felt that thoughtful dialogue may lead to more peaceful relations. While it is not the purpose of this discussion to outline the varying viewpoints on the issue, it is worth noting that little good can come from policies of isolation. Many foreign policy analysts have noted that a driving force behind Iran's foreign policy is a simple goal of attaining respect worthy of its size, population, resources, and history. That is, Iran seeks political legitimacy. Ambassador John W. Limbert, who was a hostage during the 1979 hostage crisis, suggests that as a result of this approach, Iran may come to the table with a certain combination of grandeur and grievance.[15] Thus, whoever negotiates with Iran should be prepared to face either side of the coin or, perhaps more difficult, both sides simultaneously. The best way to approach this complex situation is to simply give Iran credit for its intelligence. To some, this seems incredulous and even blasphemous, as the desire to isolate, dehumanize, and vilify "the other" has become so prominent in U.S. politics. John Limbert writes in "How to Negotiate with Iran,"

Underestimating them will only intensify the existing cycle of mistrust. There are numerous cases in recent history. In October 1979, for example, the White House thought it could placate Iranian public opinion by announcing that the United States was admitting the deposed Shah for medical treatment. Given the history of Iranian-American relations, few Iranians would have believed it. The rationale, rather than reassuring its Iranian audience, inflamed it by insulting its intelligence.[16]

Thus, the sure way to derail any progress is to make Iran feel as though it is inferior to the strength, power, might, and, most important, intelligence of the United States. As Larry Korb, a senior fellow at the Center for

American Progress, notes, part of what shaped Iran's current attitude toward the United States was such antagonism and isolation from the United States. He writes,

The Bush administration's publicly placing Iran on the Axis of Evil in January 2002, with the avowed goal of bringing about regime change. This was done in spite of the fact that Iran was one of the few Muslim countries to condemn the attacks of 9-11, had played a constructive role in Afghanistan aiding our military efforts, and had helped persuade the Northern Alliance to support the Karzai government at the Bonn Conference.[17]

As long as expectations are focused on the interests of both parties involved and not on the "evil other" that may be viewed as secretive, deceptive, and plotting to destroy, results may be possible. This, however, is not a guarantee. Engagements of this sort serve a number of positive purposes, though those who reject them outright may claim otherwise. First and foremost, meaningful and comprehensive dialogue between the United States and Iran gives both countries a better idea about what the other is thinking and doing. How could policies of isolation lead to vital information gains? Additionally, as James Dobbins notes in his 2009 *Washington Post* article "To Talk with Iran, Stop Not Talking," engaging in cooperative discussions may not solve the central problems at hand (i.e., nuclear proliferation), but it does present a unique outlet and opportunity for the possibility of cooperative engagement on other secondary issues that could lead to more amiable dialogue. Even while the central problems may remain unresolved, tension is lessened over time as both parties begin to discuss other aspects of their particular interests.[18]

The United States, unlike Iran and even Israel, has no need to reinforce its sense of political legitimacy. And, certainly, the United States has no need to display a sense of regime security. Nonetheless, when discussing topics of isolationism, increased dialogue, and cooperative engagement, it is helpful to understand how these two issues—regime security and political legitimacy—factor into the relationship between Iran and Israel and ultimately, as a result, between Iran and the United States.

When thinking about the historical trends in the relationship between Iran and the United States, it is clear that both sides have been reactive. And when we include Israel in the mix of this relationship, the sense of a reactive response is heightened. Ahmadinejad's questioning of the Holocaust and Israel's demonization of Iran as a modern-day Nazi Germany are similar to the rhetorical back-and-forth of the United States and Iran—the "Great Satan" and the "Axis of Evil."

Other cases throughout history provide paradigmatic examples of dialogues and diplomacy with countries that at the time (and perhaps still today) appeared as a threat. The United States never threatened the use of force to destroy Chinese or Soviet nuclear plants. Nor did it attack Soviet or Chinese ships supplying Vietnam with weapons. Additionally, China sent thousands of troops to aid Vietnam without repercussions from the United States in terms of military strikes. The point here is that, in these cases, Washington worked to find ways to deal with the possibilities of threats and of real threats themselves. And in some of these cases, punishment through means other than military action was needed. That should not indicate that diplomacy or soft power is "weaker" than hard strikes against a country like Iran. We can see from the above examples that the United States emerged from each case in a stable, viable, and eventually advantageous position. Many believed that the showdown with the Soviet Union during the Cold War would erode the strength of the United States to a place where it would no longer reign supreme in the array of countries at the top of the world's economic, military, and political chain. Yet today, the United States remains in a very strong position. Dobbins writes,

Taking this threat [of a military attack] off the table, and putting it in a readily available drawer, would improve the prospects for negotiation while avoiding the most likely result of the current approach, which is that in the end America either has its bluff called or finds itself launching a war it cannot win.[19]

In the case of President Carter, the military option was not taken off of the table and placed in a nearby drawer, ready to use at his disposal, but rather was disregarded and thrown out entirely. This move, as has been mentioned, has a number of important consequences, yet within the contemporary landscape of political tensions in the greater Middle East, Carter's option is worth examining from the perspective of Israeli-Iranian relations. Much has been discussed about the relationship between Israel and Iran in the preceding chapter, yet that relationship is worth examining from the perspective of lessons learned from the 1979 revolution and hostage crisis.

Tensions between Israel and Iran have grown over the past few years, and the world has seen a heightened discussion of nuclear warfare erupting between the two. Israel, despite its increased rhetoric and saber rattling, is unlikely to strike Iran. Many experts agree that such action would be the worst possible course for Israel. Take the 2006 Hezbollah War, for example. Iran successfully used a guerilla group to nearly conquer the Israeli Defense Force. Thus, for the time being, Israel is in a quagmire in which it must sit and watch Iran acquire nuclear weapons, discuss the eradication of the Israeli state, and produce a discourse of fearmongering throughout the region. The Israeli leadership would most likely prefer action to be taken by the United States to prevent Iran from enriching uranium that would lead to a nuclear bomb. As sanctions on Iran seem to have little effect, Israeli's believe that a U.S. military attack would have a much wider impact and would land a more devastating blow than anything that Israel's military could deliver. Here we may now turn back to the years of President Carter and the 1979 hostage crisis and approach the issue from a perspective of historical analysis and present-day application. Making it clear that the United States will not counter Iranian nuclear proliferation with military strikes, Iran's position is strengthened, as has been mentioned. However, a newfound strength that comes as a result of such guarantees is strength to be directed not only toward the United States but also toward the closest ally of the United States in the Middle East and longtime foe of Iran: Israel. Most recently, as of November 4, 2009, 30 years to the day after the 1979 hostage crisis, supporters of President Ahmadinejad swarmed into the streets of Iran to express continued resentment and outrage not only at the United States but also at Israel. Nick Amies of *Dutch World News* reported in an article titled "Consequences of the 1979 Hostage Crisis Still Influencing US-Iranian Relations,"

Thousands of supporters of Iranian President Mahmoud Ahmadinejad marked the 30th anniversary of the takeover of the US compound by filling the streets around the closed embassy in a state-organized anti-US rally chanting slogans such as "Death to America" and "Death to Israel."[20]

Thus, it remains quite clear that U.S. foreign policy initiatives and the relationship between the United States and Iran are still based largely on a third actor: Israel. Just as President Carter's decision to abstain from military strikes against Iran caused Iran to posture in more aggressive ways, we may infer that the same situation would be applicable to the current relationship. With threats to "wipe Israel off of the map"[21] coming from Ahmadinejad, removing the possibility of U.S. military action against Iran may in fact provide a clear path for Iran's expressed attacks on Israel. Iranian leaders would be assured that Iran would be safe from U.S. strikes, and, with Israel's military too small to produce an attack of its own against Iran, the floodgates would be left open for more nuclear development and increased aggression between Iran and Israel—yet it is safe to say that outward projections of aggression would largely be one sided.

The United States, under the new leadership of President Obama, seems to desire to erase those historical feelings of hostility and start afresh. In early November 2009, President Obama said,

I have made it clear that the United States of America wants to move beyond this past, and seeks a relationship with the Islamic Republic of Iran based upon mutual interests and mutual respect. We do not interfere in Iran's internal affairs. We have condemned terrorist attacks against Iran. We have recognized Iran's international right to peaceful nuclear power. We have demonstrated our willingness to take confidence-building steps along with others in the international community.[22]

Despite the desire to move forward on the part of the United States, one thing remains clear: the feeling is not mutual, and the 1979 hostage crisis and revolution are still very present in the minds of Iranians opposed to U.S. foreign policy today. Anthony Dworkin, a senior foreign policy fellow and expert on U.S. foreign policy at the European Council on Foreign Relations, suggests that Ahmadinejad continues to project hostile rhetoric harking back to the period of the hostage crisis. Dworkin goes on to say that, from the outside, the view is that the Iranian people feel a vested interest in stoking up feelings of anti-Americanism.[23] Supporters of the crisis and the current administration in Iran view the capture of the U.S. embassy in Tehran as an unprecedented success against the United States. The capture remains a source of pride among what many suggest is a growing U.S. hegemony. Interestingly, Ahmadinejad is said to have opposed the capture and occupation of the U.S. embassy during the 1979 hostage crisis until the Ayatollah Khomeini supported it. This anecdotal piece of history is aligned with the fact that Ahmadinejad was schooled in the same ideologies as Khomeini. Many believe that the United States is facing a second major conflict not only with Iran but also with a theological regime that projects the same displays of martyrdom, anti-Americanism, hostility, and isolationism. That is, Ahmadinejad may be viewed in the same light as Khomeini was during 1979, and thus the policy approaches taken during that time period should be examined carefully to avoid making similar mistakes today.

Aside from the increasing threat of Iran, it may be argued that the war in Iraq poses the next largest threat to instability and looming tensions in the Middle East. The war, launched in 2003 by the Bush administration, still rages some six years later, and while the Obama administration has expressed the desire to end the conflict, it does not appear that will happen in the foreseeable future. When President George W. Bush took office in 2001, Mohammad Khatami was the president of Iran. A liberal reformer with pro-Western ideals and policy postulations, Khatami stood in stark contrast to Ahmadinejad, who was elected in 2005. Khatami advocated greater freedoms of expression and speech, tolerance, and more constructive dialogues and relations with Europe, Asia, and the United States. The contrast between Khatami and Ahmadinejad could not be clearer. Thus, President Bush had a unique perspective during the eight years of his tenure, observing and interacting with a both a liberal reformer and a hard-line authoritarian leader from the Khomeini school. The political dynamics of the United States and, arguably, the entire world changed on September 11, 2001. President Bush began to lose hope in Khatami's advocacy of reforms on learning of human rights abuses and the arrests of journalists and intellectuals in Iran. Speaking before a joint session of Congress in 2002, Bush labeled Iran as part of the "axis of evil." Bush said,

Iran aggressively pursues these weapons and exports terror, while an unelected few repress the Iranian people's hope for freedom. States like these, and their terrorist allies, constitute an axis of evil, arming to threaten the peace of the world. By seeking weapons of mass destruction, these regimes pose a grave and growing danger.[24]

The Bush administration sought to make clear a link between Iran, the new threat of terrorism that had just wreaked havoc in New York, and as various subtle threats at action against Iran's nuclear ambitions surfaced, the Bush administration began to make its case for the war in Iraq. At the time, it was believed that the Israelis influenced Bush and that Iran should have not been included in the axis of evil.[25]

Many believed that the back-and-forth between the United States and Iran would eventually manifest itself into some form of physical violence or warfare, but that was not the case. Rather, in a Cold War–like fashion, the rhetoric between Iran and the United States over the course of Bush's eight years was little more than political maneuvering and posturing, with Bush, Khatami, and Ahmadinejad hanging in balance between the sweeping threats. As the war in Afghanistan came into clearer view, Iraq and the threat of weapons of mass destruction loomed in the distance. Many believed that the U.S. military was not capable of fighting on a third front—Iran—and that, if given a choice of action among the presented threats, Iraq was the clearer option. Thus, the United States invaded Iraq in March 2003.

Rather than detail the particularities of the war in Iraq, which have been elaborated on extensively by various authors and foreign policy analysts, it is important to learn how the war in Iraq affected the relationship between Iran and the United States. As the Brookings Institution reports, five years after the invasion of Iraq, senior military and government officials from the United States visited Baghdad to mark the occasion and, much to their surprise, were not greeted with "sweets and flowers" but rather blanketed under a large security detail and transported in secret transportation, and Vice President Dick Cheney was even forced to sleep on an armed plane with a reinforced trailer designed for just that. In contrast, President Ahmadinejad, visiting Baghdad for the same occasion two weeks earlier, was greeted by Iraqi leaders and counterparts to an elaborate pomp and circumstance characterized by an official state visit.[26] The report notes,

Instead of generating a liberal, secular democracy whose reverberations would drive out Iran's clerical oligarchs, the disastrous Bush policies fostered a sectarian

Iraq that has helped empower Iranian hardliners. Rather than serving as an anchor for a new era of stability and American preeminence in the Persian Gulf, the new Iraq represents a strategic black hole, bleeding Washington of military resources and political influence while extending Iran's primacy among its neighbors.[27]

This observation speaks to the underlying complexities not taken into account by the Bush administration's attempts to deal with Iraq. First, despite Iran's influence in Iraq, the large majority of Iraqis (include Shi'ites) are not pro-Iran. As Robert Dreyfuss points out in "Is Iran Winning the Iraq War?," underneath the ruling alliance in Baghdad there exists a strong undercurrent of Arab nationalism that opposes not only the U.S. occupation of Iraq but also Iran's support for religious parties in Iraq. These oppositions have manifested themselves through an outpouring of support for the country's soccer team to a fierce anger caused by efforts to privatize the Iraqi oil industry. Next, and in a somewhat of a paradox to this dynamic, the government implemented by the United States after Saddam Hussein was ousted is closer to Iran than it is the United States.[28] Dreyfuss notes,

As a result, the ayatollahs in Tehran have adroitly checkmated (a word derived from the Persian *shah mat*, "the king is dead") US efforts to install a compliant, pro-American regime in Baghdad as the anchor of Washington's interests in the oil-rich Persian Gulf. Now a proxy conflict between the United States and Iran is playing out on Iraq's complex chessboard.[29]

Dreyfuss suggests that two options remain. First, if U.S.-Iran ties improve under a new administration (as they have been projected to by President Obama), Tehran may aim to broker a deal stabilizing Iraq. This will more than likely take place in a deal that strengthens the Shia-led government and provides some kickback for Iran. Second, if the relationship between the United States and Iran continues to plummet, Iran may have the ability to end any relative periods of calm, and thus a civil war has greater chance of erupting. Compounding this complexity are Iran's extensive investments in Iraq. The former Iranian foreign minister, Manouchehr Mottaki, speaking at an international conference attended by then Secretary of State Condoleezza Rice, said that companies from the Islamic Republic of Iran were outpacing most others in their commitments to improving Iraq's economic development. Various reports surfaced shortly before Mottaki's statement suggesting that Iran had poured nearly $80 million into the Kurdistan area alone.[30]

While the large majority of Iraqi's are not pro-Iran, it would seem quite natural that a case of kin-country syndrome would emerge from this complexity. Kin-country syndrome, a term introduced by controversial political scientist Samuel Huntington in *The Clash of Civilizations and the Remaking of the World Order*, suggests that countries that share commonalities and that may be at odds with one another will come to one another's aid over an outside force before they will let an internal struggle destroy them.[31] Thus, it is plausible that Iraq would join forces with Iran were Iran faced with the threat of an outside government or military, namely, the United States. While such an option is plausible, one should ask, is it possible? Dreyfuss asks,

Can the United States make a deal with Iran to stabilize Iraq, with both Washington and Tehran ignoring their differences to support Maliki's government? Possibly? One scenario would have Washington, backed by Saudi Arabia, using its influence among the Sunnis, particularly in the burgeoning Awakening movement, to bring them to the table, while Iran would use its clout among the Shiites to convince Maliki and Hakim to make the concessions necessary to bridge the sectarian divide. That idea lay at the heart of the Iraq Study Group plan, the 2006 advisory panel chaired by James Baker and Lee Hamilton that Bush dismissed when he adopted the surge. The Baker-Hamilton plan called for negotiations with Iran (and Syria) to help stabilize Iraq.[32]

Additionally, as a result of Iran's boisterous economic investment in the region, it is unlikely that Tehran would cut its ties with Iraq. There is simply too much at stake financially for a move like this to take place. Next, with a newly installed government whose ties to the United States may not be as strong as Bush and his advisers initially perceived, Iran appears to be in a stronger position. As President Bush left office in 2008 and Barack Obama assumed the presidency, his administration was faced with the two options outlined above. In any case, Iran may appear to be largely in control of its game: if the United States is willing to renew relations with Iran and forge new political ground in a manner that is mutually beneficial, the story of Iraq may go down in the history books as a success. If the United States continues to alienate Iran and assumes a hard-line approach to foreign policy talks, it is perfectly possible that Iran will use its influence in Iraq to create a situation of perpetual warfare and endless chaos. For President Obama, who time and again has promised to create a new politics based on respect and meaningful dialogues with rogue world leaders and who has promised to end the war in Iraq in a responsible manner, the latter option may mean that he goes down in history as a one-term president. However, if Obama approaches Iran from the angle of the first option, he may very well win himself a second term. Recent events—launching test missiles, the discovery of a secret uranium enrichment facility, and the most recent announcement from Ahmadinejad saying that Iran will build ten new enrichment sites—further complicate the options for Obama and give Iran more leverage for political posturing. In effect, Iran seems to be indicating that it is setting itself up for a win-win situation, whether that is a reality or not.

In September 2009, the Bipartisan Policy Center released a report titled "Meeting the Challenge: Time Is Running Out." Authored by Senator Daniel Coats, Senator Charles Robb, and General Chuck Wald, the group suggested that in addition to economic sanctions (which, according to them, do not seem to be getting the job done), the United States should consider the possibility of military action and make it known to Iran that such things are being considered.[33] Speaking in an interview to the *New York Times* on November 30, 2009, Charles Robb said, "We want to support what would seem to be a more hawkish approach as a viable alternative to an approach that hasn't worked."[34] According to the panel, preventing Iran from obtaining nuclear capabilities through diplomatic engagement is still a priority, and while military force has been advocated, such policy choices, according to the panel, should come only as a last resort.[35] Thus, diplomacy with Iran should certainly be viewed as the recommended course of action for the time being, but a permanent system must be devised soon, and Iran provides an excellent opportunity for a new system to be introduced. However unfortunate, the fact is that past nonproliferation policy has been successful, but nearly half the world's nuclear powers now sit outside the international system, and while diplomacy may work for some of these situations, it creates no real solutions. Furthermore, diplomacy does not address the fact that those that have ratified the various nonproliferation protocols are proving reluctant to enforce them.

In the meantime, the United States cannot simply ignore the reality of a military strike. Waiting for the internal struggles in Iran to stabilize will only allow those set on obtaining and enriching more uranium to have more time to do so. Additionally, the United States should not become too complacent with small signs of progress, nor should it point to those signs as indications that Iran is committed to seriously disengaging from its nuclear ambitions. The study notes,

History suggests that the Islamic Republic will make minor diplomatic gestures in order to forestall the possibility of tougher measures and disrupt any international resolve. Any seemingly promising signals should not affect the Administration's strategy until substantive progress is made at the negotiating table.[36]

Calls for making the military option clearer come as a result of a number of factors, but perhaps the most pressing one is that, by doing do, the United States may be able to convince Israel that the threat of Iran has decreased, and thus Israel may be less likely to take military action into its own hands. Playing the diplomacy card while maintaining a serious and pressing reality of military action would also give the United States a backup plan in the event that Israel did decide to attack Iran. For these reasons, as the report indicates, it is vital to monitor Israeli perceptions of Iran and take heed of various rhetoric deployed toward the Iranian government. This back-and-forth between Israel and Iran may become increased as a result of an increased nuclear buildup in Iran. The Bipartisan Policy Center report indicates such increases, noting,

We believe that the Islamic Republic will be able to produce enough fissile material for a nuclear weapon by 2010, leaving little time for the United States to prevent both a nuclear weapons-capable Islamic Republic and an Israeli strike on Iranian nuclear facilities.[37]

If we consider the suggestions made by this report along with the current political landscape that has resulted between the United States and Iran as a result of the election of President Obama and the reelection of President Ahmadinejad, we can see largely a continuation of disinterest on the part of Iran. While the United States has certainly changed its policy positions and has taken Iran and moved it from the periphery of foreign policy objectives to the center, Iran still appears to be largely opposed to any meaningful engagements that would lead to the dissolution of nuclear sites. Prior to Obama's speech in Cairo in June 2009, Supreme Leader Khamenei said, "Even if [Obama] delivers hundreds of speeches and talks very sweetly, there will not be a change in how the Islamic countries perceive the United States."[38] This rhetoric was matched by a number of significant displays of nuclear ambition, including a digitally altered photo of missile launches depicting four missiles being fired when, in fact, only three were tested. The discovery of a hidden nuclear facility in the fall of 2009, combined with Iran's announcement of building and developing ten more, seemed to only compound the heightened sense of distrust among Americans, Europeans, and their government.[39]

After the discovery of Iran's hidden nuclear facility in the fall of 2009 and after the U.S. joint statement with France and Great Britain condemning the developments and insisting on cooperating with the International Atomic Energy Agency, Iran appeared poised to cooperate. Following a series of actions aimed at compelling Iran to cooperate, Ahmadinejad said,

The Iranian nation has from the beginning been after ... negotiations based on justice and complete respect for rights and regulations. One-sided negotiations, conditional negotiations, negotiations in an atmosphere of threat are not something that any free person would accept.[40]

It should be considered that such statements and maneuvers have been issued before. President Obama and his administration may not serve the interests of the United States well if they understand these statements from Iran as a veritable interest in changing its approach to its relationship with the United States. In fact, it may be said that Iran is buying time and that by projecting small signs of cooperating every now and then, it is buying time to use to continue building its nuclear arsenal. It is perhaps not a coincidence that after these statements, which express some sense of piety, the world learns of some increased effort on the part of Iran to enrich uranium, construct new nuclear facilities, or direct bullylike rhetoric at Israel. And each time such projections come, the United States ratchets up its rhetoric. In this manner, the relationship between the United States and Iran has been reduced to a series of back-and-forth, with each side increasing its language and its threats each time—the United States does so through discussions of sanctions, various condemnations, and subtle threats of a "possible" military strike (though Obama has not elaborated on any concrete plans for military intervention), and Iran responds to this with increased language of cooperation followed by more nuclear development.

One recent example of this exchange between the United States and Iran—and one that has been mentioned in passing as an example of Iranian posturing—is the announcement in late November 2010 that President Ahmadinejad had approved the development of ten additional nuclear enrichment facilities and the expansion of Iran's current nuclear power capability to half a million centrifuges.[41] On four occasions since Obama assumed the presidency, he has set deadlines for Iran to comply with international demands, and four times these have been largely ignored (the exception being Iran's initial agreement to open its new hidden nuclear facility to inspectors from the International Atomic Energy Agency). Various members of the Obama administration offered their criticism of the new plan for ten facilities, calling it "irresponsible" and saying that "time is running out" and that Iran should not continue to "isolate itself."

While many U.S. policymakers and government officials seek solutions to Iran's nuclear capabilities, it is necessary to consider how negotiations may be received within the Israeli government. It may be said that Israel, in considering its best interests, does not want the relationship between Iran and the United States to improve. How could this be so? To begin with, Israel's legitimacy as a democratic state and a close ally of the United States in the Middle East would be seen as diminished if Iran and the United States seek what Obama has called a "new beginning."[42] Israel considers Iran a direct threat to its security and, as a result, can legitimize various forms of political posturing, including threats of attacks on Iran and increased saber rattling. Without the threat of Iran, Israel's legitimacy as a strong, independent state and a nation capable of acting unilaterally to protect its interests is weakened. The unwavering

support of the United States adds to this. As long as the United States
takes a hard-line stance toward Iran, Israel's position toward Iran appears
more valid. In June 2010, Israeli forces attacked an international aid ship
coming from Turkey toward Gaza with relief materials. As the ship
approached the Gaza blockade, Israelis came aboard the ship, killing
some of the passengers and creating an international incident.[43] Immediately following the event, an outpouring of objection and scorn came from
the global community, all of which was directed toward Israel. Though
under pressure to condemn the act, the U.S. response was guarded, only
warning Israel not to block a second oncoming ship. Shortly after this incident, the UN Security Council approved a new round of sanctions
directed at Iran, with the full support of the Obama administration. While
many agree that the new sanctions would do little to overcome widespread doubts that Iran would halt its nuclear program, the symbolism
of the sanctions and the timing of the mild response by the United States
to the Israeli attack on the ship underscored how sensitive relations are
between these two countries. Following this event, almost immediately,
the public debate shifted to Iran. For Israel, the new round of sanctions
may have been an unexpected yet, nonetheless, welcome gift. The UN resolution allowed Israel the opportunity to comment of Iran's nuclear program, deflecting criticism and attention from their recent troubles. And,
in fact, that is exactly what happened. On June 9, 2010, the Israeli Ministry
of Foreign Affairs released a statement concerning the new sanctions,
expressing its content with the initiative to further prevent Iran from
developing nuclear weapons but also its concern and displeasure that
the sanctions did not do more to accomplish that. A portion of the statement read,

It is of high importance to implement the resolution fully and immediately. At the
same time, it should be recognized that this resolution is not sufficient in and of
itself and should be accompanied by significant steps in additional international
frameworks as well as on a national level. Only sanctions that focus on a variety
of sectors in Iran are likely to influence Iran's calculations. Broad, determined
international action is needed in order to make clear to the Iranian regime the
price tag for continuing to violate international demands. The combination of
Iran's extremist ideology together with nuclear weapons will have catastrophic
consequences.[44]

It is clear from this statement that the Israeli government is attempting to
place some pressure on the international community to seek further action
against Iran. In doing this, Israel also seeks to restore its sense of security
and align itself on the side of a global community that is pitted against
Iran. The Israeli foreign minister was not the only who believed that the
newest sanctions may be the end of the line. In fact, in October 2010,

Farideh Fari, a prominent Iranian professor from Tehran, said that the relationship between the United States, Israel, and Iran has approached an "end game."[45] "The combined US policy of sanctions and offers of talks without preconditions is having an impact, just not the intended one," she commented.[46] "The escalation has been so drastic on both sides it has made it almost impossible for both sides domestically to make compromises," she said, contending that when it comes to Iran's nuclear operations, "it actually entrenches the worst aspects of Iranian policy. I do not believe that it will change."[47] Others agreed and even took Fari's comments one step further, saying that before the latest round of economic sanctions, Iranians were largely opposed to Ahmadinejad and even outspoken about his policies. However, they noted, the public "widely supports" his tactics now, turning their anger and frustration toward the United States. Former State Department official Steven Simon weighed in on the issue, saying that both the United States and Israel have the same goal of preventing Iran from developing a nuclear bomb. He added, though, that they differ on what "a nuclear-capable Iran" means. While the United States does not want Iran to be able to quickly assemble a bomb if it chooses to, Israel's "end game" was much earlier—in the enrichment process. "The difference between those red lines leaves quite a lot of room for error," he warned.[48] Simon also offered a reminder, noting that Israel had once taken unilateral military action on Iraq's Osirak reactor in the early 1980s when it felt that the international community had turned its back on the issue. He noted, though, that he did not believe that Israel would risk its relationship with the United States over a nuclear attack. He listed several other factors that would affect an Israeli decision to attack Iran, such as whether sanctions, diplomacy, and covert actions had been exhausted; whether Israel felt it could succeed in stalling or thwarting the program at least three to five years; and whether it would have an uncontested flight plan for reaching Iran.

With specific regard to political legitimacy, it is also necessary to consider how Iran may view this statement by Israel. As has been mentioned before, statements such as the one issued above by the Israeli Ministry of Foreign Affairs are potentially risky. By suggesting that the UN resolution is not sufficient and that Iran should face further scrutiny and reprimand, Israel is openly confirming the fact that Iran is a real threat, a force to be reckoned with, and giving Ahmadinejad and others in the government reason to continue their efforts to pursue nuclear development and hurl threats at Israel and the United States. Certainly, that does not suggest that Israel should reject wholesale the validity of Iran as a rational international actor. However, Israel's legitimacy depends on the presence of a dangerous, threatening Iran.[49] Therefore, touting the need for a more peaceful Iran or an Iran that is incapable of developing nuclear weapons would possibly weaken its standing in the Middle East and would also diminish the current levels of dialogue. That is, without the spotlight on the triangular relationship of Israel, the United States, and Iran, what leverage would Israel have to project itself into the public perception as a major power that is capable of suggesting its ability to launch attacks or defend itself from threats?

Just as Israel may need Iran in order to justify its positions and legitimize its rhetorical displays of power, Iran may also need Israel—the relationship is mutual. Iran needs Israel for a number of reasons. First, Iran needs Israel in order to propagate more support for its regime. For Iran, the issue of regime security is central to its interactions with the United States and Israel. Surely, Iran does not want a Middle East that is entirely Arab (the fear here is an unlikely possibility—that the Middle East may erupt in an explosion of pan-Arab opposition). In addition, and perhaps the more central point, Iran's political and rhetorical maneuvers, though directed at Israel, are not directed at Israel exclusively: they are directed at Israel and, as a result, at the United States. The close alliance between Israel and the United States provides an easy target for Iran's saber rattling and threats without directly confronting the United States. Iran is able to temper the tone and intensity of its rhetoric by using Israel as a buffer; Iran needs Israel in order to build its case that it is a power worthy of attracting the attention of the United States and worthy of warranting serious concern. Though President Ahmadinejad may claim that he would like to see Israel "wiped off the map," the hard truth is that a world without Israel may not be exactly what he has in mind. The triangular relationship would become a straight line with Iran and the United States squaring off against each other.[50]

Certainly, it is not likely that such a possibility would arise; the relationship between the United States and Iran will continue to be somewhat indirect, with Israel always on the periphery. Just as the United States has persuaded Israel not to attack Iran, legitimizing Iran's threat in the process, by persuading Iran not to increase its nuclear weaponry for fear of retaliation by Israel, the United States in some ways legitimizes the potential Israeli response. While "Israel the state" has enjoyed a close alliance with the United States, Israeli military actions have been treated separately from statehood. Some may argue that there is, in fact, disproportionate support for "Israel the state" and Israeli military action. The strong pro-Israeli lobby within the United States has dominated support for Israel's war agenda, particularly its dealings with Iran.

Moving forward into the coming months and years, the Obama administration will have the serious task of negotiating relations between Israel and Iran and ultimately between Israel, Iran, and the United States. Israel will continue to be a strong ally of the United States in the Middle East, but a tougher stance toward Israel from Washington could jeopardize the stability of the relationship between the United States and Iran— an aggressive Iran, eager to showcase the strength of its regime and the legitimacy of its power in a region imbued with calls for a U.S.-led strike against its nuclear facilities, will cause reason for concern. Additionally, a more hawkish position toward Iran while casting a blind eye at Israel's political posturing may also entice Iran to move further in the direction of nuclear development.

Relations with Iran are important for the United States, but they do not have the same level of importance for Iran. The Islamic Republic of Iran seems to be concerned that the establishment of a long-term relationship with the United States may practically jeopardize the very existence of the regime and bring about a regime change. Tehran-based analyst Saeed Leylaz believes, "There are lot of radicals who don't want to see ordinary relations between Tehran and Washington. To convince Iran, they should send a very clear message that they are not going to try and destroy the regime."[51] By indicating that Iran's regime security is not the target of Washington policymakers and by acknowledging the security of Israel, perhaps using current Middle East peace talks as an outlet for such reminders, some ground may be gained in establishing a more stable relationship between these global actors.

CHAPTER 8

Conclusion

In July 2009, as U.S. Middle East peace envoy George Mitchell arrived in Israel for talks with Israeli and Palestinian leaders, news organizations confirmed that ahead of Mitchell's visit, President Barack Obama had sent letters to at least seven Arab and Gulf states seeking confidence-building measures toward Israel. Washington had been pressuring Israel to agree to a freeze of Jewish settlements in the West Bank and hoped to alleviate some antipathy between regional Arab states and "isolated" Israel.[1] "These letters were sent some time ago," a White House official told *Foreign Policy* magazine in late July.[2] "The president has always said that everyone will have to take steps for peace. This is just the latest instance of this sentiment."[3] A U.S. official who was familiar with the letters said they had been sent "recently" to the leaders of Bahrain, Egypt, Jordan, Saudi Arabia, and the United Arab Emirates and that they reinforced "the Mitchell message re: the need for CBMs [confidence-building measures] in exchange for [settlement] freeze and to [get] peace talks restarted."[4] Obama also sent a letter to King Mohammed VI of Morocco, urging him to "convince the parties to engage constructively," noting that he hoped Morocco would "be a leader in bridging gaps between Israel and the Arab world."[5]

Without saying so explicitly, the Obama administration appeared to have more in mind than simply stabilizing the age-old hostilities between Israel and its Arab neighbors. In fact, given the extreme complexity of the conflict, it was unlikely that fostering better relations between the regional foes was the central aim of the proposed confidence-building measures. Earlier that month, at the G-8 Summit in Italy, Obama, just six months into his presidency, amped up his rhetorical admonishments of the Iranian nuclear agenda, delivering a warning to the regime that was packaged neatly within an eloquent yet firm declaration announcing a deadline. "If Iran chooses not to walk through that door, then you have on record the G-8 to begin with, but I think potentially a lot of other countries, that are going to say we need to take further steps."[6]

This warning was much harsher than what Obama had directed to Iran and the Iranian people on the occasion of the Iranian New Year, March 19, 2009, the same year (only few months into his presidency). With no sign of coercive diplomacy and mixed with a spice of the Persian language, Obama had said,

> You, too, have a choice. The United States wants the Islamic Republic of Iran to take its rightful place in the community of nations. You have that right—but it comes with real responsibilities, and that place cannot be reached through terror or arms, but rather through peaceful actions that demonstrate the true greatness of the Iranian people and civilization. And the measure of that greatness is not the capacity to destroy, it is your demonstrated ability to build and create.[7]

It is unclear what Obama expected to achieve through that message and whether, in fact, the message had the power to bridge 30 years of disruption and bring the kind of changes he was expecting to see. Later that year in July, a strategic nuclear agreement between the United States and Russia was realized—an arms deal that aimed to reduce the ceiling on strategic warheads to 1,500 per country within seven years. The deal would also, as Sergei A. Karaganov, a Russian political scientist, noted, put increased pressure on the Iranian regime. "If you take the Georgia war, who was the winner?" he asked. "Russia, Georgia, the United States? No, it was Iran."[8]

From these episodes, it is clear that the halfway point of Obama's first year in office marked a turning point in his foreign policy objectives. As Americans became less intrigued with the new president's celebrity status and more concerned with growing tensions in the Middle East, his initiatives to mollify the rumblings between the Arabs and Israelis came into full view. It was also clear that any policy measures regarding the two competing camps would almost always include a focus on Iran—even if that focus was not overt and mentioned only in other concurrent discussions on the future of the Middle East.

Despite Obama's intentions to prompt the Arab states toward confidence-building measures directed at improving Israel's position in the Middle East, the result had the potential to isolate Iran—something that the Obama administration had long campaigned against and sought to avoid in its foreign policy initiatives. While Israel and its Arab neighbors did not come together on the conflict that has long plagued them—the dispute over the right to a sovereign Palestinian state alongside the

Jewish state—they did, as the WikiLeaks of 2010 revealed, come together
on the issue of Iran, and for the first time in a long time, Israel and its Arab
neighbors were on the same side of a hotly contested regional conflict.

Perhaps it could be said that this odd coalition—or, at a minimum, this
odd divergence of interest—is part of the confidence-building measures
that Obama hoped would evolve between the Arab states and Israel. After
all, having a common enemy, particularly one that may eventually be
capable of devastating its foes with nuclear weapons—is a powerful, unifying link. And according to Arab leaders, Iran is no longer an existential
threat to Israel alone. The Islamic Republic's nuclear program threatens
Egypt, Saudi Arabia, Jordan, and the Persian Gulf emirates as well. In
July 2009, the same month the Obama administration sealed a deal with
Russia on a nuclear ceiling and issued a warning to Iran's nuclear program, a former head of research in Israeli intelligence said, "The Saudis
are very concerned about an Iranian nuclear bomb, even more than the
Israelis."[9] Then, in late November 2010, the Saudi's became more candid
in their assessment, asking the United States to "cut the head off the
snake" and strike Iran's nuclear sites.[10] Finally, on December 10, 2010,
U.S. Secretary of Defense Robert Gates announced that the Gulf Arab
states not only backed strict sanctions on Iran but also were becoming
increasingly anxious over the "aggressive" behavior of Hezbollah in
Lebanon.[11] It became clear that Israel and the Arab states were, along with
the United States, forming a strong chorus of objection to Iran. In the process,
whether intentional or unintentional, the conflicting relationship between
Israel and its Arabs neighbors now had a common point of agreement even
though the Saudi prince said in November that Saudi Arabia would refuse
to directly or indirectly engage Israel until it leaves all the lands captured
during the 1967 Six-Day War.[12] At the end of the day, however, no matter
how badly each side may despise one another, both could agree that their
future would be bleak with an Iranian nuclear power nearby.

Another important dimension to consider with respect to the evolving
relationship between Israel, the United States, and Arab countries is
the impact that their opposition to Iran's nuclear program will have on
Tehran's perceptions of its regime security. As has been mentioned extensively in the preceding chapters, one of Iran's central objectives in dealing
with regional and international actors is to maintain the security of its
hard-line, Islamist rule. Though sharp sanctions, the long-term U.S. support of Israel, the war with Iraq and Afghanistan, and the historic
U.S. military presence in the Persian Gulf have been cited as reasons for
Iran to reject better relations with the United States and its allies, there
is one more reason that the clerical leadership of Iran does not want
to reestablish its ties with the United States, namely, the more fundamentally antagonistic conflict between the nature of the two political systems.
The fear of collapsing regime security on the part of Iran cannot be

surmounted, and the reality of a collapsing regime only increases as the United States, the Arab states, and Israel begin to form a coalition of strong opposition to Iran's nuclear ambitions.

Iran has sought to extend its regime security through the reliance on proxy groups. The Iranian regime is changing the rules of the game in its quest to become a dominant force in the Middle East by providing support to these groups, and as the country begins to feel the heat of increased international pressure, particularly from Israel and the Arab states, there is reason to believe that Iran will rely on these proxy groups for more support. Though the Iranian regime is under intense scrutiny in the international arena, it could begin to see an increase in its legitimacy as an accepted government as the popular vote and support for proxy groups such as Hezbollah and Hamas—and so many other Islamic surrogate groups—continue to rise. As Iran is on track to become a dominant leader in the region, its use of these proxy groups will serve to further legitimatize its government, maintain the security of its regime, and promote nationalism, religiosity, and Muslim brotherhood and unity around the world.

Even though Iran has sought to prove itself within the Arab and Muslim community regarding its potential ability to be a dominant force on the Islamic world, that ability is certainly not uncontested as recent events, particularly increased calls for a strike on its nuclear facilities, have shown.

Iran's attempts to unite Sunnis and Shias and its continued support for Hezbollah and Hamas will likely increase regional scrutiny and international isolation. There is little doubt that Israel will continue to maintain its military edge in the region and, in response to Iran's support of proxy groups, attempt to establish a sense of political legitimacy through continued isolation of Iran. Thus, as the policies of the Iranian government lead to its isolation, so too do the reactions to those policies by Israel and regional actors. A perpetual cycle of polarization emerges and operates as follows:

1. Iran, in seeking to advance the security of its regime, engages in a number of destructive policy measures, all of which spark the ire of the regional and international communities (ignoring nuclear deadlines and calls to halt uranium enrichment, saber rattling that is directed primarily at Israel, and offering financial and arms support to terrorist proxy groups).

2. Israel and the United States respond to Iran's belligerence through sanctions, rhetorical admonishments, and the threats of military strikes. This, in turn, undermines the security of the Iranian regime, resulting in a situation where leaders in Tehran feel inclined to counteract the response with increased confidence-building measures. The clerical leadership of Iran also believes that it is their divine responsibility to fight back against the "oppressor."

3. Iran's increased confidence-building measures are perceived as continued acts of belligerence, resulting in more sanctions, rhetorical admonishments, and threats of military action, all of which further sharpen the divisions between Israel and Iran and create a perpetual cycle of polarization that prevent an improvement in the relationship.

The longevity of the conflict between Iran and Israel has added to this cycle. The longer polarization between the two states exists, the more difficult it becomes to alleviate tensions. And neither party is able or willing to break the cycle—the regime security of Iran depends on its ability to perpetuate fear of a potential nuclear agenda. It also depends on the continued support for Hezbollah and Hamas. The groups are able to extend Iran's menacing presence out into various battlegrounds of the Middle East and temporarily divert too much attention from Iran's nuclear program. The more the Iranian leadership feels that its regime security is threatened, the more they will seek to fortify that sense of security by calling on surrogate groups to do its bidding in the region. The international community has suffered from this cycle: Iran has emerged as a country with significant regional influence that cannot be ignored and has enhanced its capability with nuclear technology even though it is still far from projecting nuclear weapons. In other words, parallel to political transformation, hostilities between Iran and the regional and international communities have transformed from controllable to uncontrollable.

It is also important to note that what frightens the Iranian system is a severe decline in the regime's support from the people. Obviously, a regime security guarantee would be what the radicals might be looking for before they accept any commitment for better relations with Israel or the United States. In addition, Iran does not seem enthusiastic about opening up contacts with United States; the outcome of an unrestricted relationship could be more harmful to the Islamic Republic of Iran though extremely useful for the people of Iran. Interestingly enough, on December 8, 2010, a poll released by the International Peace Institute found that 7 in 10 Iranians favor their country developing and producing nuclear weapons. The poll indicated that support for nuclear arms has risen almost 20 points in the past 18 months, as the international confrontation over Iran's nuclear program has deepened. Nuclear development is favored by both pro- and anti-government Iranians.[13] Thus, there appeared across-the-board support for Iranian nuclear ambitions even among those citizens who were opposed to the regime. The report also revealed that recent strategies and agreements aimed at slowing or halting Iran's plans to enrich uranium were unpopular amongst a majority of Iranian citizens:

The Iranian public also opposes two proposed international agreements to halt or slow Iran's nuclear program. The so-called "Grand Bargain"—Western security guarantees and trade normalization in return for an end to uranium enrichment, nuclear inspections, and concessions on Afghanistan, Iraq, and Palestine by Iran— is opposed by 55 percent to 27 percent. The recent Turkish-Brazilian deal, intended to slow the program and offer more time for talks by shipping half of Iran's enriched uranium abroad, was opposed by 39 percent to 34 percent, with one in four Iranians unsure.[14]

The poll also indicated that three-fifths of Iranians support aid to the anti-Israel Palestinian Hamas and Lebanese Hezbollah resistance movements.[15] Thus, with broad domestic support for an Iranian nuclear agenda and the continued reliance on Hezbollah and Hamas, the Iranian government appears to be in a position of strength moving forward despite concerns over the security of its regime.

The relationship between the Arab states and Iran has wavered over the course of the past 30 years, but even in the midst of the various ebbs and flows, Israel remained a common enemy for both. Now, as it appears that the balance has shifted, leaving Iran as the isolated party facing off against the United States, Israel, and the Arab nations, therein lies a window of opportunity for Israel to enhance its political legitimacy and its leverage over Iran. Benjamin Netanyahu, speaking about the recent news of Arab contention over Iran's nuclear program, extolled the possibilities for peace that could come as a result of the news. His remarks, void of specificity regarding the future of Arab-Israeli relations, displayed nonetheless a feeling of great pride and even vindication—the Arab leaders had enhanced his political positions and in his view justified the need to isolate Iran and strike its nuclear sites. "If leaders start saying openly what they have long been saying behind closed doors, we can make a real breakthrough on the road to peace."[16]

Netanyahu was not clear if the "road to peace" would include improved relations between Arabs and Israelis in addition to his view of a more peaceful world absent of a nuclear Iran. Even so, it is safe to say that the more Israel is able to isolate Iran and frame their desire to strike the country's nuclear sites within a narrative that exhorts a collective call from major regional actors and the international community, the more Israel's sense of security will improve. And, most important, for Israel, regional perceptions of the country's political legitimacy will improve as well.

But how would this framework improve the relationship between Israel and Iran? In short, it would not. Existing contentions between Israel and Iran (as well as existing contentions between the United States and Iran) will likely become worse. The more isolated and threatened the Iranian regime feels, the more incentive they have to continue down their current path. As the international and regional communities align themselves in opposition to Iran, the country's leadership will seek to restore a lost sense of regime security through nuclear proliferation. Even with the announcement of new, more rigid sanctions, it does not appear that the diplomatic track will produce any substantial results, particularly as long as Iran feels isolated and threatened by those who are deploying the economic punishments. More notably, while the sanctions may eventually take their toll on the people of Iran, the clerical leadership will not likely suffer, and as long as they have the reigns of power, there is little expectation that they will be motivated by the economic consequences imposed on them. And, though Iran has not been a country known to place high premium on public opinion, the recent polls showing broad support for a nuclear program and the continued relationship with Hezbollah and Hamas cannot be ignored and add a crucial element of popular backing to the regime's ambitions.

A successful resolution to the contentious relationship between Israel and Iran will have to recognize that Iran has rights to pursue its nuclear program for peaceful purpose but cannot be permitted to acquire nuclear weapons. Iran must also recognize that regaining the trust of the international community is vital to its longevity and vitality as a regional actor. Settlement over the nuclear dispute must, therefore, involve incremental confidence-building measures that ensure the absence of nuclear weaponry and the security and political legitimacy of Israel and other U.S. allies in the region but that also provide Iran with an incentive to go along with such plans. In other words, there must not be an international mandate that pits the United States and Israel against Iran, backing the Islamic Republic into a corner while deploying all-or-nothing military threats. While the continued belligerence of Iran may create an appeal for such hard-line policies, the reality is that, in end, they will only deepen the divisions between Israel and Iran and, as a result, Iran and the United States.

Particular attention must be paid to threats of a military strike against Iran, whether an Israeli strike or a U.S. strike. Calls for such actions have increased drastically even within the past year, but the reality is that a strike against Iranian nuclear sites will have devastating consequences on the Middle East and the entire international community. First, they would further polarize an already polarized region of the world and damage whatever possibilities exist for renewed relations between the United States and Iran as well as the future of the relationship between Israel and Iran. As has been noted, an isolated Iranian regime is an aggravating factor for peace talks, not a conciliatory one. In order to foster a more productive dialogue, discussions of "consequences" toward Iran as a result of their refusal to abide by international nuclear standards and guidelines must not be considered as code words for military action. After all, military vulnerability is a key part of Iran's temptation to pursue nuclear technologies in the first place, and in the event that their ambitions were realized, the situation could spin out of control with, as expected, the sum of their aggressions directed at Israel. As the recent Carmel fire in Israel has shown, the Jewish state may not be prepared for a nuclear war, which would certainly cause chaos much greater than any fire.[17] Whether Israeli leaders want to admit it or not, Iran is a part of the long-term strategy of the United States in the Middle East, and the current standoff, therefore, must not be viewed simply in terms of taking down a defiant regime and disabling Iran's nuclear capabilities. Certainly, those measures are viewed as important, but they are not a guarantee that 5, 10, or even 20 years from now Iran will cooperate with Western policymakers. In other words, the nuclear standoff is the pressing issue of our time but will be considered historically as one episode in a long history of rocky relations. Looking at the domestic situation in Iran, there is a strong possibility that the regime will alter from within sooner or later, and since there is little support for a more severe shift to the extreme right, the changes must be toward more compatibility with Western values and standards. That is not to say that the West must stand by idly while Iran continues down its current path—especially as Iran's government gives the international community every reason to believe that it is not pursuing traveling down the nuclear path for peaceful, energy-producing purposes.

On December 13, 2010, Iranian President Mahmoud Ahmadinejad abruptly fired Manouchehr Mottaki, the Iranian foreign minister, while Mottaki was traveling on official business in Senegal. Mottaki was replaced with Ali Akbar Salehi, Iran's nuclear chief and secretary of the Supreme National Security Council.[18] Mottaki had been, as discussed in the previous chapters, one of the public faces of Iran's nuclear program, maintaining that it existed for peaceful purposes. Compared to Ahmadinejad, Mottaki was considered relatively moderate, and it was no secret that the two did not see eye to eye. Ali Ansari, professor of Iranian studies at St. Andrews University in Scotland, notes that while personal differences between the two may have come to the fore from time to time, the dismissal was "about who is in charge of running Iranian foreign policy . . . and these disputes have little to do with a hard-line view or a difference in a hard-line view."[19] Recently, a series of events unfolded that Ahmadinejad interpreted as defeats for Mottaki and, as a direct result, for Iran. The foreign minister was blamed for failing to thwart the UN resolution condemning Iran's violation of human rights as well as failing to gain an Iranian seat on the UN Women's Rights Panel. Then, news broke that Iran had sent illegal weapons to Nigeria, and while Mottaki traveled to the country to stop the political bleeding, it was too late. These events appeared to have given Ahmadinejad the foundation on which to make the case to Khamenei for Mottaki's dismissal.

The move indicated that Ahmadinejad aims to homogenize the government and, in the midst of revived nuclear talks and increased scrutiny from the international community, make the nuclear issue the main pillar of the Iranian government. And who better to lead the way than the nuclear chief? Salehi sparked the ire of world leaders at the Geneva Conference in December 2010, bolstering Tehran's bargaining power by announcing that his nation had achieved the ability to produce yellow cake—a uranium-based powder that is used to create nuclear fuel. Salehi noted that as a result of this achievement, Iran would not need to rely on imported uranium. "The enemies and ill-wishers have always tried to create despair and disappointment among our youth, academicians, engineers and our nation, but today we witness the delivery of the first batch of yellowcake which is produced inside the country," he said.[20] If Iran hoped to advance skepticism of its nuclear ambitions and further provoke the West, their mission was accomplished. The White House responded immediately. Michael Hammer, a spokesman for the National Security Council, said that since Iran's uranium supply is "not enough for a peaceful nuclear energy program, this calls into further question Iran's intentions."[21]

With Salehi out front, Iran's message is clear: Iranian foreign policy and the nuclear issue are one in the same and, despite the grave consequences, understandably so. Militarily, Iran is weaker than other regional states and pales in comparison to the militaries of Israel and the United States; the regime security of Tehran is not enhanced by a robust military. Economically, Iran is on the weak end as well, thus the country's bargaining power—its wedge or leverage, so to speak—is the fear that it strikes in the hearts of world leaders by continuing down its current nuclear path. Perhaps more symbolic than anything, Mottaki's replacement was a grim message to the world: the person heading Iranian foreign policy is also the person in charge of Iran's nuclear program.

The international community has the right to expect Iran's cooperation per its contractual obligations as part of the Nuclear Non-Proliferation Treaty, but considerations must also be made regarding ways to foster a sense of Iranian security that is not the result of the government's support for terrorism or the development of nuclear weapons. However unlikely it may be, the international community has the right to expect that Iran recognizes the state of Israel and does not deploy threats of striking it. The longer the rhetorical saber rattling continues, the more difficult it will be to ease the cleavage of tensions and anxieties that result from the back-and-forth threat leveling between the states. When small steps can be taken to fortify the political legitimacy of Israel and the stability and security of a nuclear-free Iran, perhaps there will be a clearer way out of what has been a long and contentious standoff in the Middle East.

Notes

CHAPTER 1

1. "Says Iran: 'Greatest Challenge" to Region's Stability,' *Al Arabiya*, October 19, 2010, http://www.alarabiya.net/articles/2010/10/19/122724.html.

2. Ibid.

3. "Israeli-Palestinian Peace Will Isolate Iran, Suggests Peres," *Open Democracy*, October 22, 2010, http://www.opendemocracy.net/opensecurity/security_briefings/221010.

4. Ibid.

5. European Security and Defense Assembly, "Recommendation 854: Iran and the Middle East," http://www.assembly-weu.org/en/documents/sessions_ordinaires/rpt/2010/2068.php?PHPSESSID=e6239caad4525cfc51876e05ea23e1e4.

6. "U.S. Pessimistic on Iran Overtures," *BBC News*, July 23, 2009, http://news.bbc.co.uk/2/hi/middle_east/8165265.stm.

7. Mazal Mualem, "Kadima Leader Livni: Israel Can Save Itself from Global Isolation," *Haaretz*, June 6, 2010, http://www.haaretz.com/news/national/kadima-leader-livni-israel-can-save-itself-from-global-isolation-1.294704.

8. Ibid.

9. Ibid.

10. D. N. Hadiyan, "Iran-US Cold War," *Iran Review*, May 8, 2010, http://www.iranreview.org/content/view/5608/36.

11. Ibid.

12. M. Bard, "Potential Threats to Israel: Iran," February 20, 2009, http://www.jewishvirtuallibrary.org/jsource/threats to israel/Iran.html.

13. A. Press, "Iran Accelerating Missle Work, U.S. Says," *USAToday.com*, January 16, 2008, http://www.usatoday.com/news/world/2008-01-16-iranmissiles_N.htm.

14. Associated Press, "Israel Threatens Iran over Nuclear Program," September 24, 2004, http://www.foxnews.com/story/0,2933,133899,00.html.

15. Roy Anderson, Robert Seibert, and John Wagner, *Politics and Change in the Middle East* (Upper Saddle River, NJ: Pearson, 2009), 106.

16. Ian Bickerton and Carla Klausner, *A History of the Arab-Israeli Conflict* (Englewood Cliffs, NJ: Prentice Hall, 2010), 374.

17. Brigitte L. Nacos, *Terrorism and Counterterrorism* (New York: Longman, 2008), 120.

18. Ted Galen Carpenter and Malou Innocent, "The Iraq War and Iranian Power," *Survival* 49, no. 4 (Winter 2007–2008), http://www.cato.org/pubs/articles/carpenter_innocent_the_iraq_war_and_iranian_power.pdf.

CHAPTER 2

1. J. Rosenberg, *Inside the Revolution* (Carol Stream, IL: Tyndall House, 2009), 54.

2. Ibid., 57.

3. Ibid.

4. Ibid., 61.

5. M. Budeiri, "The Nationalist Dimension of Islamic Movement in Palestinian Politics," *Journal of Palestinian Studies* 24, no. 3 (2009): 91.

6. J. Sharp, "The United States and Iran," October 24, 2005, http://www.pri.org/theworld/?q=node/3565.

7. M. Bard, "Potential Threats to Israel: Iran," February 20, 2009, http://www.jewishvirtuallibrary.org/jsource/threats to israel/Iran.html.

8. Associated Press, "Iran Accelerating Missle Work, U.S. Says," *USAToday*, January 16, 2008, http://www.usatoday.com/news/world/2008-01-16-iranmissiles_N.htm.

9. Associated Press, "Israel Threatens Iran over Nuclear Program," September 24, 2004, http://www.foxnews.com/story/0,2933,133899,00.html.

10. M. Mualem, "Kadima Leader Livini: Israel Can Save Itself from Global Isolation," *Haaretz*, July 6, 2010, http://www.haaretz.com/news/national/kadima-leader-livni-israel-can-save-itself-from-global-isolation-1.294704.

11. Change.Gov: The Office of the President-Elect, "The Obama-Biden Plan," July 28, 2010, http://change.gov/agenda/foreign_policy_agenda.

12. A. Ganji, "Commentary: World Should Shun Iranian Leader," *CNN.com*, September 22, 2009, http://www.cnn.com/2009/WORLD/meast/09/22/ganji.iran.ahmadinejad/index.html.

13. Nasser Hadiyan, "Iran-US Cold War," *Iran Review*, June 6, 2010, http://www.iranreview.org/content/view/5608/36.

14. Ibid.

15. F. Amuzegar, "Iran's Crumbling Revolution," *Foreign Affairs* 82, no. 1 (2003): 44–57.

16. H. C. Metz, "Iran: A Country Study," 1987, U.S. Library of Congress, http://countrystudies.us/iran/82.htm.

17. G. Tezc and T. Azadarmak, "Religiosity and Islamic Rule in Iran," *Journal for Scientific Study of Relgion* 47, no. 2 (2008): 211–24.

18. Ibid.

19. R. Amiri, "The Politics of Polarization: Iran's Elections: Why Arab Leaders Want Ahmadinejad to Win," April 10, 2009, http://www.globalresearch.ca/index.php?context=va&aid=13135.

20. Ganji, "Commentary."

21. Ibid.

22. Ibid.

23. Ibid.

24. A. Naeymi-Rad, "Possible Outcomes for Future of Iran," April 20, 2010, http://www.examiner.com/x-45737-Chicago-Government-Examiner~y2010m4d20-Possible-Outcomes-for-Future-of-Iran.

25. Andrei Naeymi-Rad, "Possible Outcomes for Future of Iran," April 20, 2010, http://www.examiner.com/government-in-chicago/possible-outcomes-for-future-of-iran

26. A Asraf and A. Banuazizi, "Iran's Tortuous Path toward 'Islamic Liberalism,'" *International Journal of Politics, Culture, and Society* 15, no. 2 (2001): 237.

27. M. Ispahani, "Varieties of Muslim Experience," *The Wilson Quarterly* 14 (1989): 63–72.

28. M. Shuster, "The Origins of the Shia-Sunni Split," February 12, 2007, http://www.npr.org/templates/story/story.php?storyId=7332087.

29. M. Wurmser, "The Iran-Hamas Alliance," October 4, 2007, https://www.hudson.org/index.cfm?fuseaction=publication_details&id=5167.

30. Central Intelligence Agency, *World Factbook*, https://www.cia.gov/library/publications/the-world-factbook/geos/ir.html.

31. "Iran Urges Muslim Unity against Israel," *Press TV*,May 30, 2010, http://edition.presstv.ir/detail/128369.html.

32. "Iran Urges World Muslim 'Resistance' against Israel," AFP, April 4, 2010, http://www.breitbart.com/article.php?id=CHG21c84721b2a4459b107dfbfbada315a.2fl.

33. "Muslim Scholars Urge for Shia-Sunni Unity," Abdhul Bayt News Agency, February 8, 2010, http://www.abna.ir/data.asp?lang=2&id=180098.

34. Islamic Ummah and Opressed People Agenda, "Muslim Alims Urge for Shia-Sunni Unity," March 4, 2010, http://www.islamidavet.com/english/2010/03/04/muslim-alims-urge-for-shia-unity.

35. Ibid.

36. Abdhul Bayt News Agency, "Muslim Scholars Urge for Shia-Sunni Unity."

37. *New York Times*, "Iran's Nuclear Program," April 15, 2010, http://www.nytimes.com/info/iran-nuclear-program/?inline=nyt-classifier.

38. Ibid.

39. Ibid.

40. Amos Jordan, William J. Taylor, Jr., and Michael J. Mazarr, *American National Security* (Baltimore, Maryland: The Johns Hopkins University Press, 2009), 424.

41. "Profile: Mahmoud Ahmadinejad," *BBC News*, June 16, 2009, http://news.bbc.co.uk/2/hi/middle_east/4107270.stm.

42. Donna Miles, "Diplomacy Best Way to Confront Iran's Nuclear Programs, Gates Says," American Forces Press Services, June 2, 2007, http://www.globalsecurity.org/wmd/library/news/iran/2007/iran-070602-afps01.htm.

43. Jacquelyn S. Porth, "Iran Moving Forward to Master Uranium Enrichment Capability: US Envoy Says There Is Still Time for Diplomacy but Not Complacency," *USINFO*, June 11, 2007, http://www.globalsecurity.org/wmd/library/news/iran/2007/iran-070611-usia01.htm.

44. "Iran Welcomes Active Role of Various States in N-Case," Islamic Republic News Agency, June 6, 2007, http://www.globalsecurity.org/military/library/news/2007/06/mil- 070606-voa03.htm.

45. "Larijani: 'Precise Steps' Can Prevent New Resolution," Islamic Republic News Agency, June 6, 2007, http://www.globalsecurity.org/wmd/library/news/2007/iran-070606-irnao1.htm.

46. "Iran Welcomes Active Role of various States in N-Case."

47. Mills, "Diplomacy Best Way to Confront Iran's Nuclear Programs, Gates Says."

48. Breffni O'Rourke, "US Warns Tehran of Tough New Sanctions," Radio Free Europe/Radio Liberty, June 13, 2007, http://www.globalsecurity.org/wmd/library/news/iran/2007/iran-070612-referl02.htm.

49. "IAEA Chief Warns against Military Attack on Iran," *VOA News*, June 22, 2007, http://www.globalsecurity.org/wmd/library/news/iran/2007/iran-070 614-voa01.htm.

50. Julia Damionova, "Nuclear Negotiations with Iran end in Failure," *The Los Angeles Times*, January 23, 2011, http://articles.latimes.com/2011/jan/23/world/la-fg-iran-nuclear-20110123.

51. Limor Simhony and Roni Bart, "John McCain and Barack Obama: The Middle East and Israel," *Strategic Assessment* 11, no. 1 (June 2008), http://www.inss.org.il/publications.php?cat=21&incat=&read=1939 &print=1.

52. Ibid.

53. Robert Kagan, "America's Crisis of Legitimacy," *Foreign Affairs* 83, no. 2 (2004): 66–67.

54. Quoted in Mills, "Diplomacy Best Way to Confront Nuclear Programs, Gates Says."

55. Kagan, "America's Crisis of Legitimacy," 81–82.

56. Joanna Spear, "Organizing for Internationalism Counterproliferation: NATO and US Nonproliferation Policy," in *Ultimate Security: Combating Weapons of Mass Destruction*, ed. Janne E. Nolan, Bernard I. Finel, and Brian D. Finlay (New York: Century Foundation Press, 2003), 218–20.

57. Ibid., 29.

58. Kagan, "America's Crisis of Legitimacy," 87.

59. David Sanger and Thom Shanker, "Gates Says U.S. Lacks a Policy to Thwart Iran," *New York Times*, April 17, 2010, http://www.nytimes.com/2010/04/18/world/middleeast/18iran.html?scp=2&sq=gates&st=cse.

60. Ibid.

61. Nicholas Blanford, "Lebanon Resumes Defense Talks on Hezbollah's Military Wing," *Christian Science Monitor*, March 10, 2010, http://www.csmonitor.com/World/Middle-East/2010/0310/Lebanon-resumes-defense-talks-on-Hezbollah-s-military-wing.

62. Kim Ghattas, "US Concerned about Syrian Intentions over Hezbollah," *BBC News*, April 15, 2010, http://news.bbc.co.uk/2/hi/8621405.stm.

63. Khair el-Din Haseeb, ed, *Arab-Iranian Relations* (Beirut: Centre for Arab Unity Studies, 1998), 510.

64. Ibid.

65. "Iran Gives Weapons to Re-Arm Hezbollah, Pentagon Says," *Bloomberg*, April 20, 2010, http://www.businessweek.com/news/2010-04-20/iran-gives-weapons-funds-to-help-lebanese-hezbollah-re-arm.html.

66. "Iran Leader Urges Destruction of 'Cancerous' Israel," *CNN.com*, December 15, 2000, http://archives.cnn.com/2000/WORLD/meast/12/15/mideast.iran.reut.

67. Brigitte L. Nacos, *Terrorism and Counterterrorism* (New York: Longman, 2008), 119.

68. Blanford, "Lebanon Resumes Defense Talks on Hezbollah's Military Wing."

69. "Military," *Globalsecurity.org*, http://www.globalsecurity.org/military/world/iran/intro.htm.

70. Ibid.

71. Ibid.

72. Farhad Pouladi, "Iran Guards Test Missiles as War Games End: State Media," *SMH News*, April 26, 2010, http://news.smh.com.au/breaking-news-world/iran-guards-test-missiles-as-war-games-end-state-media-20100426-tlw3.html.

73. Ibid.

74. "Iran Test-Fires Five Missiles," *RTT News*, April 25, 2010, http://www.rttnews.com/ArticleView.aspx?Id=1279833.

75. Pouladi, "Iran Guards Test Missiles as War Games End."

76. Ted Galen Carpenter and Malou Innocent, "The Iraq War and Iranian Power," *Survival* 49, no. 4 (Winter 2007): 72, http://www.cato.org/pubs/articles/carpenter_innocent_the_iraq_war_and_iranian_power.pdf.

77. Pouladi, "Iran Guards Test Missiles as War Games End."

78. Carpenter and Innocent, "The Iraq War and Iranian Power," 67.

79. Ibid., 71.

80. Amos Jordan, ed., *American National Security* (Baltimore: Johns Hopkins University Press, 2009), 320.

81. Carpenter and Innocent, "The Iraq War and Iranian Power," 70.

82. Jordan, *American National Security*, 320.

83. David Sanger, "Decrying U.S., Iran Begins War Games," *New York Times*, April 21, 2010, http://www.nytimes.com/2010/04/22/world/middleeast/22iran.html.

84. Ibid.

85. Central Intelligence Agency, *World Factbook*, https://www.cia.gov/library/publications/the-world-factbook/rankorder/2001rank.html?countryName=Iran&countryCode=ir&regionCode=me&rank=17#ir.

86. "Middle East: Iran," *CIA.gov*, April 21, 2010, https://www.cia.gov/library/publications/the-world-factbook/geos/ir.html.

87. Ibid.

88. Ibid.

89. Ibid.

90. "Are Iran's Leaders Hiding a Severe Economic Downturn?," *Time*, March 3, 2010, http://www.time.com/time/world/article/0,8599,1969390,00.html.

91. "Middle East: Iran."

92. "Middle East: Saudi Arabia," *CIA.gov*, April 22, 2010, https://www.cia.gov/library/publications/the-world-factbook/geos/sa.html.

93. Ibid.

94. "Middle East: Turkey," *CIA.gov*, April 22, 2010, https://www.cia.gov/library/publications/the-world-factbook/geos/tu.html.

95. Robert Worth, "Iran Mutes a Chorus of Voices for Reform," *New York Times*, April 19, 2010, http://www.nytimes.com/2010/04/20/world/middleeast/20iran.html.

96. "Military."

97. Bill Roggio, "Coalition and Afghan Forces Kill Taliban Commander Linked to Iran, Al-Qaeda," *Long War Journal*, November 22, 2010, http://www.long warjournal.org/archives/2010/11/coalition_and_afghan_1.php.

98. "Talib" means seminary school's pupil, and hence the term "Taliban" signifies that the group recruits its members from pupils of that study at such schools. The order was originally established by Pakistan in seminary schools.

99. Payvand quoting Iranian government news agency in "Karzai: Iran's Help Has Contributed to Afghanistan Development," Islamic Republic News Agency, December 27, 2005, http://www.payvand.com/news/05/dec/1216.html.

100. Afghanistan News Center, "Afghanistan Seeks Iran's Majlis Experience," December 27, 2005, http://www.afghanistannewscenter.com/news/2005/december/dec272005.html.

101. "Iran Arming Taliban, U.S. Claims," *CNN News*, June 13, 2007, http://www.cnn.com/2007/WORLD/asiapcf/06/13/iran.taliban/index.html.

102. "Iran 'Arming Taliban with Roadside Bombs,'" *The Telegraph*, October 4, 2007, http://www.telegraph.co.uk/news/worldnews/1565106/Iran-arming-Taliban-with-roadside-bombs.html.

103. "Afghanistan Skeptical Iran Arming Taliban," United Press International, October 19, 2007, http://www.upi.com/Top_News/2007/10/19/Afghanistan-skeptical-Iran-arming-Taliban/UPI-44601192797584.

104. Kate Clark, "Iran Sending Weapons to Taliban," *BBC News*, September 15, 2008, http://news.bbc.co.uk/2/hi/7616429.stm.

105. Ibid.

106. Yochi Dreazen and August Cole, "Gates Says Taliban Have Momentum in Afghanistan," *Wall Street Journal*, May 26, 2009, http://online.wsj.com/article/SB124329472631452687.html.

107. "Karzai Congratulates Ahmadinejad in Phone Call," *Jerusalem Post*, June 14, 2009, http://www.jpost.com/servlet/Satellite?cid=1244371093896&pagename=JPost%2FJPArticle%2FShowFull.

108. "Karzai Congratulates Ahmadinejad in Phone Call," *Tehran Times*, September 21, 2009, http://www.tehrantimes.com/index_View.asp?code=203574.

CHAPTER 3

1. "U.S. Rejects Israel Call for Armed Threat against Iran," *Al-Arabiya News*, November 8, 2010, http://www.alarabiya.net/articles/2010/11/08/125279.html.

2. Ibid.

3. Ibid.

4. Ibid.

5. Ibid.

6. Ibid.

7. Ibid.

8. Barak Ravid, "Netanyahu: WikiLeaks Cables Prove Israel Is Right on Iran," *Haaertz.com*, November 29, 2010, http://www.haaretz.com/news/diplomacy -defense/netanyahu-wikileaks-cables-prove-israel-is-right-on-iran-1.327653.

9. Ibid.

10. Heather Langan, "Egypt Sought Spies in Iraq, Syria to Stop Iran, WikiLeaks Shows," *Businessweek*, November 30, 2010, http://www.businessweek.com/news/ 2010-11-30/egypt-sought-spies-in-iraq-syria-to-stop-iran-wikileaks-shows.html.

11. Ibid.

12. Dana Allin and Steven Simon, *The Sixth Crisis: Iran, Israel, America, and the Rumors of War* (Oxford: Oxford University Press, 2010), 51.

13. Asher Arian, *The Second Republic: Politics in Israel* (New York: Chatham House, 2005), 19.

14. Ibid.

15. Israeli Central Bureau of Statistics, "Last Produced for Monthly Bulletin of Statistics No. 11/2010," http://www.cbs.gov.il/www/yarhon/b1_e.htm.

16. Ibid.

17. Ibid.

18. Ibid.

19. Quoted in Uri Bialer, *Between East and West: Israel's Foreign Policy Orientation 1948–1956* (Cambridge: Cambridge University Press, 1990), 59.

20. Ibid., 23.

21. Ibid., 26.

22. Aaron S. Klieman, *Israel and the World after 40 Years* (Washington, DC: Pergamon-Brassey, 1990), 43–44.

23. Raymond Cohen, "Israel's Starry-Eyed Foreign Policy," *Middle East Quarterly* 1, no. 2 (June 1994), http://www.meforum.org/221/israels-starry-eyed -foreign-policy.

24. Ibid.

25. Quoted in Walter Eytan, *The First Ten Years* (New York: Simon & Schuster, 1958), 10.

26. Alastaire Crooke, "The Strange Tale of Iran and Israel," *Le Monde Diplomatique*, February 5, 2009, http://nondediplo.com/2009/02/05iran.

27. Quoted in Avi Shlaim, "Israel, the Great Powers and the Middle East Crisis of 1958," *Journal of Imperial and Commonwealth History* 12 (May 1999): 2.

28. Ibid.

29. Ibid.

30. http://www.jewishvirtuallibrary.org/jsource/History/casualty_table.html.

31. Robert Rabil, *Embattled Neighbors: Syria, Israel, and Lebanon*, (New York: Rienner, 2003), 14.

32. Andrew Borowiec, *Modern Tunisia: A Democratic Apprenticeship* (New York: Greenwood, 1998), 107.

33. Cohen, "Israel's Starry-Eyed Foreign Policy."

34. Daniel Ammann, *The King of Oil: The Secret Lives of Marc Rich*, (New York: St. Martin's, 2009), 27.

35. Quoted in Trita Parsi, *The Treacherous Alliance: The Secret Dealings of Iran, Israel, and the United States* (New Haven, CT: Yale University Press, 2007), 30.

36. Ibid.

37. Ibid.

38. "The Arab Oil Embargo: What Happened and Could It Happen Again?," *HeatingOil.com*, August 5, 2009, http://www.heatingoil.com/wp-content/uploads/2009/09/the_arab_oil_embargo.pdf.

39. William D. Smith, "Price Quadruples for Iranian Crude Oil at Auction," *New York Times*, December 12, 1973.

40. John J. Mearsheimer and Stephen M. Walt, "The Israel Lobby and US Foreign Policy," *Middle East Policy* 13, no. 3 (Fall 2006): 31.

41. According to the "Greenbook" of the U.S. Agency for International Development, which reports "overseas loans and grants," Israel has received $140,142,800,000 (in constant 2003 dollars) from the United States through 2003; http://qesdb.cdie.org/gbk, November 8, 2005.

42. Trita Parsi, "The Post Revolution Period," *Encyclopedia Iranica*, http://www.iranica.com/articles/israel-i-relations-with-iran.

43. Ibid.

44. Ibid.

45. Ibid.

46. Quoted in ibid.

47. For all intents and purposes, the war of 1973 may be viewed as the last great war in the Middle East. Wars that followed, such as the Lebanon War of 1982, were seen largely as fragmented in the region. Israel faced an Arab state opponent(s) in 1948, 1956, 1967, 1968–1971, and 1973.

48. Astrid Scharf, "The Arab-Israeli Peace Process: From Madrid to Oslo and Beyond," *Studies in Contemporary History and Security Policy* 3 (1999): 3.

49. Ibid.

50. Ibid.

51. Lenore Martin, "Assessing the Impact of U.S.-Israeli Relations on the Arab World," Strategic Studies Institute Report, July 2003, http://www.strategicstudiesinstitute.army.mil/pdffiles/PUB104.pdf.

52. Ibid.

53. Ibid.

54. G. Harms and T. Ferry, *The Palestine-Israel Conflict: A Basic Introduction* (London: Pluto, 2005), 153.

55. Quoted in "Netanyahu: 'America Is a Thing You Move Easily,'" *CheckPoint Washington*, July 2010, http://voices.washingtonpost.com/checkpoint-washington/2010/07/netanyahu_america_is_a_thing_y.html.

56. Martin, "Assessing the Impact of U.S.-Israeli Relations on the Arab World."

57. Ibid.

58. Speech at Tel Aviv University, quoted by Josh Mitnick, "Israel Warms to Obama's Pledge of Talks with Iran," *Washington Times*, November 26, 2008.

59. Ibid.

60. Alex Fishman, "Existential Threat," *Yedi'ot Aharonot*, February 16, 2009.

61. Roni Sofer, "Israel Takes Part in NATO Intelligence Discussions," December 5, 2008, http://www.ynetnews.com/articles/0,7340,L-3683004,00.html.

62. Carol Migdalovitz, "Israel: Background and Relations with the United States," April 2, 2009, http://www.fas.org/sgp/crs/mideast/RL33476.pdf.

63. Ibid.

64. Ibid.

65. Arian, *The Second Republic*, 4.

66. Ibid., 6.

67. Ibid.

68. "Poll: Most Israelis Could Live with a Nuclear Iran," *Haaretz*, June 14, 2009, http://www.haaretz.com/news/poll-most-israelis-could-live-with-a-nuclear-iran-1.277908.

69. Ibid.

70. "Israeli Ambassador on Nuclear Iran: 'No Way,'" *USAToday*, September 30, 2010, http://www.usatoday.com/news/opinion/forum/2010-09-30-column30_ST_N.htm.

71. "CIA: Iran Could Be Two Years from Nuclear Bomb," *ABC News*, June 27, 2010, http://blogs.abcnews.com/politicalpunch/2010/06/cia-iran-could-be-two-years-from-nuclear-bomb.html.

72. Ibid.

73. Barry Posen, "We Can Live with a Nuclear Iran?," *New York Times*, February 27, 2006, http://www.nytimes.com/2006/02/27/opinion/27posen.html.

74. Ibid.

75. Ibid.

76. "CIA."

77. A. Shavit, "Barak: It's Clear That the Calm Was Not a Mistake: We Have No Interest in War" (in Hebrew), *Haaretz*, December 18, 2008, 1.

78. Matthew Bunn and Anthony Wier, "Terrorist Nuclear Weapon Construction: How Difficult?" Chapter in *Confronting the Spector of Nuclear Terrorism*, Philadelphia: The Annals of the American Academy of Political and Social Science, September 2006, 133-139.

79. Chuck Freilich, "The Armageddon Scenario: Israel and the Threat of Nuclear Terrorism," *Mideast Security and Policy Studies No. 84*, April 2010, http://www.biu.ac.il/Besa/MSPS84.pdf.

80. Ibid.

81. C. D. Ferguson and W. C. Potter, "The Four Faces of Nuclear Terrorism," Center for Nonproliferation Studies, Monterey Institute of International Studies, 2004, 37; U.S. Government, "World at Risk: Report of the Commission on the Prevention of WMD Proliferation and Terrorism," 2008, Part One: Biological and Nuclear Risks.

82. R. Mowatt-Larssen, "Al Qaeda Weapons of Mass Destruction Threat: Hype or Reality?," Belfer Center, Harvard Kennedy School, January 2010, 2; D. Byman, "Do Counterproliferation and Counterterrorism Go Together?," *Political Science Quarterly* 122, no. 1 (Spring 2007): 38; P. D. Zimmerman and J. G. Lewis, "The Bomb in the Backyard," *Foreign Policy* 157 (November/December 2006): 32–39; Graham Allison, *Nuclear Terrorism: The Ultimate Preventable Catastrophe*, (New York: Times Books, 2004), 11–12; Michael Levi, *On Nuclear Terrorism*, (Cambridge, Massachusetts: Harvard University Press, 2007), 29; Bunn, "Securing the Bomb," 3; Ferguson and Potter, "The Four Faces of Nuclear Terrorism," 17.

83. Freilich, "The Armageddon Scenario."

84. Ibid.

85. Ibid.

86. Martin Beck, "Regional Politics in a Highly Fragmented Region: Israel's Middle East Policies," http://www.giga-hamburg.de/dl/download.php?d=/content/publikationen/pdf/wp89_beck.pdf.

87. Ibid.

88. Ibid.

89. Ibid.

90. Avner Cohen, "Israel Missing a Chance at Nuclear Global Legitimacy," *Haaretz*, April 11, 2010, http://www.haaretz.com/print-edition/opinion/israel -missing-a-chance-at-nuclear-global-legitimacy-1.771.

91. Ibid.

92. Ibid.

93. Zvi Bar'el, "Iran Is Regional Superpower Even without Nukes," *Haaretz*, February 12, 2010, http://www.haaretz.com/print-edition/opinion/iran-is -regional-superpower-even-without-nukes-1.266031.

94. Ibid.

95. Ibid.

96. "Iran FM: Israel Root Cause of ME Woes," *Press TV*, December 9, 2010, http://www.presstv.ir/detail/154663.html.

97. "Clinton Loses Iran Minister at 'Hello,'" *MSNBC News*, December 4, 2010, http://www.msnbc.msn.com/id/40504360/ns/world_news-mideast/n_africa.

98. "Iran Calls for Constructive Approach in Geneva Talks," *Xinhuanet News*, December 7, 2010, http://news.xinhuanet.com/english2010/world/2010-12/07/ c_13637601.htm.

99. "Iran Greatest Threat, Will Have Nukes by '99," Reuters, October 25, 1992, quote available in Parsi, *The Treacherous Alliance*, 163.

100. Benjamin Netanyahu, *Fighting Terrorism: How Democracies Can Defeat the International Terrorist Network* (New York: Farrar, Straus & Giroux, 2005), 121.

101. Gil Hoffman and Tovah Lazaroff, "Iran Can Produce Nuclear Bomb by 2005—IDF," *Jerusalem Post*, August 5, 2003, http://www.highbeam.com/doc/ 1P1-77155497.html.

102. Quoted in Jeffrey Goldberg, "The Point of No Return," *The Atlantic*, September 2010, http://www.theatlantic.com/magazine/archive/2010/09/ the-point-of-no-return/8186.

CHAPTER 4

1. "Israel Official: Hamas Rockets Can Reach Tel Aviv," Associated Press, November 14, 2010, http://news.in.msn.com/international/article.aspx ?cp-documentid=4577570.

2. "IDF Arrests Top Hamas Official in Ramallah," *Jerusalem Post*, November 10, 2010, http://www.jpost.com/Israel/Article.aspx?id=194710.

3. John Gambrell, "Nigeria: Shipper Confirms Weapons Came from Iran," October 30, 2010, http://www.boston.com/news/world/africa/articles/2010/ 10/30/nigeria_shipper_confirms_weapons_came_from_iran.

4. Quoted in *BNO News*, "Nigeria Seizes Iranian Weapons Cache Allegedly Headed for Gaza," October 28, 2010, http://wireupdate.com/wires/11714/ nigeria-seizes-iranian-weapons-cache-allegedly-headed-for-gaza.

5. Gambrell, "Nigeria."

6. Quoted in Barak Ravid, "Iran's African Adventure Could End Badly at the UN," *Haaretz*, November 23, 2010, http://www.haaretz.com/news/international /analysis-iran-s-african-adventure-could-end-badly-at-the-un-1.326406.

7. "Gambia Cuts Ties with Iran and Orders Diplomats to Go," *BBC News*, November 23, 2010, http://www.bbc.co.uk/news/world-africa-11819143.

8. M. Herzog, "Can Hamas Be Tamed?," *Foreign Affairs* 85, no. 2 (2006): 83–94.

9. M. Wurmser, "The Iran-Hamas Alliance," October 4, 2007, https:// www.hudson.org/index.cfm?fuseaction=publication_details&id=5167

10. Ibid.

11. "Ahmadinejad: Iran Will Support Hamas until Collapse of Israel," *Haaretz.com*, December 9, 2008, http://www.haaretz.com/news/ahmadinejad -iran-will-support-hamas-until-collapse-of-israel-1.253714.

12. Herzog, "Can Hamas Be Tamed?," 83.

13. Wurmser, "The Iran-Hamas Alliance."

14. Ibid.

15. "Iran Urges World Muslim 'Resistance' against Israel," *Breitbart*, March 4, 2010, http://www.breitbart.com/article.php?id=CNG.21c84721b2a4459b107dfbfb 9ada315a.2f1.

16. The author will indifferently use both "the Gulf" and "the Persian Gulf" where the flow of the writing requires. This should not be interpreted as a political preference.

17. See, among others, Bjørn Møller, *Conflict Theory*, Working Paper No. 122, Research Center on Development and International Relations, Alborg University, 26.

18. Eighty-six members of the Assembly of Experts are elected from a government-screened list by direct vote to eight-year terms.

19. Imam Ruhollah Khomeini, *Islam and Revolution: Writings and Declarations of Imam Khomeini*, trans. Hamid Algar (Berkeley, CA: Mizan Press, 1981), 59.

20. It was only in the 1980s and by accepting Eduard Shevardnadze, then the Soviet minister of foreign affairs, that he realized that breaking the alliance with both East and West was probably a mistake.

21. In 2001, Khamenei issued a decree known as "Farman hasht made'h-ee," or "eight articles decree," to combat against economic corruption. The text was considered equal to the text of law and branded as "governmental decree." For an analysis of the decree (in the Persian language), see the Iranian parliament Web site at http:// www.majlis.ir/mhtml/modules.php?name=News&file=article&sid=396.

22. Mashaei's daughter is married to Ahmadinejad's son.

23. "Leader Tells Ahmadinejad to Undo VP Choice, as Quoted by Press TV," http://www.presstv.com/detail.aspx?id=101259&sectionid=351020101.

24. Alireza Ronaghi, "Big Shoes to Fill," October 22, 2007, http://english .aljazeera.net/news/middleeast/2007/10/2008525173547951705.html.

25. For further detail and elaboration on the intricacies of the political situation in Iran, see the thoughtful reports published recently by Ali Ansari, "Iran under Ahmadinejad: Populism and Its Malcontents," in *International Affairs* (2008), and "The Revolution Will Be Mercantilized," in *The National Interest*, at http:// www.nationalinterest.org/PrinterFriendly.aspx?id=22602, http://www.merip.org /mer/mer252/farhi.html, and http://www.merip.org/mero/mero120809.html.

26. Reuters report from Clinton's statement in Qatar: http://www.reuters.com/article/idUSTRE61E1FR20100215. See also Amir Taheri, "Iran's Emerging Military Dictatorship," *Wall Street Journal*, February 16, 2010, http://online.wsj.com/article/SB20001424052748704431404575067193404330842.html.

27. Faisal Bin Salma Al-Saud, *Iran, Saudi Arabia and the Gulf: Power Politics in Transition* (New York: I. B. Tauris, 2004), 30.

28. "Bahrain Halts Gas Talks in Protest," *Iranian Daily*, February 19, 2009, http://www.iran-daily.com/1387/3345/html/national.htm#s364737.

29. Jasim M. Abdulghani, *Iraq and Iran: The Years of Crisis* (London: Croom Helm, 1984), 87.

30. Jeffrey Fleishman, "Iran Supreme Leader's Son Seen as Power Broker with Big Ambitions," *Los Angeles Times*, June 25, 2009, http://articles.latimes.com/2009/jun/25/world/fg-iran-khamenei-son25.

31. Abbas Maleki, "Decision Making in Iran's Foreign Policy: A Heuristic Approach," http://www.caspianstudies.com/article/Decision%20Making%20in%20Iran-FinalDraft.pdf.

32. Kenneth Katzman, "Iran: U.S. Concerns and Policy Responses," report to Congressional Research Service, August 6, 2009, 28, http://www.fas.org/sgp/crs/mideast/RL32048.pdf.

33. Ibid.

34. Dasetan Dowlat, "The Story of Government" (in Persian), http://www.hamshahrionline.ir/hamnews/1384/840520/world/siasatw.htm.

35. These people form a Council of Foreign Relations type of institution that functions in parallel with the government's Ministry of Foreign Affairs and keeps Khamenei and his office current on international issues.

36. "Khamenei: Hamas and Hezbollah Spread Islamic Revolution's Principles," *Naharnet News*, February 9, 2008, http://www.naharnet.com/domino/tn/News Desk.nsf/Lebanon/26BCE7D668EECDD3C2257557004F4DDA?OpenDocument.

37. Ibid.

38. Hala Jaber, *Hezbollah: Born with a Vengeance* (New York: Columbia University Press, 1997), 8.

39. Ibid.

40. Naim Qassem, *Hezbollah* (London: Saqi, 2005), 13.

41. Ibid., 13–16.

42. Jaber, *Hezbollah*, 10–11.

43. Ibid., 11.

44. Qassem, *Hezbollah*, 18.

45. http://www.cfr.org/publication/9155/hezbollah_aka_hizbollah_hizbullah.html.

46. Qassem, *Hezbollah*, 20.

47. Ibid., 21–50.

48. Ibid., 20.

49. Jaber, *Hezbollah*, 20.

50. Ibid., 19–20.

51. Ibid., 20–21.

52. Ibid., 29.

53. Ibid.

54. "Hezbollah," *New York Times*, June 8, 2009, http://topics.nytimes.com/top/ reference/timestopics/organizations/h/hezbollah/index.html?scp=1-spot&sq =hezbollah&st=cse.

55. "Iran Gives Weapons to Re-Arm Hezbollah, Pentagon Says," *BusinessWeek*, April 20, 2010, http://www.businessweek.com/news/2010-04-20/iran-gives -weapons-funds-to-help-lebanese-hezbollah-re-arm.html.

56. "Hezbollah."

57. Amir Oren, "Next Israel-Hezbollah War Will Be Worse, Says U.S. Analyst," September 9, 2010, http://www.haaretz.com/print-edition/news/next-israel -hezbollah-war-will-be-worse-says-u-s-analyst-1.314880.

58. Ibid.

59. Ibid.

60. Ibid.

61. ldquo;Understanding the Iran-Hezbollah Connection," *USIP.org*, September 2006, http://www.usip.org/resources/understanding-iran-hezbollah -connection.

62. Roy Anderson, Robert Seibert, and John Wagner, *Politics and Change in the Middle East* (Upper Saddle River, NJ: Pearson, 2009), 106.

63. Ian Bickerton and Carla Klausner, *A History of the Arab-Israeli Conflict* (Englewood Cliffs, NJ: Prentice Hall, 2010), 374.

64. Ibid., 375.

65. Ibid.

66. "Hezbollah."

67. "Hezbollah (a.k.a. Hizbollah, Hizbu'llah)," July 15, 2010, http://www .cfr.org/lebanon/hezbollah-k-hizbollah-hizbullah/p9155.

68. Brigitte Nacos, *Terrorism and Counterterrorism* (New York: Longman, 2008), 120.

69. Ted Galen Carpenter and Malou Innocent, "The Iraq War and Iranian Power," *CATO.org*, Winter 2007–2008, http://www.cato.org/pubs/articles/ carpenter_innocent_the_iraq_war_and_iranian_power.pdf.

70. Esther Pan, "Lebanon's Weak Government," *CFR.org*, July 20, 2006, http:// www.cfr.org/publication/11135.

71. "Hezbollah (a.k.a. Hizbollah, Hizbu'llah)."

72. "Lebanon Resumes Defense Talks on Hezbollah's Military Wing," *CSmonitor.com*, March 10, 2010, http://www.csmonitor.com/World/Middle-East/ 2010/0310/Lebanon-resumes-defense-talks-on-Hezbollah-s-military-wing/ (page)/2.

73. "Hezbollah (a.k.a. Hizbollah, Hizbu'llah)."

74. "Hezbollah Takes Over West Beirut," *BBC News*, May 9, 2008, http:// news.bbc.co.uk/2/hi/7391600.stm.

75. Jeremy Sharp, "Lebanon: The Israel-Hamas-Hezbollah Conflict," Congressional Research Service, September 15, 2006, http://fas.org/sgp/crs/ mideast/RL33566.pdf.

76. "Iran Gives Weapons to Re-Arm Hezbollah, Pentagon Says."

77. Nacos, *Terrorism and Counterterrorism*, 82.

78. "Hezbollah (a.k.a. Hizbollah, Hizbu'llah)."

79. "Lebanon Resumes Defense Talks on Hezbollah's Military Wing."

80. Amos Jorda et al., eds., *American National Security* (Baltimore: Johns Hopkins University Press, 2009), 438.

81. Ibid.

82. Ibid.

83. Ibid.

84. Nacos, *Terrorism and Counterterrorism*, 49.

85. Ibid., 118.

86. Ibid., 118–19.

87. Ibid., 49.

88. Khair el-Din Haseeb, ed., *Arab-Iranian Relations* (Beirut: Centre for Arab Unity Studies, 1998), 520–21.

89. Ibid.

90. Ibid., 27–28.

91. Gwen Ackerman, "Israel's Ayalon Says Iran Must Be Kept from 'Meddling' in Egypt," *Bloomberg.com*, February 14, 2011, http://www.bloomberg.com/news/2011-02-14/israel-s-ayalon-says-iran-must-be-kept-from-meddling-in-egypt.html.

92. Jonathan Wright, "Change in Egypt To Ratchet Pressure on Israel," February 18, 2011, http://af.reuters.com/article/tunisiaNews/idAFLDE71G20Y20110218?pageNumber=1&virtualBrandChannel=0.

93. "Iran: Mubarak's Fall A Great Achievement," February 15, 2011, http://www.presstv.ir/detail/165304.html.

94. Ibid.

95. Richard Boudreaux, "Israel Official Says Iran Ship Is 'Provocation,'" *Wall Street Journal*, February 17, 2011.

96. Ibid.

97. Edmund Sanders, "Hamas Sees Opportunity in Change in Egypt," *Los Angeles Times*, February 18, 2011.

98. "Many Israelis Worry About The 'New Egypt,'" *Radio Free Europe*, February 16, 2011, http://www.rferl.org/content/israel_egypt/2311114.html.

99. "Iran's Top Leader: Mubarak Betrayed His People," February 4, 2011, http://www.google.com/hostednews/ap/article/ALeqM5jO3vg3f7Da1NBw2oPvIUvClGSqog?docId=6167be63e8e245a29546ae1097b4e08f.

100. For a good historical analysis of oil prices, see http://www.wtrg.com/prices.htm.

101. Haroutiun Khachatrian, "Armenia and Iran Agree on New Communication Projects," Central Asia-Caucasus Institute, January 14, 2009, http://www.cacianalyst.org/?q=node/5016.

102. Brenda Shaffer, "Iran's Role in the South Caucasus and Caspian Region: Diverging Views of the U.S. and Europe," in *Iran and Its neighbors: Diverting Views on a Strategic Region*, ed. Eugene Whitlock (Berlin: German Institute for International and Security Affairs, 2003), 17–22.

103. Khachatrian, "Armenia and Iran Agree on New Communication Projects.""

104. "Russia-Iran: Cooling Relations?," *BBC News*, February 24, 1998, http://news1.thdo.bbc.co.uk/low/english/world/analysis/newsid_59000/59404.stm.

105. "Russia Defends Iran Exports in Talks with U.S.," *CNN World News*, January 21, 2002, http://www.cnn.com/2002/WORLD/meast/01/21/rU.S.sia.U.S.a.reut/index.html.

106. "Unclassified Report to Congress on the Acquisition of technology Relating to Weapons of Mass Destruction Munitions, 1 January through 30 June 2000," http://ftp.fas.org/irp/threat/bian_feb_2001.htm.

107. "Russia Offers Another Reactor to Iran," *BBC News*, September 4, 2001, http://news.bbc.co.uk/hi/english/world/europe/newsid_1525000/1525095.stm.

108. Since 2007, rumors have resurfaced about Russia selling the S-300 missile system to Iran. It seems that a contract has been signed, but no delivery has been made because of international pressures on Russia to cancel the deal.

109. Michael T. Klare, *Blood and Oil: The Dangers and Consequences of America's Growing Dependency on Imported Petroleum* (New York: Metropolitan Books, 2004) 160, 171–73.

110. See http://www.srir.ru.

111. See http://www.farsnews.com/newstext.php?nn=8803030428.

112. Nikolai Novichkov, "Russian Firms Accord with Iran," *Jane's Defence Weekly* 36, no. 15 (2001): 31.

113. Ibid.

114. "Iran Says Tests Own Model of Russian S-300 Missile," *Reuters*, November 18, 2010, http://www.reuters.com/article/2010/11/18/us-iran-military-missile idUSTRE6AH2YW20101118.

115. Ed Blanche, "Russia: The Tehran Factor," *Jane's Defence Weekly* 36, no. 22, (2001): 37.

116. See, e.g., Leonard S. Spencer's testimony to the U.S. Congress, June 2003, "Russian Exports of Sensitive Equipment and Technology," http://cns.miis.edu/testimony/testspec.htm.

117. "Iran, Russia and the U.S. Nonproliferation Efforts," http://www.acus.org/new_atlanticist/iran-russia-and-us-nonproliferation-efforts.

118. Aviel Magnezi, "Russia Moving Closer to Hezbollah Too," May 13, 2010, http://www.ynetnews.com/articles/0,7340,L-3888893,00.html.

119. Ibid.

120. Ibid.

121. Ibid.

122. J. Gunning, "Peace with Hamas? The Transforming Potential of Political Participation," *International Affairs* 80, no. 2 (2004): 233–55.

123. Ibid., 233–34.

124. Ibid., 234–38.

125. Wurmser, "The Iran-Hamas Alliance."

126. Ibid.

127. D. Byman, "Should Hezbollah Be Next?," *Foreign Affairs* 82, no. 6 (2003): 54.

128. Z. Schiff, "Israel's War with Iran," *Foreign Affairs* 85, no. 6 (2006): 23.

129. Ibid., 31.

130. Byman, "Should Hezbollah Be Next?," 55.

131. Herzog, "Can Hamas Be Tamed?"

132. Ibid.

133. Byman, "Should Hezbollah Be Next?," 62.

134. Ibid., 64.

135. "Several Scenarios, Not All Bright, Could Result from Iran's Tumult," *Wall Street Journal*, June 19, 2009, http://online.wsj.com/article/SB12453510958 7828517.html.

136. M. Fischer, "Scenario Building for Iran," http://www.pbs.org/wgbh/ pages/frontline/tehranbureau/2010/01/scenario-building-for-iran.html.

137. R. Amiri, "The Politics of Polarization: Iran's Elections: Why Arab Leaders Want Ahmadinejad to Win," April 10, 2009, http://www.globalresearch.ca/ index.php?context=va&aid=13135.

138. Ibid.

139. G. Bruno, "Iran's Revolutionary Guards," June 22, 2009, http://www .cfr.org/publication/14324/irans_ revolutionary_guards.html.

140. Ibid.

141. F. Wehrey, J. Green, B. Nichiporuk, A. Nader, L. Hansell, R. Nafisi, et al., *The Rise of the Pasadarn: Assessing the Domestic Roles of Iran's Islamic Revolutionary Guard Corps*, 2009, RAND Corporation, http://www.rand.org/pubs/monographs/ 2008/RAND_MG821.pdf.

142. A. Naeymi-Rad, "Possible Outcomes for Future of Iran," April 20, 2010, http://www.examiner.com/x-45737-Chicago-Government- Examiner~y2010m4d20-Possible-Outcomes-for-Future-of-Iran.

143. M. Bard, "Potential Threats to Israel: Iran." February 20, 2009, http:// www.jewishvirtuallibrary.org/jsource/threats to israel/Iran.html.

144. Naeymi-Rad, "Possible Outcomes for Future of Iran."

145. Ibid.

146. M. Burns, "Maintaining Distance from Iran," June 29, 2009, http://www .fpif.org/articles/maintaining_distance_from_iran.

CHAPTER 5

1. "Text of Mahmoud Admadinejad's Speech," *New York Times*, October 30, 2005   http://www.nytimes.com/2005/10/30/weekinreview/30iran.html ?_r=1&ex=1161230400&en=26f07fc5b7543417&ei=5070.

2. "Revealed: Israel Plans Nuclear Strike on Iran," *The Sunday Times*, January 7, 2007, http://www.timesonline.co.uk/tol/news/world/article1290331.ece.

3. 2006 National Security Strategy, http://georgewbush-whitehouse. archives.gov/nsc/nss/2006/sectionV.html.

4. Parisa Hafezi, "Obama Taking 'Wrong' Path over Israel," March 4, 2009, http://uk.reuters.com/article/idUKTRE5231B120090304.

5. G. Bruno, "Iran's Nuclear Program," March 10, 2010, http://www.cfr.org/ publication/16811/irans_nuclear_program.html#.

6. Ibid.

7. Associated Press, "Iran, Syria continuing nuke projects," *The Jerusalem Post*, February 20, 2009. http://www.jpost.com/servlet/Satellite?cid =1233304834205 &pagename=JPost%2FJPArticle%2FShowFull

8. Bruno, "Iran's Nuclear Program."

9. Ibid.

10. William Broad and David Sanger, "Iran Said to Have Nuclear Fuel for One Weapon," *New York Times*, November 19, 2008, http://www.nytimes.com/2008/

11/20/world/middleeast/20nuke.html?_r=1&scp=1&sq=iran%20said%20to%20have %20nuclear&st=cse.

11. Bruno, "Iran's Nuclear Program."

12. Sam Gardiner, "The Israeli Threat: An Analysis of the Consequences of an Israeli Strike on Iranian Nuclear Facilities," Sweedish Defense Research Agency, Stockholm, Sweden, Report, March 2010.

13. "Iran Drills Simulate Defense of Nuclear Sites," *Payvand Iran News*, November 23, 2009.

14. "Hezbollah Threatens Weapon Buildup," *Wall Street Journal*, November 30, 2009.

15. "Iran Can Now Produce a Nuclear Bomb," *Jerusalem Post*, September 9, 2009.

16. Sam Gardiner, "The Israeli Threat."

17. Ibid.

18. Ibid.

19. Michael Gordon, ""U.S. Says Exercise by Israel Seems Directed at Iran," *New York Times*, June 20, 2008, http://www.nytimes.com/2008/06/20/world/africa/20iht-20iran.13846577.html.

20. Sam Gardiner, "The Israeli Threat."

21. Hilary Krieger, "Bolton: 'Military Strikes Only Way to Stop Iran Nukes,'" *Jerusalem Post*, November 30, 2010, http://www.jpost.com/International/Article.aspx ?id=197422.

22. Peter Baker, "Quieter Approach to Spreading Democracy Abroad," *New York Times*, February 21, 2009, http://www.nytimes.com/2009/02/22/weekin review/22baker.html.

23. Ibid.

24. J. Gunning, "Peace with Hamas? The Transforming Potential of Political Participation," *International Affairs* 80, no. 2 (2004): 233–55.

25. Ibid., 233–34.

26. Ibid., 234–38.

27. M. Wurmser, "The Iran-Hamas Alliance," October 4, 2007, https://www.hudson.org/ndex.cfm? fuseaction=publication_details&id=5167.

28. Ibid.

29. D. Byman, "Should Hezbollah Be Next?," *Foreign Affairs* 82, no. 6 (2003), 54.

30. Z. Schiff, "Israel's War with Iran," *Foreign Affairs* 85, no. 6 (2006), 23.

31. Byman, "Should Hezbollah Be Next?," 55.

32. M. Herzog, "Can Hamas Be Tamed?," *Foreign Affairs* 85, no. 2 (2006): 83–94.

33. Karl P. Mueller, Jasen J. Castillo, Forrest E. Morgan, Negeen Pagahi, and Brian Rosen, *Striking First: Preemptive and Preventative Attack in US National Security Policy* (Santa Monica, CA: RAND Corporation, 2006), 216.

34. U.S. Department of State, "State Sponsors of Terrorism," November 20, 2007, http://www.state.gov/s/ct/c14151.htm.

35. See, e.g., U.S. Department of State, "Chapter 3: State Sponsors of Terrorism," *Country Reports on Terrorism* (Washington, DC: Government Printing Office, April 2007).

36. See, e.g., Lolita Baldor, "General: Iran Training Shiite Insurgents," *WashingtonPost.com*, August 23, 2006, and Thom Shanker and Steven Weisman, "Iran Is Helping Insurgents in Iraq, US Officials Say," *New York Times*, September 20, 2004.

37. "Vice President's Remarks to the World Affairs Council of Dallas/Fort Worth," http://www.whitehouse.gov/news/releases/2007/11/print/200711002 -13.html.

38. Shanker and Weisman, "Iran Is Helping Insurgents in Iraq, US Officials Say."

39. Nabih Sonboli, "Challenges to Iran as an Emerging Regional Power" (title translated from the Persian text), http://www.ipis.ir/index.php?newsid=344.

40. Kate Clark, "Iran 'Sending Weapons to Taliban,'" September 15, 2008, http://news.bbc.co.uk/2/hi/7616429.stm.

41. Director General of the IAEA, "Implementation of the NPT Safeguards Agreement in the Islamic Republic of Iran," August 30, 2007, and "Iran Generally Honest on Nuclear Program, IAEA Inspectors Say," *Global Security Newswire*, November 15, 2007.

42. British American Security Information Council and Paul Ingram, "Changing the Frame of the International Debate over Iran's Nuclear program," 2 (full text available at http://www.basicint.org/pubs/Papers/08iran01.pdf).

43. The Treaty on the Non-Proliferation of Nuclear Weapons (NPT)," http://www.un.org/events/npt2005/npttreaty.html.

44. Ayatollah Kashani, "Ayatollah Kashani: Nuclear-Bomb Production Religiously Forbidden," *Islamic Republic News Agency*, November 9, 2007.

45. "Iran's Statement at IAEA Emergency Meeting," *Mehr News Agency*, August 10, 2005.

46. See Ayatollah Sanei with the Iranian Canadian filmmaker Maziar Bahari (detained by the Islamic Republic of Iran after the recent election in Tehran), http://www.youtube.com/watch?v=-BoP8aOamyY.

47. Sharon Squassoni, "Iran's Nuclear Program: Recent Developments," *CRS Report to Congress*, March 8, 2007, 2.

48. "Ahmadinejad Boasts of Iran's Nuclear Gear," *United Press International Online*, November 7, 2007, http://www.redorbit.com/news/international/ 1134134/ahmadinejad_boasts_of_irans_nuclear_gear/index.html and Sean Yoong, "Ahmadinejad: Destroy Israel, End Crisis," *Washington Post*, August 3, 2006, http://www.washingtonpost.com/wp-dyn/content/article/2006/08/03/ AR2006080300629.html.

49. "US Intel Chief Says 'No Iran Nukes Possible Before 2013,'" *The Christian Science Monitor*, August 10, 2009, http://www.csmonitor.com/World/Global -News/2009/0810/us-intel-chief-says-no-iran-nukes-possible-before-2013.

50. Steven Lee Myers, "American Release Iranian Detainees to Iraq," *New York Times*, July 9, 2009, http://www.nytimes.com/2009/07/10/world/middleeast/09 release.html.

51. "Iran Says It Is Holding American Hikers," *CNN World News*, August 11, 2009, http://edition.cnn.com/2009/WORLD/meast/08/11/iran.detained .americans.

52. "Clinton Says Iran Trials 'Sign of Weakness,'" *Television Washington*, http:// televisionwashington.com/floater_article1.aspx?lang=en&t=3&id=12889.

53. Daniel Dombey, "Clinton Fears Regional Conflict without Accord on Iran Sanctions," *Financial Times*, April 19, 2010, http://www.ft.com/cms/s/0/ 66c4dd94-4b4a-11df-a7ff-00144feab49a.html.

54. "US Pessimistic on Iran Overtures," *BBC News*, July 23, 2009, http://news.bbc.co.uk/2/hi/middle_east/8165265.stm.

55. "Obama White House May Send Letter to Unfreeze US-Iran," *The Guardian*, January 28, 2009, http://www.guardian.co.uk/world/2009/jan/28/barack-obama-iran-us-letter.

56. Elliot Abrams, "For Arab Nations, the Threat of Nuclear Iran Puts Israel in a New Light," *Washington Post*, August 6, 2010, http://online.wsj.com/article/SB10001424052748703748904575411162454395320.html?mod=WSJASIA_hpp_MIDDLE SecondNews.

57. Ibid.

58. Ibid.

59. Ibid.

60. Ibid.

CHAPTER 6

1. Jeremy Pressman, *The United States and the Israel-Hezbollah War*, Middle East Brief (Waltham, MA: Crown Center for Middle Eastern Studies, 2006).

2. Mark Perry, interview by Margaret Warner, "Israel, Hezbollah Claim Victories after Weeks of Fighting," Public Broadcasting Service, August 4, 2006, http://www.pbs.org/newshour/bb/middle_east/ july-dec06/victory_08-04.html.

3. Ibid.

4. Congressional Research Service, *Lebanon: The Israel-Hamas-Hezbollah Conflict*, CRS Report for Congress (Washington, DC: Congressional Research Service, 2006).

5. Mark Perry and Alastair Crooke, "Asia Times: Middle East News," October 12, 2006, *Asia Times*, http://www.atimes.com/atimes/middle_east/hj12ak01.html.

6. David Makovsky and Jeffrey White, "Lessons and Implications of the Israel-Hizballah War: A Preliminary Assessment," Policy Focus (Wahington, DC: Washington Institute for Near East Policy, 2006), 1–72.

7. Gal Luft, interview by Margaret Warner, "Israel, Hezbollah Claim Victories after Weeks of Fighting," Public Broadcasting Service, August 4, 2006, http://www.pbs.org/newshour/bb/middle_east/ july-dec06/victory_08-04.html.

8. Perry, "Israel, Hezbollah Claim Victories after Weeks of Fighting."

9. Anthony Cordesman, *Lessons of the 2006 Israeli-Hezbollah War* (Washington, DC: Center for Strategic and International Studies, 2007), 5.

10. Matt Matthews, *We Were Caught Unprepared: The 2006 Hezbollah-Israeli War*, Long War Series Occasional Paper 26 (Fort Leavenworth, KS: U.S. Army Combined Arms Center Combat Studies Institute Press, 2006).

11. Cordesman, *Lessons of the 2006 Israeli-Hezbollah War*.

12. Gary Gambill, "Implications of the Israel-Hezbollah War," *Global Politician*, April 17, 2007, http://www.globalpolitician.com/22630-israel-hizballah.

13. Ibid.

14. UN Security Council, *Report of the Secretary-General on the United Nations Interim Force in Lebanon*, Report to Congress (New York: UN Security Council, 2006).

15. Ibid., 13.

16. Matthews, *We Were Caught Unprepared*, 11.

17. Gary Gambill, "Implications of the Israel-Hezbollah War," September 6, 2006, http://www.mideastmonitor.org/issues/0609/0609_2.htm.

18. Ehud Olmert, "Olmert Announces Intent to Resign," July 8, 2008, http://www.jewishvirtuallibrary.org/jsource/History/OlmertResign073008.html.

19. Daniel Helmer, "Not Quite Counterinsurgency: A Cautionary Tale for US Forces Based on Israel's Operation Change of Direction," *Armor*, January 2007, 10.

20. Matthews, *We Were Caught Unprepared*, 28.

21. Makovsky and White, "Lessons and Implications of the Israel-Hizballah War," 49.

22. Ibid.

23. Cordesman, *Lessons of the 2006 Israeli-Hezbollah War*, 17.

24. George Bush, "President Bush Meets with Bipartisan Members of Congress on the G8 Summit," July 18, 2006, http://georgewbush-whitehouse.archives.gov/news/releases/2006/07/20060718-4.html.

25. Pressman, *The United States and the Israel-Hezbollah War*, 91.

26. Bashar al-Assad, "Speech of President Bashar al-Assad at Journalists Union 4th Conference," August 15, 2006, http://www.sana.sy/eng/21/2006/08/15/57835.htm.

27. Emily Landau, "Red Light, Green Light: Establishing US Levers of Pressure on Iran," July 13, 2009, http://www.israelpolicyforum.org/blog/red-light-green-light-establishing-us-levers-pressure-iran.

28. Quoted in "'Wipe Israel Off the Map' Iranian Says," October 27, 2005, http://www.nytimes.com/2005/10/26/world/africa/26iht-iran.html.

29. Alfonso Serano, "Iran President: Israel Will Soon Disappear," CBS News, October 20, 2006, http://www.cbsnews.com/stories/2006/10/20/world/main2110011.shtml.

30. "Iran to Supply Hezbollah with Missiles: Report," *China Post*, August 5, 2006, http://www.chinapost.com.tw/international/detail.asp?ID=87223&GRP=D.

31. Ibid.

32. "Iran Special Weapons Facilities," *Globalsecurity.org*, http://www.globalsecurity.org/wmd/world/iran/natanz.htm.

33. Uzi Mahnaimi, "Israel Plans for War with Iran and Syria," *The Times*, September 3, 2006, http://www.timesonline.co.uk/tol/news/world/article626630.ece.

34. Abid Mustafa, "White House: Between Rhetoric and Reality over Iran," *Global Politician*, November 26, 2006, http://www.globalpolitician.com/22332-foreign-iran-israel.

35. Mahnaimi, "Israel Plans for War with Iran and Syria."

36. Ibid.

37. Seymour Hersh, "Watching Lebanon," *The New Yorker*, August 21, 2006, http://www.newyorker.com/archive/2006/08/21/060821fa_fact.

38. Ibid.

39. Ron Ben-Yashi, "Security Experts: Iran to Be Bombed in 2007," *Israel News*, April, 11, 2006, http://www.ynetnews.com/articles/0,7340,L-3238806,00.html.

40. David Samuels, "Why Israel Will Bomb Iran," *Slate*, April 9, 2009, http://www.slate.com/id/2215820/pagenum.

41. "FNS Roundtable on Global Hotspots," *Fox News Sunday Transcripts*, October 5, 2009, http://www.foxnews.com/story/0,2933,560000,00.html.

42. Ibid.

43. Pressman, *The United States and the Israel-Hezbollah War*.

44. Simon McGregor-Wood, "Tensions Build between Israel and Syria," ABC News, April 3, 2008, http://abcnews.go.com/International/story?id=5241767&page=1&page=1.

45. Ibid.

46. Mark Tran, "US Claims Video Shows North Korea Helped Build Syrian Reactor," *The Guardian*, April 24, 2008, http://www.guardian.co.uk/world/2008/apr/24/usa.korea.

47. White House, "Statement by Press Secretary," April 24, 2008, http://georgewbush-whitehouse.archives.gov/news/releases/2008/04/20080424-14.html.

48. "UN: Hezbollah Has Increased Military Strength since 2006 War," *Haaretz*, October 25, 2007, http://www.haaretz.com/hasen/spages/916759.html.

49. Ibid.

CHAPTER 7

1. "U.S., Israel Claim Iran Serious Problem in Near East," http://www.aysor.am/en/news/2010/10/19/usa-israel-iran, October 19, 2010.

2. At any given time, there were more than two players. For instance, in the 1953 coup, the British were involved. Throughout the Cold War, various players were factors, and after the Cold War and until recently, Iraq was a factor. After the 2003 invasion of Iraq, the new Iraq became a part of the triangle, and now the relationship between Iran, Israel, and the United States is the latest form of a triangular relationship.

3. David W. Lesch, *The Middle East and the United States: A Historical and Political Reassessment* (Boulder, CO: Westview Press, 2003), 52.

4. Kenneth Pollack, *The Persian Puzzle: The Conflict between Iran and America* (New York: Random House, 2004.)

5. David Kadavar, "Mossadegh at the La Hague Court of Justice Defends Iran's Interests (1951)," *Iranian.com*, July 24, 2009, http://www.iranian.com/main/blog/darius-kadivar/pictory-mossadegh-la-hague-court-justice-defends-irans-interests-1951.

6. Mark Gasiorowski and Malcom Byrne, *Mohammad Mosaddeq and the 1953 Coup in Iran* (Syracuse, NY: Syracuse University Press, 2004).

7. Nikki R. Keddie, *Modern Iran: Roots and Results of Revolution* (New Haven, CT: Yale University Press, 2003).

8. Ibid.

9. Ibid.

10. "Carter Defends His Handling of Iran Hostage Crisis," November 16, 2009, *USA Today*, http://www.usatoday.com/news/world/2009-11-16-carter-thailand-housing_N.htm.

11. "Obama Reaches Out to Muslim World," BBC News, January 27, 2009, http://news.bbc.co.uk/2/hi/middle_east/7852650.stm.

12. Janine Zacharia, "Obama Urged to Ready Tougher Iran Sanctions, Military Strike," September 15, 2009, http://www.bloomberg.com/apps/news?pid=20601103&sid=aGXuRWqsEFos.

13. French Atomic Pique, September 30, 2009, http://www.wakeupamerica.com/french-atomic-pique.

14. Ross Colvin, "U.S. Says All Options on Table to Deal with Iran," Reuters, January 20, 2009, http://www.reuters.com/article/GCA-GCA-iraq/idUSTRE50S6LZ20090130.

15. "Former Embassy Hostage Says He Was 'Wrong about Iran's Revolution,'" Radio Free Europe, December 1, 2009, http://www.rferl.org/content/Former_Embassy_Hostage_Says_He_Was_Wrong_About_Irans_Revolution/1380567.html,

16. John Limbert, "How to Negotiate with Iran," *Foreign Policy Magazine*, March 2008, http://www.foreignpolicy.com/story/cms.php?story_id=4220&page=0.

17. Larry Korb, "How Should the United States Respond to Iran?," http://security.nationaljournal.com/2009/02/obamas-approach-to-iran-how-sh.php.

18. James Dobbins, "To Talk with Iran, Stop Not Talking," *Washington Post*, March 3, 2009, http://www.washingtonpost.com/wp-dyn/content/article/2009/03/02/AR2009030201951_pf.html.

19. James Dobbins, "Dealing with Iran: The Case for Talking," *New York Times*, June 30, 2008, http://www.nytimes.com/2008/06/30/opinion/30iht-edobbins.1.14099056.html.

20. Nick Amies, "Consequences of 1979 Hostage Crisis Still Influencing US-Iran Relations," April 11, 2009, *Dutch World News*, http://www.dw-world.de/popups/popup_printcontent/0,,4859884,00.html.

21. Nazila Fathi, "Wipe Israel 'Off the Map' Iranian says," *New York Times*, October 27, 2005, http://www.nytimes.com/2005/10/26/world/africa/26iht-iran.html.

22. "Iran Boosts Output of Uranium Mine," Global Security News Wire, November 4, 2009, http://www.globalsecuritynewswire.org/gsn/nw_20091104_4328.php.

23. Amies, "Consequences of 1979 Hostage Crisis Still Influencing US-Iran Relations."

24. "Bush State of the Union Address Transcript," *CNN.com*, January 29, 2002, http://transcripts.cnn.com/2002/ALLPOLITICS/01/29/bush.speech.txt.

25. Tony Jones, "French Foreign Minister Outraged by Axis of Evil Speech," *Lateline*, February 2, 2002, http://www.abc.net.au/lateline/stories/s486647.htm.

26. Suzanne Maloney, "How the Iraq War Has Empowered Iran," *Brookings Institute Report*, March 21, 2008, http://www.brookings.edu/opinions/2008/0321_iraq_maloney.aspx.

27. Ibid.

28. Robert Dreyfuss, "Is Iran Winning the Iraq War?," *The Nation*, February 21, 2008, http://www.thenation.com/doc/20080310/dreyfuss.

29. Ibid.

30. Ibid.

31. Samuel Huntington, *The Clash of Civilizations and the Remaking of the World Order* (New York: Simon and Schuster, 1998), 20.

32. Ibid.

33. Daniel R. Coats, Charles Robb, and General Charles F. Wald, "Meeting the Challenge: Time Is Running Out," September 15, 2009, Bipartisan Policy Center, http://www.bipartisanpolicy.org/library/report/meeting-challenge-time-running-out.

34. Quoted in John Vinocur, "Obama Vow, Iran's Stance and the Options," *New York Times*, November 30, 2009, http://www.nytimes.com/2009/12/01/world/middleeast/01iht-politicus.html.

35. Ibid.

36. Ibid.

37. Ibid.

38. Thomas Erdbrink and William Branigin, "Supreme Leader of Iran: Muslim Nations 'Hate America,'" *Washington Post*, June 4, 2009, http://www.washingtonpost.com/wp-dyn/content/article/2009/06/04/AR2009060402305.html.

39. Karen DeYoung and Michael Shear, "U.S., Allies Say Iran Has Secret Nuclear Facility," *Washington Post*, September 25, 2009, http://www.washingtonpost.com/wp-dyn/content/article/2009/09/25/AR2009092500289.html.

40. "Iran Opens Nuclear Fuel Facility," BBC News, April 9, 2009, http://news.bbc.co.uk/2/hi/7991282.stm.

41. Thomas Erdbrink, "Ahmadinejad Vows Dramatic Expansion of Iran's Nuclear Program," *Washington Post*, November 30, 2009, http://www.washingtonpost.com/wp-dyn/content/article/2009/11/29/AR2009112900992.html.

42. BBC News, "Obama Offers Iran 'New Beginning,'" BBC News, March 20, 2009, http://news.bbc.co.uk/2/hi/7954211.stm.

43. "Israel Attacks Gaza Aid Fleet," *Al-Jazeera*, May 13, 2010, http://english.aljazeera.net/news/middleeast/2010/05/201053133047995359.html.

44. Israeli Ministry of Foreign Affairs, "Israel's Response to the UN Security Council Resolution 1929 on Sanctions against Iran," June 9, 2010, http://www.mfa.gov.il/MFA/The+Iranian+Threat/Nuclear+threat/Israeli_response_Security_Council_Resolution _1929_sanctions_Iran_10_Jun_2010.htm, June 11, 2010.

45. Hilary Krieger, "US, Israel, and Iran Have Approached the 'End Game,'" *Jerusalem Post*, October 21, 2010, http://www.jpost.com/IranianThreat/News/Article.aspx?id=192187.

46. Ibid.

47. Ibid.

48. Ibid.

49. Raghida Dergham, "The Message of the Washington Summit to Syria and Iran," *Al-Arabiya*, September 3, 2010, http://www.alarabiya.net/views/2010/09/03/118406.html.

50. Raghida Dergham, "Iran and Israel Are in Need of Mutual Enmity," *Dar al-Hayat*, October 15, 2010, http://www.daralhayat.com/portalarticlendah/192262.

51. Robert Tait and Ewen Macaskill, "Revealed: The Letter Barack Obama's Team Hope Will Heal Iran Rift," The Guardian, January 28, 2009, http://www.guardian.co.uk/world/2009/jan/28/barack-obama-letter-to-iran

CHAPTER 8

1. Laura Rozen, "In Letters, Obama Asked Arab States for Confidence-Building Measures toward Israel," *Foreign Policy*, July 26, 2009, http://thecable

.foreignpolicy.com/posts/2009/07/26/in_letters_obama_asks_arab_states_for
_confidence_building_measures_towards_israel.

2. Ibid.

3. Ibid.

4. Ibid.

5. "Obama: Build on Arab Plan for Mideast Peace," *Haaretz*, July 5, 2009, http://
www.haaretz.com/news/obama-build-on-arab-plan-for-mideast-peace-1.266802.

6. Quoted in Stephen Dinan, "Obama Gives Iran Deadline on Nuclear Program," *Washington Times*, July 10, 2009, http://www.washingtontimes.com/
news/2009/jul/10/obama-gives-iran-deadline-nuclear-program.

7. Barack Obama, "A New Year, a New Beginning," White House Blog,
March 19, 2009, http://www.whitehouse.gov/Nowruz.

8. Clifford Levy and Peter Baker, "U.S.-Russia Nuclear Agreement Is First Step
in Broad Effort," *New York Times*, July 6, 2009, http://www.nytimes.com/2009/07/
07/world/europe/07prexy.html.

9. Uzi Mahnaimi and Sarah Baxter, "Saudis Give Nod to Israeli Raid on Iran,"
Sunday Times, July 5, 2009, http://www.timesonline.co.uk/tol/news/world/
middle_east/article6638568.ece.

10. Ross Colvin, "'Cut Off Head of Snake' Saudis Told U.S. on Iran," Reuters,
November 29, 2010, http://www.reuters.com/article/idUSTRE6AS02B20101129.

11. "U.S. Defense Secretary: Gulf Arab States Back Iran Nuclear Sanctions,"
Haaretz, December 10, 2010, http://www.haaretz.com/news/international/
u-s-defense-secretary-gulf-arab-states-back-iran-nuclear-sanctions-1.329922.

12. Glenn Kessler, "Saudi Prince Rules Out Engagement with Israel until Arab
Land Is Returned," *Washington Post*, November 5, 2010, http://www.washington
post.com/wp-dyn/content/article/2010/11/04/AR2010110406840.html.

13. International Peace Institute, "Iran, Lebanon, Israelis and Palestinians:
New IPI Opinion Polls," December 8, 2010, http://www.ipacademy.org/news/
general-announcement/209-iran-lebanon-israelis-and-palestinians-new-ipi-opinion
-polls.html.

14. Ibid.

15. Ibid.

16. Barak Ravid, "Netanyahu: WikiLeaks Cables Prove Israel Is Right on Iran,"
Haaretz, November 29, 2010, http://www.haaretz.com/news/diplomacy
-defense/netanyahu-wikileaks-cables-prove-israel-is-right-on-iran-1.327653.

17. Aluf Benn, "Carmel Inferno Proves Israel Can't Afford War with Iran,"
Haaretz, December 3, 2010, http://www.haaretz.com/news/national/carmel
-inferno-proves-israel-can-t-afford-war-with-iran-1.328529.

18. "Reports: Iranian President Removes Foreign Minister," *CNN*, December 13,
2010, http://www.cnn.com/2010/WORLD/meast/12/13/iran.foreign.minister.

19. Robert Tait, "Mottaki Doomed by Personal Animus, Not Political Visions,"
Globalsecurity.org, December 14, 2010, http://www.globalsecurity.org/wmd/
library/news/iran/2010/iran-101214-rferl01.htm.

20. Quoted in Paul Richter and Ramin Mostaghim, "Iran Announces Breakthrough on Eve of Talks," *Los Angeles Times*, December 6, 2010, http://
articles.latimes.com/2010/dec/06/world/la-fg-iran-talks-20101206.

21. Ibid.

Bibliography

Abdulghani, Jasim M. *Iraq and Iran the Years of Crisis*. London: Croom Helm, 1984.

Allin, Dana, and Steven Simon. *The Sixth Crisis: Iran, Israel, America, and the Rumors of War*. Oxford: Oxford Press, 2010.

Allison, Graham. *Nuclear Terrorism: The Ultimate Preventable Catastrophe*. New York: Times Books, 2004, 11–12.

Al-Saud, Faisal Bin. *Iran, Saudi Arabia and the Gulf: Power Politics in Transition*. New York: I. B. Tauris, 2004.

Ammann, Daniel. *The King of Oil: The Secret Lives of Marc Rich*. New York: St. Martin's Press, 2009.

Amuzegar, F. "Iran's Crumbling Revolution." *Foreign Affairs* 82, no. 1 (2003): 44–57.

Anderson, Roy, Robert Seibert, and John Wagner. *Politics and Change in the Middle East*. Upper Saddle River, NJ: Pearson, 2009.

"The Arab Oil Embargo: What Happened and Could It Happen Again?" *HeatingOil.com*. August 5, 2009. http://www.heatingoil.com/wp-content/uploads/2009/09/the_arab_oil_embargo.pdf.

Arian, Asher. *The Second Republic: Politics in Israel*. Chatham, MA: Chatham House, 2005.

Asraf, A., and A. Banuazizi. "Iran's Tortuous Path toward 'Islamic Liberalism.'" *International Journal of Politics, Culture, and Society* 15, no. 2 (2001): 237.

Beck, Martin. "Regional Politics in a Highly Fragmented Region: Israel's Middle East Policies." GIGA Research Program: Violence, Power, and Security. Working Paper. http://www.giga-hamburg.de/dl/download.php?d=/content/publikationen/pdf/wp89_beck.pdf.

Bialer, Uri. *Between East and West: Israel's Foreign Policy Orientation 1948–1956*. Cambridge: Cambridge University Press, 1990.

Bickerton, Ian, and Carla Klausner. *A History of the Arab-Israeli Conflict*. Englewood Cliffs, NJ: Prentice Hall, 2010.

Borowiec, Andrew. *Modern Tunisia: A Democratic Apprenticeship*. New York: Green-wood, 1998.

Budeiri, M. "The Nationalist Dimension of Islamic Movement in Palestinian Poli-tics." *Journal of Palestinian Studies* 24, no. 3 (2009): 91.

Matthew Bunn and Anthony Wier, "Terrorist Nuclear Weapon Construction: How Difficult?" Chapter in *Confronting the Spector of Nuclear Terrorism*, Philadelphia: The Annals of the American Academy of Political and Social Science, September 2006, 133-139.

Byman D. "Do Counterproliferation and Counterterrorism Go Together?" *Political Science Quarterly* 122, no. 1 (2007): 25–46.

Byman, D. "Should Hezbollah Be Next?" *Foreign Affairs* 82, no. 6 (2003): 54–66.

Carpenter, Ted Galen, and Malou Innocent. "The Iraq War and Iranian Power." *Survival* 49, no. 4 (Winter 2007): 67–84. http://www.cato.org/pubs/articles/carpenter_innocent_the_iraq_war_and_iranian _power.pdf.

Cohen, Raymond. "Israel's Starry-Eyed Foreign Policy." *Middle East Quarterly* 1, no. 2 (June 1994). http://www.meforum.org/221/israels-starry-eyed -foreign-policy.

Eytan, Walter. *The First Ten Years*. New York: Simon and Schuster, 1958.

Ferguson, C. D., and W. C. Potter. *The Four Faces of Nuclear Terrorism*. Monterey, CA: Institute of International Studies, 2004.

Freilich, Chuck. "The Armageddon Scenario: Israel and the Threat of Nuclear Terrorism." *Mideast Security and Policy Studies* 1, no. 84 (2010). http://www.biu.ac.il/Besa/MSPS84.pdf.

Gardiner, Sam. "The Israeli Threat: An Analysis of the Consequences of an Israeli Strike on Iranian Nuclear Facilities." FOI Report. March 2010. http://www.foi.se/upload/nyheter/2010/FOI_Rapport%20G5_NY2_med%20omslag.pdf.

Gasiorowski, Mark, and Malcom Byrne, *Mohammad Mosaddeq and the 1953 Coup in Iran*. Syracuse, NY: Syracuse University Press, 2004.

Gunning, J. "Peace with Hamas? The Transforming Potential of Political Participa-tion." *International Affairs* 80, no. 2 (2004): 233–55.

Harms, Gregory, and Tom Ferry. *The Palestine-Israel Conflict: A Basic Introduction*. London: Pluto Press, 2005.

Haseeb, Khair el-Din, ed. *Arab-Iranian Relations*. Beirut: Centre for Arab Unity Studies, 1998.

Herzog, M. "Can Hamas Be Tamed?" *Foreign Affairs* 85, no. 2 (2006): 83–94.

Huntington, Samuel. *The Clash of Civilizations and the Remaking of the World Order*. New York: Simon and Schuster, 1998.

Ispahani, M. "Varieties of Muslim Experience." *Wilson Quarterly* 14 (1989): 63–72.

Israeli Central Bureau of Statistics. "Last Produced for Monthly Bulletin of Statis-tics No. 11/2010." http://www.cbs.gov.il/www/yarhon/b1_e.htm.

Jaber, Hala. *Hezbollah: Born with a Vengeance*. New York: Columbia University Press, 1997.

Jordan, Amos, ed. *American National Security*. Baltimore: Johns Hopkins University Press, 2009.

Kagan, Robert. "America's Crisis of Legitimacy." *Foreign Affairs* 83, no. 2 (2004): 66–67.

Katzman, Kenneth. "Iran: U.S. Concerns and Policy Responses." CRS Report 32048 to Congress. August 6, 2009. http://www.fas.org/sgp/crs/mideast/RL32048.pdf.

Keddie, Nikki R. *Modern Iran: Roots and Results of Revolution*. New Haven, CT: Yale University Press, 2003.

Khomeini, Imam Ruhollah. *Islam and Revolution: Writings and Declarations of Imam Khomeini*. Translated by Hamid Algar. Berkeley, CA: Mizan Press, 1981.

Klare, Michael T. *Blood and Oil: The Dangers and Consequences of America's Growing Dependency on Imported Petroleum*. New York, Metropolitan Books, 2004.

Klieman, Aaron S. *Israel and the World after 40 Years*. Washington, DC: Pergamon-Brassey, 1990.

Lesch, David W. *The Middle East and the United States: A Historical and Political Reassessment*. Boulder, CO: Westview Press, 2003.

Levi, Michael. *On Nuclear Terrorism*. Cambridge, Massachusetts: Harvard University Press, 2007, 29.

Martin, Lenore. "Assessing the Impact of U.S.-Israeli Relations on the Arab World." Strategic Studies Institute Report. July 2003. http://www.strategicstudiesinstitute.army.mil/pdffiles/PUB104.pdf.

Matthews, Matt. "We Were Caught Unprepared: The 2006 Hezbollah-Israeli War." The Long War Series Occasional Paper 26. Fort Leavenworth, KS: U.S. Army Combined Arms Center Combat Studies Institute Press, 2006. http://carl.army.mil/download/csipubs/matthewsOP26.pdf.

Mearsheimer, John J., and Stephen M. Walt. "The Israel Lobby and US Foreign Policy." *Middle East Policy* 13, no. 3 (Fall 2006): 29–87.

Metz, Helen Chapin, ed. *Iran: A Country Study*. Washington, DC: Government Printing Office for the Library of Congress, 1987. http://countrystudies.us/iran/82.htm.

Migdalovitz, Carol. "Israel: Background and Relations with the United States." CRS Report 33476 for Congress. April 2, 2009. http://www.fas.org/sgp/crs/mideast/RL33476.pdf.

Mueller, Karl P., Jasen J Castillo, Forrest E Morgan, Negeen Pagahi, and Brian Rosen. *Striking First: Preemptive and Preventative Attack in US National Security Policy*. Santa Monica, CA: RAND. 2006.

Nacos, Brigitte L. *Terrorism and Counterterrorism*. New York: Longman, 2008.

Netanyahu, Benjamin. *Fighting Terrorism: How Democracies Can Defeat the International Terrorist Network*. New York: Farrar, Straus and Giroux, 2005.

Nolan, Janne, E. Bernard I. Finel, and Brian D. Finlay, eds. *Ultimate Security: Combating Weapons of Mass Destruction* New York: Century Foundation Press, 2003).

Novichkov, Nikolai. "Russian Firms Accord with Iran." *Jane's Defence Weekly* 36, no. 15 (2001): 31.

Parsi, Trita. *The Treacherous Alliance: The Secret Dealings of Iran, Israel, and the United States*. New Haven, CT: Yale University Press, 2007.

Pollack, Kenneth. *The Persian Puzzle: The Conflict between Iran and America*. New York: Random House, 2004.

Pressman, Jeremy. *The United States and the Israel-Hezbollah War*. Waltham, MA: Crown Center for Middle Eastern Studies, 2006.

Qassem, Naim. *Hezbollah*. London: Saqi Press, 2005.

Rabil, Robert. *Embattled Neighbors: Syria, Israel, and Lebanon*. New York: Lynne Rienner, 2003.

Rosenberg, Joel. *Inside the Revolution: How the Followers of Jihad, Jefferson and Jesus Are Battling to Dominate the Middle East and Transform the World*. Carol Stream, IL: Tyndall House, 2009.

Scharf, Astrid. "The Arab-Israeli Peace Process: From Madrid to Oslo and Beyond." *Studies in Contemporary History and Security Policy* 3 (1999): 53–76.

Schiff, Z. "Israel's War with Iran," *Foreign Affairs* 85, no. 6 (2006): 23–31.

Shaffer, Brenda. "Iran's Role in the South Caucasus and Caspian Region: Diverging Views of the U.S. and Europe." In *Iran and Its Neighbors: Diverting Views on a Strategic Region*, edited by Eugene Whitlock. Berlin: German Institute for International and Security Affairs, 2003, 17–22.

Sharp, Jeremy. "Lebanon: The Israel-Hamas-Hezbollah Conflict." CRS Report 33566 to Congress. September 15, 2006. http://fas.org/sgp/crs/mideast/RL33566.pdf.

Shlaim, Avi. "Israel, the Great Powers and the Middle East Crisis of 1958." *Journal of Imperial and Commonwealth History* 12 (May 1999): 177–92.

Spear, Joanna. "Organizing for Internationalism Counterproliferation: NATO and US Nonproliferation Policy." In *Ultimate Security: Combating Weapons of Mass Destruction*, edited by Janne E. Nolan, Bernard I. Finel, and Brian D. Finlay. New York: Century Foundation Press, 2003. 218–20

Tezc, G., and T. Azadarmak. "Religiosity and Islamic Rule in Iran." *Journal for Scientific Study of Relgion* 47, no. 2 (2008): 211–24.

Wehrey, F., J. Green, B. Nichiporuk, A. Nader, L. Hansell, and R. Nafisi. *The Rise of the Pasadarn; Assessing the Domestic Roles of Iran's Islamic Revolutionary Guard Corp*. Monograph. RAND Corporation. 2009. http://www.rand.org/pubs/monographs/2008/RAND_MG821.pdf.

Wurmser, M. "The Iran-Hamas Alliance." *InFocus*, no. 2 (Fall 2007). https://www.hudson.org/index.cfm?fuseaction=publication_details&id=5167.

Zimmerman, P. D., and J. G. Lewis. "The Bomb in the Backyard." *Foreign Policy*, no. 157 (2006): 32–39.

Index

About the Authors

JALIL ROSHANDEL is associate professor and director of the Security Studies Program at the Department of Political Science, East Carolina University. He received his PhD in political science at the Université Toulouse I, France, and was the deputy dean of the Faculty of Law and Political Science at the University of Tehran-Iran. Roshandel has since been a researcher and professor at many leading universities and research institutions in Europe and the United States, including the Copenhagen Peace Research Institute; Stanford University; the University of California, Los Angeles; and Duke University. His recent publications include *Jihad and International Security* (2006) and *The United States and Iran, Policy Challenges and Opportunities.* (2010).

NATHAN CHAPMAN LEAN received an MA in international studies with a concentration in Middle Eastern studies from East Carolina University in 2010. His graduate thesis, "Islam and the West: Problematizing a Discourse of Dualism," was nominated for a thesis prize with the Conference of Southern Graduate Schools. Under the auspices of a State Department scholarship, he gained advanced proficiency in Arabic during the summer of 2009 in Tunisia. His research interests include Islam, international security, American foreign policy, and cultural diplomacy. He is a contributing writer on national politics and global affairs at PolicyMic.